SOLIDUS

SOLIDUS

A NEW MODEL FOR UNDERSTANDING THE RELATIONSHIP BETWEEN HUMANS AND GOD

(SECOND EDITION)

A Commentary from a Christian Perspective

Chris L Abreo

Copyright © 2016 by Chris L. Abreo

All rights reserved. No part of this publication may be reproduced, stored in or introduced into a retrieval system, or transmitted, in any form, or by any means – electronic, mechanical, photocopying, recording, or otherwise – except for brief quotations in printed reviews, without the prior written permission of the copyright owner.

Unless otherwise noted all scripture quotations are from the King James Version (KJV) of the Holy Bible.

Second Edition, June 2016

Cover image: MacKenzie Falls, Grampians National Park, Victoria, Australia. © 2008 (Reflections: Matthew 7:24-25, 1Corinthians 10:4).

Requests for information should be addressed to:

>   Solidus Publications
>   P. O. Box 383
>   Hurst, Texas 76053

>   *SolidusPublications.com*

Library of Congress Control Number: 2016910355

ISBN-13: 978-0-9965884-0-9 *(ppb)*
ISBN-10: 0-9965884-0-X *(ppb)*

Let me pass through thy land:
I will go along by the high way,
I will neither turn unto the right hand nor to the left.

Deuteronomy 2:27

Dedication

In its entirety this book is first dedicated to:
God the Father, the Lord Jesus Christ,
and the Holy Spirit.

This is then dedicated to our neighbor.
It is to help empower the individual who
chooses to build upon faith in Jesus so that
we as His Body may become further instilled
with the Wisdom and Grace of God,
and move according to His Will.

Table of Contents

TABLE OF CONTENTS	VII
LIST OF ILLUSTRATIONS	VIII
LIST OF TABLES	VIII
PREFACE	IX

I.	**INTRODUCTION**	**1**
II.	**DIVERSITY VS. SENSE OF BELONGING**	**3**
III.	**DEFINING PARTS OF A WHOLE**	**9**
A.	EXPLORING COMMON KNOWLEDGE	9
	1. Understanding	9
	2. Brain Function: Perspective	12
	3. Laterality: East & West, Left & Right	17
	4. Id, Ego, Super-Ego: North & South	23
B.	EXPLORING THE BIBLE IN BRIEF	26
	1. Great Commandment	27
	2. Important Terms to Know	38
IV.	**HUMAN UNDERSTANDING AND DEVOTION**	**43**
A.	BASIS FOR SOLIDUS	44
	1. HUHD Model	44
	2. Quadra-Circumplex Model	76
	3. Stratum Model	101
B.	APPLICATIONS OF SOLIDUS	105
	1. Socio-Ideological Tendencies Table	107
	2. Functional Alignments Table	200
	3. Church & State as Parents: Fatherhood & Motherhood	210
V.	**CONCLUSION**	**213**
VI.	**EPILOGUE**	**217**
VII.	**APPENDICES**	**219**
	APPENDIX A – NOTEWORTHY TERMINOLOGY	220
	1. Contents	220
	2. Purpose	220
	3. Heart and Soul	221
	4. Faith and Believing	224
	5. Objects of Knowing	225
	APPENDIX B – HUHD MODEL	227
	1. Contents	227
	2. Northward	227
	3. Southward	232
	APPENDIX C – QUADRA-CIRCUMPLEX MODEL	236
	1. Contents	236

2. Just, Weight, Balance, Scales 237
3. Falling.. 238
4. Arising.. 244

SELECTED BIBLIOGRAPHY 255

List of Illustrations

FIGURE	PAGE	DESCRIPTION
FIGURE 1	9	CURRENT PROPOSITIONS MODEL FOR EPISTEMOLOGY
FIGURE 2	11	NORTHWARD HUHD MODEL (TRIQUETRA HIGHLIGHTED)
FIGURE 3	18	CHRIST PANTOCRATOR IMAGE AT SAINT CATHERINE'S MONASTERY
FIGURE 4	19	EQUAL-ARM BALANCE (SHOWN WEIGHED ON ONE SIDE)
FIGURE 5	24	SIGMUND FREUD'S ID, EGO, AND SUPER-EGO
FIGURE 6	37	EQUAL-ARM BALANCE (SHOWN BALANCED)
FIGURE 7	45	NORTHWARD HUHD MODEL (COMPLETE)
FIGURE 8	61	SOUTHWARD HUHD MODEL (COMPLETE)
FIGURE 9	76	QUADRA-CIRCUMPLEX MODEL
FIGURE 10	81	THE MARK FIGURATIVELY AS NINES & SIXES
FIGURE 11	100	CROOKED MOVEMENTS OF TEMPLES
FIGURE 12	102	STRATUM MODEL

List of Tables

TABLE	PAGE	DESCRIPTION
TABLE 1	15	FUNCTIONS OF HUMAN CEREBRAL HEMISPHERES
TABLE 2	21	BASIC COMPARISON OF CHRISTIAN REASONING
TABLE 3	108	SOCIO-IDEOLOGICAL TENDENCIES TABLE
TABLE 4	201	FUNCTIONAL ALIGNMENTS TABLE
TABLES 5-10	APPENDIX A – NOTEWORTHY TERMINOLOGY	
TABLES 11-24	APPENDIX B – HUHD MODEL	
TABLES 25-52	APPENDIX C – QUADRA-CIRCUMPLEX MODEL	

Preface

My main objective in writing this book was to help empower individuals with understanding of various principles derived from Biblical Truth so that they can—even in this very secular world—make their presence known on behalf of God. I wrote the book from an all-inclusive Christian perspective, an approach I came to appreciate at LeTourneau University. There I had the pleasure of taking *Old Testament Principles* and *New Testament Principles*, two classes in which I not only learned about scripture itself, but also about the significance of historical and archeological findings with respect to Christianity and the Bible. But more than this, I found that there was more to the issue of faith than meets the eye. There were real implications of the belief that God exists, and that faith in Him is vital for salvation. After this realization, life itself made better sense.

My thinking on these matters has been formed by life events. At the age of four, I became crippled and unable to walk. This was the result of a bicycle accident that shattered the femur head (the uppermost portion of the thigh bone) of my left leg. I used crutches to help get around and was soon fitted with braces on both legs—the braces were connected with a metal bar in-between to keep my legs stabilized and to help with the healing process. Because I could not walk, I had much time available to watch others enjoy normal lives, and simply to reflect on human behavior. After two years, medical results indicated that there was no sign of healing, so now there was the threat of amputating my left leg. In my mind it was by the grace of God that I was finally healed by the age of eight.

During those years, my parents divorced. My mother (who I lived with) remarried a couple of years later. And then, around 1971, we found ourselves living in North Central Texas.

With hindsight, I believe that God's influence moved my mother and father to seek out answers beyond the norm for my healing. This included seeking the advice of other physicians even in neighboring New Mexico. Around the same time, one day my father, along with a close friend of his, took turns carrying me on each of their backs up the long uphill journey (and then back down) of Mount Cristo Rey in Sunland Park, New Mexico. Even with the weight of braces they managed to make it to the top to make a spiritual appeal for the Lord to heal. In reflecting on how my mother and step-father carried me with braces up and down flights of stairs of our apartment complex during those years, and how my father carried me as well—and even reflecting on how people help carry others in more ways than one—I realize how vital human effort is over the long haul, along with faith in God, in order to overcome the impossible.

As a child, to be freed from the shackles of braces is a very humbling experience. From that point on, life wasn't about walking, it was about running. In retrospect, though, I will also suggest that there are inherent risks when running with that kind of persistent motivation—one may easily take wrong paths that only lead to futility, particularly when God is not high in one's mind.

As a left-hander who made average grades during school, it was in my 20s when I realized I enjoyed advanced mathematics, and it would be in my 30s that I became more capable with writing. And although I am not known as a joke-teller, I enjoy the company of family and friends—those with a sense of humor, those who are realists, and those who view life as a glass half full.

I have attempted various business ventures, most pursuits requiring little to no upfront capital; hence, much time and effort was spent on research and development. It was my last venture that I liked the most and knew he could do well – the salsa manufacturing business. Long story, short, I wanted this business to help fund efforts to benefit those crippled and left behind. But as certain critical opportunities came and went during the start-up stage, I began to wonder if this was really what God wanted me to do now, or if it should wait until later.

It was early in 2007 (now in my 40s) that, after reflecting on the behavioral tendencies of people from all walks of life, I became increasingly aware that there was no simple way to explain why individuals and groups of like-minded people do the things that they do. While I knew that there were countless books and other resources available on human understanding and behavior, it seemed there were few if any that provided a tandem discussion of both objective facts and subjective truths. By differentiating objective facts from larger subjective truths (according to the mind's ability to reason), I realized that one model can be used to frame a discussion that explains much about the human condition in relation to Biblical Truth. Thus I decided to write this book.

In the course of writing the first edition I visited local churches affiliated with various Christian denominations. Though the denomination in which my wife and I grew up was meeting our spiritual needs, I felt an urge to venture out and learn more about other denominations. So in late 2007 we began to test the waters of local churches with the goal of identifying those closely aligned with the religious beliefs that I had grown to understand and appreciate. At the time I had no idea where those efforts would ultimately lead us—toward another church or back to the one we were comfortable with. One thing I knew: At that point in my life it was important to find a local body that was centered more on biblical teachings, not only as heard but also as read. It was also important to find a church that recognized that even after one was baptized, one could spiritually fall from grace after a change of heart. It was essential to find a community that demonstrated a natural desire for missionary involvement (i.e., one that was outreach-oriented). Lastly, it was important to find a church whose leader not only led with strong conviction but also humbly attempted to bridge the gap of understanding between biblical truths and life issues.

We found that all the churches we visited had a sincere approach to God, as well as warm and gracious people. It really came down to personal preference combined with sifting the beliefs and practices of each on an issue-by-issue basis. ReligionFacts.com was a useful tool in my research. In reviewing such information, though, I discovered how easy it is to become disillusioned with the many ways religious issues can be interpreted – the terminology alone seemingly requires advanced education.

After months of research and visitation we found our beliefs aligned more with groups that base a portion of their theology on prevenient grace—a view similar to Wesleyan Arminianism. It was this, as well as an emphasis on Biblical teachings and the art of music—each regarded as an expression of faith when shared with others—that made the difference. So we settled into a church of another denomination.

What I learned in the process is that most (perhaps all) Christian groups genuinely approach God and invoke the Holy Spirit from a unique perspective, and each possesses particular strengths that build the Body stronger.

In June 2008, a year into the writing of this book on a part-time basis, I took the leap of faith by leaving a secure job with benefits to devote myself to researching and writing full-time. I simply felt that there was an important message for me to share with others and felt certain that God helped instill the motivation to respond as I did. From that point on, though, it was a constant battle to clear various hurdles while also having to contend with mounting financial burdens. Even so, with God above and my wife by my side, I was able to maintain the course with hope and determination.

I gratefully thank my wife and the rest of my family for being so patient with me over the years, particularly in recent times. Though I have explained the basics of this project to various family members, I can see how the tremendous amount of time I spent researching and writing could have been construed as an attempt to create distance. This was simply not the case. I hope now that my mother and father, my daughter and her family, and other family members will read it and know how much I love them. This is a love that has only strengthened as a result of God's grace.

Beyond this, I realize that each and every person I have known has had some impact on how I approached this project. My parents were there for me in good times and in difficult times. Though most blood family members were hundreds of miles away, my step family was also close to my heart. In this family it was my Grandma who consistently demonstrated warmth, good humor, and social graces that really made an impact on how I view family and friends. I have also been blessed over the years with friends from all walks.

During the course of my life, I have listened to, watched, and learned from leaders of various Christian persuasions. The guidance of each of these leaders has had some impact on how my faith-journey has progressed. Many thanks go out to all those who are moved by the Spirit of God in making remarkable changes in the lives of others.

I must also mention the many fine Internet sites that I used in my research; sites that have compiled biblical information in resourceful ways. For a number of reasons I consistently found myself going back to BlueLetterBible.org, a website that is not only easy to use when researching but offers information on various lexicons that most other sites do not.

And finally, it is important to note that after publishing the first edition of Solidus in May 2010, I came to realize that it would be necessary to dedicate more time to the book. For this second edition my aim was to simplify the overall discussion while also making it more complete. Though I hope this book will be a useful stepping stone for non-believers to help them move toward the Christian community, my main hope is that it will help affirm the Christian faith among believers and thus strengthen Christianity as a whole.

I. Introduction

Where should one begin when discussing the relationship between humans and God? Consider for the moment how much has been written and conveyed through oral tradition throughout the centuries about religion, spirituality, philosophy, and science. In our day, the Internet provides ready access to this whole collective body of thought. Yet we might ask: Even with all of this information literally at our fingertips, are we any more capable of spiritually growing toward God than our ancestors were? Can modern folks achieve a condition more pleasing to God? At this point in time it certainly appears that believers are fighting a losing battle against the decadence that is eroding *all* human cultures. It seems clear that more knowledge does not always equate to higher morality.

The Internet serves to diversify thinking so that opinion becomes part of the collective consciousness. Everybody has an opinion, and many believe that any opinion is as valid as any other, as tolerance is hailed as the virtue of pluralism. In truth, who could muddle through all the information about every system of thought and expect to find the right path? Despite these difficulties, we must persevere, as salvation depends on the individual's choosing the best possible truth, and thus rising above the opinions of others.

The law of the LORD [is] perfect, converting the soul:
the testimony of the LORD [is] sure, making wise the simple.
Psalm 19:7

Regardless of what socio-ideological or political persuasion you hold, I wrote this book to help you make sense of the full gamut of issues involving conflict, persecution, love and hate, peace and war, and so on. I will explore our nature as human beings relative to one another on the plane of humanity/reality, and in relation to and in communion with God on the plane of spirituality.

At first some readers may regard *Solidus* as an intellectual exercise concerning a matter not accessible to the intellect: the issue of faith. While this book is geared to appeal to the intellectually inquisitive, my goal is not to provide an intellectual argument for faith. Rather it is to explain the different yet mutually supporting roles played by *Logic* on one hand and *Intuition* on the other in opening the way to a Purpose directed toward God. From the overall discussion I hope to affirm God's existence and humanity's position within His creation.

Don't worry if you are not well-versed in scripture. At first, try reading *Solidus* without the commitment of time normally given to reading passages. For most readers, this will make the flow of discussions smoother. It is vital to note, though, that each discussion is possible only because of the biblical Truth that appears immediately before it. When you go back and read the book a second time, you will find that each referenced passage takes on additional meaning, and is offered from a perspective that sheds greater light on faith-based reasoning from a Christian perspective.

Solidus might at first seem to be just another opinion competing with other equally valid opinions, but bear with me. I think that you will find significant differences between this argument and most others. At times, I will use terms that are technical or might be new to you, but rest easy: I will define each one. They will actually make the concepts easier to understand. So take a deep breath, and let's begin our study.

II. Diversity vs. Sense of Belonging

I applied mine heart to know, and to search, and to seek out wisdom, and the reason [of things], and to know the wickedness of folly, even of foolishness [and] madness.
Ecclesiastes 7:25

It is easy to see that the human race is beset by distrust, disunity, and hatred. The problem seems to be getting worse. Many adults recall a time when people young and old gathered together to socialize. Enjoying each other's company was a unifying experience that further solidified the community.

We all share the human desire to form long-lasting and meaningful relationships with others based on common beliefs and traditions—a shared worldview. Sure we're all of one nation or one world, but it's difficult to find a sense of belonging on such a grand scale. In attempting to do so, we may actually lose our sense of belonging and ultimately experience feelings of detachment. Trying to find common ground with everyone can lead us to a basis of (a certain) unity that only gets shallower and shallower. All the while we find that tolerance is being pressed upon us as a virtue.

While it is certainly good to be tolerant, some advocates of tolerance have taken the idea too far, seeking to use the notion that intolerance is bad to force others to accept every unconventional viewpoint and behavior as legitimate. Embracing all viewpoints might seem good, but is it really healthy to support destructive belief systems and behaviors? Automatic tolerance of everything in deference to a socio-cultural dogma can lead us to places where we don't want to go. If instead we seek as individuals to become pleasing to God, we will naturally become tolerant where appropriate; this, while retaining a sense of the importance of distinguishing between cases where tolerance is appropriate and those where it is not. In this book, I will explain how, in this kind of case and in others, the practice of specific kinds of behavior commonly regarded as good, such as tolerance, does not necessarily result in peace and harmony. Instead, it's the motivations behind those behaviors that are important.

It's a common view that no one should have to sacrifice his or her individuality to comply with another's opinion for what is considered acceptable. So what can be done to help people who value their differences from the mainstream to lower their guard long enough to see that there may indeed be a commonality among the diverse which might lead to a natural coming together? To help others see this, we must first recognize that commonalities such as race, culture, and religion are trivial in comparison to what we all have in common as human beings.

Efforts to unite must be for the greater good and His greater glory, not to serve our own interests. But selfless acts are often subjected to harsh scrutiny by those who think differently, giving rise to deeper divisions. Believers are often mocked and ridiculed because they have acted contrary to the standards of others. Should believers of God consistently allow themselves to be treated like this? Let's see what Jesus said:

> *Ye have heard that it hath been said,*
> *An eye for an eye, and a tooth for a tooth: But I say unto you,*
> *That ye resist not evil: but whosoever shall smite thee on thy*
> *right cheek, turn to him the other also.*
> *Ye have heard that it hath been said,*
> *Thou shalt love thy neighbour, and hate thine enemy.*
> *But I say unto you, Love your enemies, bless them that curse*
> *you, do good to them that hate you, and pray for them which*
> *despitefully use you, and persecute you;*
> *That ye may be the children of your Father which is in*
> *heaven: for he maketh his sun to rise on the evil and on the*
> *good, and sendeth rain on the just and on the unjust.*
> Jesus, Matthew 5:38-39, 43-45

For some, these words (of Truth) seemingly defy the real world. They wonder why Jesus would suggest these things, realizing that His followers from that point on would be placing their own lives in the hands of those who have evil intent. To non-believers, Christianity may seem only to demonstrate weakness by accepting the abuse of others. They argue that if Jesus were truly the Son of God then His Father would have done something (anything!) to prevent Jesus' death. Further, they reason that because Jesus was weak, those who follow Him are also weak. How can believers understand Jesus' (seeming) willingness to subject His followers to such harm? There simply have to be valid reasons.

> *Then said Jesus, Father, forgive them;*
> *for they know not what they do.*
> *And they parted his raiment, and cast lots.*
> Luke 23:34

The above passage may contain the most profound reason why Jesus said "love your enemies... and pray for them which despitefully use you, and persecute you."[1] Simply stated, most people who persecute others do so because they are unknowing – clueless as to why they do the things they do. To them, believers are the enemy. Believers, however, are indeed the knowing group and realize that those who persecute are lost and will lash out against anyone who is perceived as the enemy. Keep in mind though that all believers were once non-believers, so the point is not really to attack those who persecute believers but rather to teach them.

In essence, God-inspired Truth is not only the way for believers to gain everlasting life but is also a source of real strength during one's time on earth. This idea is confusing to non-believers who only understand physical strength, and perhaps ordinary emotional strength, but not spiritual strength. Thus, many non-believers look upon Christians as weak and timid people who back away from any sort of fight. The truth, however, is that Jesus' statements show a profound *inward* strength – a strength that actually helps guide those who share it toward the truest forms of wisdom and grace, qualities Jesus wanted His followers to cultivate in themselves and thus, in others.

> *For God hath not given us the spirit of fear;*
> *but of power, and of love, and of a sound mind.*
> 2 Timothy 1:7

God wants believers to be strong and happy, to defend the truth if and when necessary, and to move according to His will—not to

---

[1] Matthew 5:44

suffer at the hands of people who waste their time and energy pursuing self and greed.

When believers do defend the truth, they may be seen as arrogant and opinionated and as attempting to impose their will on others. Reflecting on our own sins against God and against others, though, remember that we too have needed help to find the way. If we go about it the right way, seeking to teach first rather than to condemn first, and showing others the way through our own behavior, we will often be more persuasive as to what others in need ought to learn. Such ways will also help to deflect the kind of criticism that comes with Christian forthrightness.

Having a circle of others who are (in the truest sense) wise,[2] responsible, and caring can help us make good decisions about when it's important to take a stand and how best to do so, as well as help us to remain patient and hopeful.

We can expect some non-believers to scoff at the teachings of Christianity as farfetched notions that perhaps sound good but can never be proven. Don't be discouraged – scoffing has been around since the beginning! Everyone must be shown the spiritual way toward God, but not everyone will choose to follow it. Our task as Christians is to live our lives in a way that shows the strength of the Spirit within each of us and to keep trying to show the way to others, despite the many obstacles in our path. In doing so, we will provide the best possible evidence of God's existence. Just as the physical body shows the existence of the mind that gives order to its movements, we, as the Body of Christ show His existence as the Head when we (by faith) allow ourselves to be guided by Him. The proof of God's existence is the manifestation of all things good by the natural response to faith.

Because the Church serves as the Body of Christ as well as being instrumental in providing inspiration, it is important for believers to be affiliated with their own church community or religious-based group. Where else can they go to find wise people who share their religious convictions? If your family lives a long way off, where else can you go to find caring others who will help with thoughts,

---

[2] Proverbs 13:20

prayers, and other forms of assistance at a moment's notice? It is the church community that provides the greatest opportunities for that sense of belonging and security that we all long for. By bringing others into that community, we can help them to achieve the same sense of belonging and begin to overcome differences that are ultimately superficial.

> *Then said they unto him, Where is thy Father? Jesus answered, Ye neither know me, nor my Father: if ye had known me, ye should have known my Father also.*
> John 8:19

This book emphasizes every person's need for a personal relationship with God based on faith. In order to know God the Father, one must first know the Son. When we discover our purpose in God, we become increasingly capable of understanding life issues from the perspective of God's Truth. This enables us to distinguish true strength from true weakness, both in ourselves and in others.

Reflect on the parent-child relationship: The parent knows what's best for the child. Often the child has no idea that the parent is consistently trying to help (directly or indirectly) save the child from his or her own actions. In his immaturity, the child will be easily influenced by what the world offers, pressures and enticements that fill the child with a false sense of identity, a false sense of security, a false sense of expectation for self and others, and thus, a false sense of reality with respect to what is truly good.

Children often resist parents' interference with these influences, but typically come to appreciate what their parents have done as they grow into adults.

> *And said, Verily I say unto you, Except ye be converted, and become as little children, ye shall not enter into the kingdom of heaven.*
> Jesus, Matthew 18:3

Similarly, we can hope that every physical and spiritual child will one day realize the tremendous efforts God (the believer's Father) makes to instruct us and keep us from danger. While God loves all human beings and has been encouraging each of us to respond to His call, His appeal, and His blessings ever since the beginning, not everyone will respond to Him in faith. Instead, many will choose to perish rather than to be born (again) into life. While fear of their ultimate fate can motivate people to turn toward Him, those who do so will ultimately come to understand that a precious union with God can be achieved out of love for God, not simply out of fear. Because non-believers risk the eternal loss of God's gracious gift of salvation, God desires strong believers of "sound mind"[3] to help awaken others from their unconscious state. The inward strength of believers is greater than any force in the physical realm. Those who persecute others may appear to be strong, but inwardly they are weak; only those who are inwardly strong are indeed capable of turning the other cheek.

As the strong begin to awaken more and more people to realize the majesty of God's love and grace, and to see Him as the higher authority, the differences that now divide us will come to seem trivial, and ultimately there will be greater commonality among the diverse.

---

[3] 1 Timothy 1:7

III. Defining Parts of a Whole

I begin by discussing selected parts of understanding (as driven either by common knowledge or by inspiration) in order to provide an account of the greater whole of human understanding. "Solidus" – the name of this book – is derived from a mathematical fraction slash (/) representing the sum of parts equal to the whole (as in 4/4=1). In this section, I will lay the groundwork for a new model of understanding human relationships by first identifying the parts and then showing how they fit together in the model.

A. Exploring Common Knowledge

1. Understanding

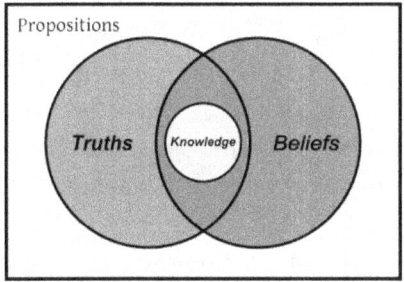

Figure 1

The traditional model of the relationship among truths, beliefs, and knowledge is shown in Figure 1. This model suggests that knowledge requires the intersection of two major categories: Truths and Beliefs. It shows that there are *truths* we don't believe (truths outside the belief circle) and *beliefs* that are not true (beliefs outside the truth circle). True beliefs – as validated between Truths and Beliefs – are in the area where the two large circles overlap, thus forming knowledge (an area regarded as integrated).

This model represents the relationship among the concepts, but does not address how we acquire knowledge. In this chapter, I will introduce a model of how we acquire knowledge through the mind's ability to apprehend ideas both objectively and subjectively using two independent forms of human understanding.

In order to arrive at a more broad and yet rational concept of how we arrive at knowledge, we must add the element of Purpose – that is, the orientation of the purpose-driven individual with respect to God – to the model. So we move from a two-part model to a three-part model, or the Solidus model (shown in Figure 2). To be able to wrap our minds around the concept of "integrated" Knowledge, we must first appreciate that there are two forms of "truth" that we routinely negotiate in the mind when reasoning. The thought process goes something like this: What one knows to be true in the objective sense is a *fact*, and what one knows to be true in the subjective sense is a *truth*.

Notice how one can ultimately *know* both forms of truth. When one does become knowing in the broadest sense, then it is said that he or she has "true beliefs." Since two forms of truth forming knowledge are what give rise to true beliefs, then for purposes of illustration and discussion we will focus on *facts* according to Logic (e.g., what appears in reality as "true"); and *truths* according to the Intuitive (e.g., the unseen of influential or spiritual "truths").

So we transition from a two-part Propositions Model involving "Truths and Beliefs" to a three-part Solidus model involving "Facts and Truths." Between the two models, notice the placement of the term Truths. The two-part model regards Truths more objectively, while the three-part model will regard Truths more subjectively.

Without appreciating the significance of the objective and the subjective of "truths" (generally-speaking), one may easily become overly influenced by the realities of this world deemed true, factual, and physically apparent. In other words, while thinking of truth as fact-based does seem most logical, it can end up hindering the mind from accepting the influences of unseen truths – those "truths" that counterbalance Logic with the Intuitive.

When Purpose is directed upward toward God we will refer to the model as a Northward Model of Human Understanding and Human Devotion (HUHD) (see Figure 2); and when Purpose is directed downward we will refer to it as a Southward HUHD Model (as later discussed).

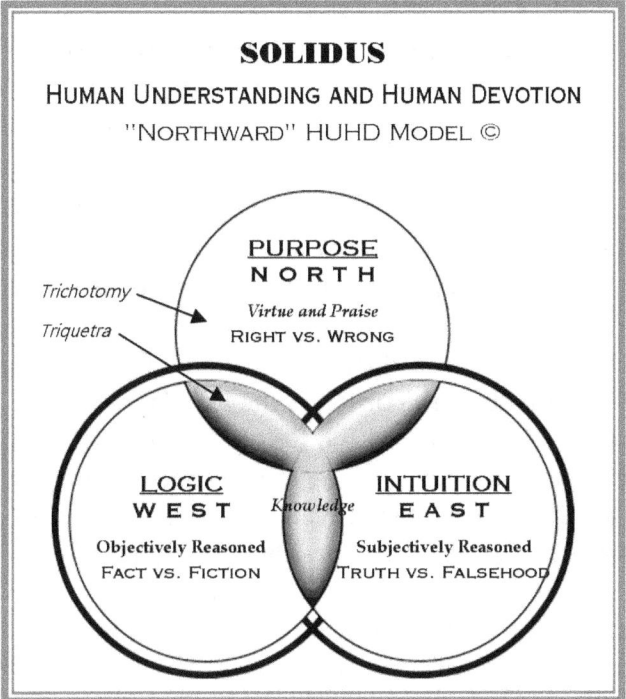

Figure 2

Note: A *trichotomy* inherently contains a *triquetra* – mathematically speaking and relevant to this discussion, it is action (represented by the "heart-shaped" triquetra) that is a derivative of thought (represented by the trichotomy). As the mind thinks thus the body moves.

The Purpose element contains the qualities of virtue and praise (as first induced by faith in God), which look above the human plane to higher aspirations and a higher authority. From Northward Purpose derive principles, morals, and ethics, each realized by righteousness gained from the upward Purpose element. If one's Purpose is directed upward toward God, then a triquetra is formed representing one's heart; if Purpose is directed downward to the plane of human beings or even further below, then an upside-down heart is formed. Generally speaking, if one's Purpose is not centered Northward (toward God), then it will be centered Southward on self.

2. Brain Function: Perspective

Perspective is very important in this model. Broadly speaking, there are two main thought perspectives: Western and Eastern.

Some may think: Since this discussion will be about brain function why replace conventional terms like *left-brained* and *right-brained* with unconventional terms of *Western* and *Eastern*, respectively? There are a few reasons for this.

Let's start with this: Just like viewing a map, most persons will understand that the left portion of the map is toward the West while the right portion is toward the East. What if, though, the reader of the map—a passenger in, let's say, a motor home, rotating on a swivel chair—says to the driver: "The lake is toward the right." Without any gestures by the passenger, will the driver know which way to turn? No. In and of themselves terms *left* and *right* are insufficient descriptions of coordinates and direction, particularly when matters of orientation and perspective are important.

This is even the case with linguistics (e.g., the study of human language). In an article called *Does Your Language Shape How You Think?*[4], Guy Deutscher writes:

> Some 50 years ago, the renowned linguist Roman Jakobson pointed out a crucial fact about differences between languages in a pithy maxim: "Languages differ essentially in what they *must* convey and not in what they *may* convey." This maxim offers us the key to unlocking the real force of the mother tongue: if different languages influence our minds in different ways, this is not because of what our language *allows* us to think but rather because of what it habitually *obliges* us to think about.

Deutscher, an Israeli linguist, uses these statements as the basis for various discussions about how one's mother tongue ultimately shapes his or her thinking. One such discussion deals with

---

[4] Deutscher, Guy. (2010, August 26). Does Your Language Shape How You Think? *The New York Times*. Retrieved July 3, 2013, from http://www.nytimes.com

orientation. He suggests that there are two ways humans can describe the same route or object position: (1) by *egocentric* means (e.g., left, right, front, and back) which depend much on one's oriented body; and (2) by *geographic* means (e.g., north, south, west, and east) which is a fixed coordinate system no matter what the individual's orientation.

While various languages, including English, do cater to both coordinate systems, some are more geographically based than others. Interestingly, Guugu Yimithirr, a language found in north Queensland Australia is said to utilize *only* geographic coordinates. "It has been estimated that as much as 1 word in 10 in a normal Guugu Yimithirr conversation is 'north,' 'south,' 'west,' or 'east,' often accompanied with hand gestures," notes Deutscher. He also states: "Indeed, speakers of geographic languages seem to have an almost-superhuman sense of orientation."

Of course the labels *left-brained* and *right-brained* are in themselves fixed coordinates about the brain, but not the terms *left* and *right*. So even if left-brained and right-brained terms were used principally in our discussion, their employment would become problematic, particularly when attempting to integrate North and South coordinates as well. So the utilization of West and East as descriptions of brain function makes it easier to discuss and perceive orientation on a non-egocentric basis.

Recognize that the language of God as conveyed by the Holy Bible provides hundreds of geographic coordinates. These coordinates provide greater detail about the multitude of Biblical accounts. At this point it must be asked: When we read or hear Biblical stories like these, and then visualize them as big-picture accounts within the mind, what effect does this have on our innate sense of orientation? Throughout our discussion I hope to demonstrate how the Bible transforms the perception, awareness, and even consciousness of believers from the horizontal plane of human understandings into the vertical plane of divine understandings. In other words, with greater Biblical understandings, one's thinking and response is progressively raised from the cardinal earthly orientation and into the celestial divine orientation.

While Western and Eastern thought perspectives are negotiated within the "one mind" of one's brain, both sides of the mind will be regarded as interdependent in brain function. In essence, *logic or intellect* (e.g., the Western portion of mind) and *intuition* (the Eastern portion of mind) are mutually dependent outputs of brain function.

When reflecting on the model during our discussion, it will be easier to think of it from the perspective of one's own mindset, or the mindset of another when viewed from behind or even alongside. In this way the Western mind will consistently be on the left and Eastern mind will consistently be on the right. If, however, the person whose mindset is being viewed turns to face the reader, then clearly the Western mind of what is being viewed will be on the right side and the Eastern mind will be on the left side.

So while recognizing the importance of maintaining West-East perspective in alignment with one's mindset, let's turn our attention to brain function that gives rise to Western and Eastern thoughts and perspectives.

Functions of Human Cerebral Hemispheres:
Cerebral Hemispheres, Lateralization of Brain Function,
and The Human Brain

Table 1

Left Brain (Western Mind)	Right Brain (Eastern Mind)	Ref
Logical, intellectual	Intuitive	a,d
Verbal	Imagistic, visual, tactile, kinesthetic creative	a,d
Sequential, analytical, objective	Simultaneous, holistic, relational, subjective	a,d
Linear algorithmic processing	Holistical algorithmic processing	a
Language: grammar /words, pattern perception, literal	Language: intonation/emphasis, prosody, pragmatic, contextual	a
Mathematics (exact calculation, numerical comparison, estimation); left hemisphere only: direct fact retrieval	Mathematics (approximate calculation, numerical comparison, estimation)	b,c
Responds to logic	Responds to emotion	d
Responds to word meaning	Responds to word pitch, feeling	d
Recalls people's names	Recalls people's faces	d

$a^5\ b^6\ c^7\ d^8$

---

[5] Taylor, Insep, and Taylor, M. Martin (1990) "Psycholinguistics: Learning and using Language". p.367

[6] Dehaene S, Spelke E, Pinel P, Stanescu R, Tsivkin S. Sources of mathematical thinking: behavioral and brain-imaging evidence. Science. 1999 May 7;284(5416):970-4. PMID 10320379.

[7] Stanislas Dehaene, Manuela Piazza, Philippe Pinel, and Laurent Cohen. Three parietal circuits for number processing. Cognitive Neuropsychology, 20:487-506

[8] The Human Brain: The Left and Right Brains. Wright State University. Retrieved on 2008-09-30.
<http://www.wright.edu/academics/honors/institute/brain/leftright.html>

The thought process of the Western mind appears to be more analytical or linear whereas the thought process of the Eastern mind is more relation-based or holistic. The Western mind or *Logic* attempts to understand the parts, while the Eastern mind or *Intuition* attempts to understand the whole. The two sides of mind must integrate or work together to arrive at Knowledge.

The side of Logic distinguishes fact from fiction through objective, deductive reasoning, examining the soundness of premises and the logic of arguments. This requires critical thinking skills, which appeal to those who are more logically inclined. Conversely, the side of Intuition distinguishes truth from falsehood on a subjective, inductive basis. This requires creative thinking skills, which appeal to those who are more intuitively inclined. We will see later that facts and truths are the domain of those who are Knowing, while those who possess fiction and falsehood are Unknowing.

The more notable scientific breakthroughs in history began with holistic imagining or wondering (asking questions such as "what if?" or "why?"), and the hypotheses thus generated were then linearly proven (or disproven) by experimenting with the parts. In a sense, the efforts of the West realize the efforts of the East, thus substantiating facts and truths.

> *But as for me, I will walk in mine integrity:*
> *redeem me, and be merciful unto me.*
> Psalm 26:11

> *He layeth up sound wisdom for the righteous:*
> *[he is] a buckler to them that walk uprightly.*
> Proverbs 2:7

I will use the words *soundness* and *integrity* from time to time to represent wholeness or uprightness of one's understanding (thoughts) or one's walk (action or behavior). We will consider that a person possesses a sound mind when he or she knows facts and truths about the multitude of issues that affect the human condition. With a sound mind one is better capable of making reliable decisions. With an unsound mind the individual will more easily accept fiction and falsehood. Since the body moves according to the decisions of the mind, the integrity of one's walk is critically dependent on the soundness of his or her mind. We do well to remember that the quantity of knowledge is less important than its quality.

3. Laterality: East & West, Left & Right

Let's add another dimension to the discussion of thought and action: laterality. Laterality refers to preference for one side of the body over another and the fact that each side is controlled by the opposite side of the brain (i.e., the right hemisphere controls the left side of the body and vice versa).

> *A wise man's heart [is] at his right hand; but a fool's heart at his left. Yea also, when he that is a fool walketh by the way, his wisdom faileth [him], and he saith to every one [that] he [is] a fool.*
> Ecclesiastes 10:2-3

Scriptural passages that compare one hand to another are certainly interesting clues to what is viewed as good or bad, but there may be more to these passages than meets the eye. Jesus makes a similar statement in Matthew 25:31-46 when He proclaims that the sheep on His right hand are righteous and welcomed into everlasting life whereas the goats on the left are rejected from the kingdom.

Keep in mind that those for whom the Western mind (Logic) is dominant will be more naturally proficient in using the right side of the body, whereas those for whom the Eastern mind (Intuition) is dominant will be more naturally proficient in using the left side of the body. The passage above certainly places the good on the right and the bad on the left, but no one can know the true motivations of another person simply by observing whether he or she is left- or right-handed. More on this later, but for now, let's say that one's motivations and intentions are revealed only by the natural expression of thoughts in words or actions.

The Christ Pantocrator[9] image (see Figure 3)[10] produced some time between the 6th and 7th centuries is located at Saint Catherine's Monastery on Mt. Sinai. Recall the issue of perspective: While the Solidus model and overall discussion cater to one's own West-East perspective, this image of Jesus faces the audience, so that His Eastern mind is toward the left side of the page as His Western mind is toward the right side of the page. For the sake of maintaining perspective, take a moment to imagine going around to the back side of the image of Christ, so as to think of one's self following Jesus.[11]

After reflecting on this, let's now come back around to view the front side of the image for discussion purposes.

This image is a fine example of inspirational art relevant to this study. There are other Christ Pantocrator images, but this image shows lateralization in a way that most others do not. For instance, the left side of Christ's body appears dominant in the image. His left eye, with its raised eyebrow, appears dominant, and the whole left side of His presence appears to be raised, full, and confident.

Figure 3

---

[9] Pantocrator is defined as: almighty ruler. pantocrator. Webster's Third New International Dictionary, Unabridged. Merriam-Webster, 2002. http://unabridged.merriam-webster.com (1 Nov. 2009).
[10] Image found at: Christ Pantocrator. In *Wikipedia, the free encyclopedia*. Retrieved April 30, 2009, from http://en.wikipedia.org/wiki/Christ_Pantocrator
[11] Matthew 16:24

Further, the Christ Pantocrator image appears to embody characteristics of a balance scale, such as that shown in Figure 4. Christ is shown as strong, with a physical presence that is indicative of a certain strength of mind – in this case, the Eastern mind, the side of Intuition. Thus, Jesus' faith, originating from the Eastern mind, becomes evident in his actions, moving from the Word as written on one hand and into the Word as revealed (with the act of blessing) on the other hand.

Figure 4

Gather not my soul with sinners, nor my life with bloody men:
In whose hands [is] mischief,
and their right hand is full of bribes.
Psalm 26:9-10

This passage from Psalms substantiates the idea that not everyone who is right-handed is good, and correspondingly, we may assume that not everyone who is left-handed is bad. So what is the link between the two passages above and the Christ Pantocrator image? Most Christian theologians would agree that righteousness is dependent upon one's response in faith in God and is not a result of handedness. Left-right comparisons in the Bible do not indicate that one physical side is holier than the other, but rather help explain the relationship between thought and action.

The thought-action process itself can be expressed in terms of handedness. Based on science we have a better understanding that actions by the left physical side are predominately driven by the right brain or Eastern mind, whereas actions by the right physical side are predominately driven by the left brain or Western mind: hence, lateralization. If holistic notions begin in the Eastern mind and such notions are then linearized by the Western mind, then one has effectively developed understandings forming Knowledge. Passages that suggest that *righteousness* is associated with the right hand therefore imply that proper *action* responses are the result of such integrated understandings.

All life issues (not only issues of faith) need to be understood, considered, and then decided. If one's thought-process relies chiefly on holistically/intuitively believing or disbelieving, then one is not exercising logic in order to make better sense of such matters.

To linearize issues of faith, though, is not a matter of blending the subjective of truth with the objective of facts—this would be similar to intellectualizing faith. Rather it is to increase the depth of one's understanding of Biblical Truth in order to draw from Truth to make sense of reality.

God has gifted mankind with two hemispheres of the brain (West and East) so that our understanding of objective facts and subjective truths—as derived from independent objective and subjective reasoning processes—can result in a walk of integrity.

As we gain knowledge from understandings that integrate Western and Eastern thought processes, the wisdom and grace of God can more easily develop within us. Think about how understandings today are derived more from taking a stance against another; that is, West vs. East or Left vs. Right in philosophies, ideologies, and religions. Each group suggests that it has a superior message while denigrating the other. Left vs. Right (horizontal) views like these have only caused divisiveness and even war. While each side devises ways to enhance its own image, the true enemy continues to advance in those who remain unaware. While most humans think of themselves as being aware in the physical sense, many continue to be unaware in the spiritual sense. To be made aware in the spiritual sense so that there is less divisiveness in the physical sense, humans must become responsive to God. When we don't incorporate both objective and subjective reasoning into our views, facts and truths become blended and obscured.

Let's examine the laterality issue in the differences between Western and Eastern Christian persuasions.

Basic Comparison of Christian Reasoning

Table 2

West-Dominant	East-Dominant
The side of Justice as more notably conveyed by the Father.	The side of Mercy as more notably conveyed and exemplified by the Son.
West-dominant people have a natural tendency to reason objectively; most will interpret Scriptural meaning in more literal or exacting thoughts and ways; the more West-dominant the more quick to dismiss holistic East.	East-dominant people have a natural tendency to reason subjectively; most will interpret Scriptural meaning in more figurative or symbolic thoughts and ways; the more East-dominant the more quick to dismiss linear West.
West-dominant people may decide to increase merciful understandings from the East as driven by Truths in order to balance their foundation.	East-dominant people may decide to increase just understandings from the West as driven by Facts in order to balance their foundation.

This table assumes there are two distinct mind-sets to compare and contrast; that is, a West-dominant and an East-dominant, each aspiring toward God from its own perspective. While each side has unique strengths, one without the other causes an imbalance. The ultimate goal is equilibrium between both sides, so that one's foundation is level and his or her path is made straight.

Take my yoke upon you, and learn of me; for I am meek and lowly in heart: and ye shall find rest unto your souls.
Jesus, Matthew 11:29

As it applies to the issues of equilibrium or balance, let's consider how the term *yoke*[12] applies while reflecting on the following definition:

---

[12] yoke. (2009). In Merriam-Webster Online Dictionary. Retrieved May 4, 2009, from http://www.merriam-webster.com/dictionary/yoke

1 a: a wooden bar or frame by which two draft animals (as oxen) are joined at the heads or necks for working together b: an arched device formerly laid on the neck of a defeated person c: a frame fitted to a person's shoulders to carry a load in two equal portions d: a bar by which the end of the tongue of a wagon or carriage is suspended from the collars of the harness

West-dominant people become yoked into a Northward progression only after accepting merciful Christ as Lord and Savior. Getting to that point, though, may be a challenge because West-dominant people are less capable than the East-dominant when reasoning out why faith in God makes sense. Many West-dominants have the tendency to over-intellectualize religion, perhaps even needing proof of God's existence before steps are taken.

East-dominants will more readily accept merciful Christ because they have natural affinity with such emotional, subjective thinking; however, they will have a certain imbalance because they are often hesitant (or perhaps resistant) to objectively applying their understanding of faith into action. This is due in part to their thinking that objective reasoning and response of religious matters is performance-driven. East-dominants may therefore be inclined to distance themselves from those who are more religiously objective, whereas West-dominants will distance themselves from those who are more religiously subjective.

Even though both West and East approach God prayerfully and with sincerity, instead of becoming yoked together, many decide to step away and even reject the functional qualities of the other side. Again, though some groups within the Church are distinctly West-dominant or East-dominant, many individual Christians and collaborative groups are well-balanced between objective and subjective modes of reasoning regarding Christian matters and life issues.

In the Christ Pantocrator image, Jesus is shown to be East-dominant with left-side physical strengths. For some this may contradict our discussion on one's becoming balanced between Eastern and Western mind. Before reaching this conclusion, however, reflect on the overarching implication of this image.

Defining Parts of a Whole

Even the righteousness of God [which is] by faith of Jesus Christ unto all and upon all them that believe: for there is no difference: For all have sinned, and come short of the glory of God; Being justified freely by his grace through the redemption that is in Christ Jesus:
Romans 3:22-24

In order to believe in Christ Jesus one must choose to have faith in Him. In essence, He becomes the object of faith so that by faith human intellect (West) becomes yoked with and responsive to the intuitive of Christ (East).

Thus, the Christ Pantocrator image does not simply demonstrate the strength of faith that Christ possessed, it also demonstrates that He is a source of strength for those who have faith in Him. This strength was a quality that Jesus undoubtedly had and wanted future believers to possess as well.

As long as we can avoid the trap of overly intellectual or purely intuitive thinking, each of which runs counter to God's message of love, wisdom, and grace, aligning oneself Northward may simply be a matter of choosing to balance the foundation after accepting God as the higher, divine authority. Both sides—West and East yoked together—are necessary for proper balance[13] and spiritual growth. Once the two are yoked, we can increasingly know God in the truest sense.

4. Id, Ego, Super-Ego: North & South

Now that we have laid the groundwork for the mind's West-East relationship, let's incorporate some North-South dynamics. Sigmund Freud's model of the human psyche has three parts: Id, Ego, and Super-Ego (see Figure 5)[14]. Keep in mind that these labels represent functions of the mind, not parts of the brain.

---

[13] Job 31:6
[14] Image found in the article: Freud's Structural and Topographical Models of Personality. Retrieved December 26, 2009, from http://allpsych.com/psychology101/ego.html

Id: In layman's terms the instinctive id seeks physical gratification that begins with satisfying basic drives such as for water, food, sex, etc. The id is illogical, amoral, and egocentric. It contains the libido, and without another force to counter its impulses, the id will persistently seek pleasure and gratification at all costs.

Ego: Above the id is the ego, which is associated with the normal cognitive processes of the brain. The ego thinks, reasons, and remembers. Since it also attempts to make sense of the real world, the ego is where the mind's conscious awareness is found. Much of our behavior is the result of deliberations by the ego.

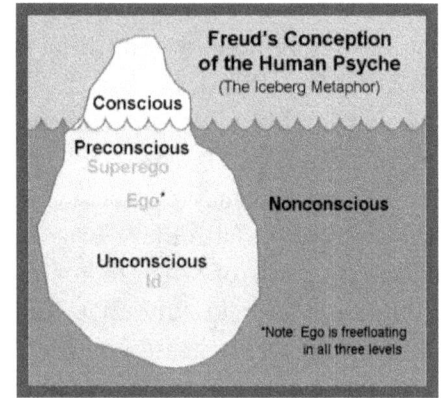

Figure 5

Super-ego: Finally, the super-ego is the moral and critical function of mind, with goals and aspirations that are of higher consciousness.

In general, the id and super-ego have entirely opposing roles. In everyday decisions each will have an influence on how the ego decides. For example, because the id responds to basic drives, it will urge us to eat the most gratifying kinds of food whenever we are hungry. The super-ego will remind us of other considerations: we need to think about our health, consider the needs of others, and weigh the importance of eating at any particular moment against other things we have to take care of. The ego makes the decision about how to balance these two influences. Keep in mind that it is also the ego's job to consider the influences of the outside world when making decisions. We established above that the West and East functions of mind reason together to form Knowledge. As discussed earlier, the third intangible element, called Purpose, is positioned above or below the West-East hemispheres.

Defining Parts of a Whole

> *For to be carnally minded [is] death; but to be spiritually minded [is] life and peace. Because the carnal mind [is] enmity against God: for it is not subject to the law of God, neither indeed can be.*
>
> Romans 8:6-7

Let's examine the overlap between our discussion and Freud's three parts of the human psyche. Some important concepts of Freud's views include: (1) the id is regarded as amoral and egocentric; hence, "carnally-minded" as explained in Romans above; (2) the super-ego reflects spiritual goals and provides a sense of morality; (3) the id and the super-ego are opposed to each other; and (4) the ego attempts to strike a balance between the two vertical extremes while also having to negotiate the influences of the external world.

In our Solidus model, the vertical element of Purpose may pull either Northward (toward God) or Southward (away from God) depending on many factors. The cumulative effect of pull in one direction or the other leads to either the arisen state or the fallen state. For instance, if Purpose is directed Northward, the mind (through the ego) is attempting to advance the super-ego (arising), but only if the ego is capable of resisting the impulses of the id (recall that the id also contains the libido). Keep in mind, though, Northward Purpose first requires a conscious decision to respond to God in faith.

By contrast, Southward Purpose (falling) requires little or no conscious decision because if the ego does not resist, the id will easily lead it to pursue basic gratifications. The more the id is strengthened, the more easily the ego will comply with its will. If the ego's job of mediating between the id and super-ego wasn't hard enough, consider how difficult it must be for it to handle the influences of the outside world as well. The ego's job becomes particularly burdensome when individuals decide to place themselves in situations that are id-driven and conducive to future sin. As more sins are committed, the id becomes even stronger, further diminishing the role of the super-ego.

One with Southward Purpose may (unconsciously) give more time and attention to the id, but the id itself does not become the element of Purpose. The mind with Southward Purpose will seek out ways to satisfy the id, though, increasing its sway over the individual's behavior.

B. Exploring the Bible in Brief

> *All scripture [is] given by inspiration of God,*
> *and [is] profitable for doctrine, for reproof, for correction,*
> *for instruction in righteousness: That the man of God may be*
> *perfect, throughly furnished unto all good works.*
> 2 Timothy 3:16-17

There are dozens of English translations of the Bible to choose from.[15] While there are various reasons for referring to one translation over another, the passages cited in this book are drawn only from the King James Version (KJV). A literal translation like the KJV is necessary because it is a sound basis to draw from when discussing the realities of life relative to Biblical Truth.

The various translations of the Bible serve different purposes. While it would be convenient to have one translation that suits all purposes, all levels of spiritual growth, and all denominations, there is an inherent disparity in how scripture is absorbed between those who reason more objectively and those who reason more subjectively. The rationale for this contention will follow, but for now, let's say that those who reason objectively will naturally seek word-for-word translations, while those who reason subjectively will seek thought-for-thought translations (or even paraphrases).

The Holy Bible is premised on true inspiration that makes all other forms of truth pale, and is thus trustworthy and authoritative.[16] On the subject of versions, the New Revised Standard (NRS) is known to have "wide acclaim and broad support from academics and church leaders as a Bible for all Christians."[17] This may be due

---

[15] Best Known Translations (n.d.). Retrieved March 14, 2009, from http://biblestudy.crosswalk.com/bibles/

[16] GotQuestions.org. (n.d.). *Does the inerrancy of the Bible only apply to the original manuscripts?* Retrieved May 6, 2009, from http://www.gotquestions.org/Bible-inerrancy.html

[17] New Revised Standard (NRS) (n.d.). Retrieved November 25, 2009, from http://biblestudy.crosswalk.com/bibles/translation/new-revised-standard/nrs/

(in part) to the fact that the NRS offers a balance between word-for-word and thought-for-thought translation. For our purposes it was important to cite passages from a reliable word-for-word translation like the KJV.

> *Buy the truth, and sell [it] not; [also] wisdom,*
> *and instruction, and understanding.*
> Proverbs 23:23

The above passage may be taken one of two ways: (1) do not attempt to profit from what is known to be good; or (2) do not sell off (and thus lose) anything you have that contains known good. Men have written countless books about God as they understood and/or experienced Him. I hope this book will also help believers in the edification process.

1. Great Commandment

> *Jesus said unto him, Thou shalt love the Lord thy God with all*
> *thy heart, and with all thy soul, and with all thy mind. This is*
> *the first and great commandment. And the second [is] like*
> *unto it, Thou shalt love thy neighbour as thyself. On these two*
> *commandments hang all the law and the prophets.*
> Jesus, Matthew 22:37-40

These words of Jesus make it clear how believers should interpret their relationship with God and others. In the passage, Jesus identifies two commandments in order of importance, as He responds to the question: "Master, which [is] the great commandment in the law?"[18] Jesus instructs His followers (believers) first and foremost to love God, and to do so with all their heart, soul, and mind. Notice that he places the heart first. The passage also identifies a second commandment, "Love thy neighbor as thyself," which we will discuss later.

---

[18] Matthew 22:36

a. Grace and Truth

Everything else, including the laws of Moses and the words of the prophets, is secondary to these two commandments, as John states:

> *For the law was given by Moses,*
> *[but] grace and truth came by Jesus Christ.*
> John 1:17

This is important because many non-Christians believe that subjecting themselves to the law and the prophets is sufficient to demonstrate their allegiance to God and others. Many others believe that simply conforming to the laws of man is enough to make them good. The laws of man and the words of prophets may be good, but it's likely that some of them are bad. Believers in Christ Jesus know the Truth and can easily see whether movements provoked by certain laws and prophets are leading humanity toward God or away from God. Believers should not evaluate themselves on the basis of the judgment of other persons on their works or actions. Such judgments may easily be wrong and in extreme cases, can lead to oppression and tyranny.

> *Knowing that a man is not justified by the works of the law,*
> *but by the faith of Jesus Christ, even we have believed in*
> *Jesus Christ, that we might be justified by the faith of Christ,*
> *and not by the works of the law:*
> *for by the works of the law shall no flesh be justified.*
> Galatians 2:16

Each believer's personal relationship with God is unique and does not require works (good deeds) as such. Instead, what is required foremost is that we love God. Our love for Him and for others will lead us to perform good deeds. All we need to do is to become more responsive to Him by faith.[19]

If you go about doing what you see as good for others without first having faith in God, you may easily be doing those works for

---

[19] Romans 3:20-26, Galatians 5:4, Titus 3:7

reasons other than love for God. You may be trying to curry favor with God, to impress other people, or to gain some earthly reward such as praise or recognition. Depending on the motivation and persistence in doing such things, this may be an indication of Southward Purpose, centered on the self.

In society as a whole, where the commitment to love God first does not predominate, the lawless grow in number and are strengthened; where that commitment does predominate, the lawful grow in number and are strengthened. It would be ridiculous to suggest that human laws be banned. But compliance with human laws is no part of the basis for judging whether a person loves God or has a deepening relationship with Him. This is because as the love for God predominates one's mind, there is a natural desire to comply with His Law, a Law that, in terms of goodness, trumps all laws imposed by man. For those who choose not to believe in God, or even for believers who have strayed, human laws are necessary in order to maintain some level of civility.

He that loveth father or mother more than me is not worthy of me: and he that loveth son or daughter more than me is not worthy of me.
Jesus, Matthew 10:37

Legalism: Over the centuries much religious and philosophical thought has been linearized from the East into the West in the form of legalistic prescriptions; that is, one is required to do this or not to do that to conform to human expectations, or, worse, in an attempt to earn God's approval and resulting salvation. Natural, loving conformity among believers grows out of a God-first approach, not a neighbor-first approach or family-first approach. Loving others is certainly important—and in fact is essential to progressing Northward in spiritual growth and maturity—but the type of true love Jesus was talking about comes only after a God-first relationship.

SOLIDUS

*For kings, and [for] all that are in authority; that we may
lead a quiet and peaceable life in all godliness and honesty.*
1 Timothy 2:2

Reflect on what happened to Jesus, the Apostles, and countless other prophets and saints who said and did things because of their love for God first. History has shown that leaders of State and even of Church—particularly in the larger institutions—are easily threatened by those who move according to the will of One greater than any ruler on earth. In nearly every case of persecution and martyrdom, the one martyred was perceived as a threat to an earthly power because of his or her expression of love, freedom, and liberty – expressions that (seemingly) challenged prevailing earthly authorities. So this sort of walk would be a threat to any leader who elevated him- or herself to the point of encouraging (or even demanding) the submission of others – such elevations of power are the result of man's laws apart from God's Law. This is called oppression, and those who oppress (sometimes unconsciously) loathe democracy, freedom, and liberty among citizens. This is not to suggest that all leaders are oppressive, but rather that those leaders who are not rightly Purposed in God have a propensity to become oppressive.

Such oppressive schemes serve to further empower the leadership of institutions while effectively impeding each individual's direct pursuit of a path toward God.

*They profess that they know God;
but in works they deny [him], being abominable,
and disobedient, and unto every good work reprobate.*
Titus 1:16

It is easy to understand why oppressive leaders of the State and the Church (among virtually all religions throughout history) have used performance not only as a basis for inclusion or exclusion, but also to identify those persons who may pose a future threat to existing custom or tradition. For instance, because of Jesus' loving ways, which were unorthodox for that time period, He was not only rejected by His own, He was deemed a threat to institutions filled with elitists who were driven more by self-interest than by interest in

God. Although customs and traditions of God are very important, in many cases failure to follow such practices has paradoxically been used as a basis for eliminating the "threat" of those who exemplified true righteousness, a pure and intimate relationship with God. The most noteworthy victim of this kind was, of course, Jesus.

As it was in Jesus' day so it is today: Many are striving for more power, ostensibly on behalf of God. Churches and States of practically every stripe have attempted to increase their power. The power-hungry (past and present) have typically cited evidence of God's favor for them, instead of seeking to humble themselves before God in the eyes of citizens. This becomes particularly evident when God's name is invoked in promoting certain agendas or broadcasting propaganda to justify or excuse unethical or immoral behavior. Simply put, the power-driven will think of themselves as the center or hub by which any and all decisions become final without true consideration for God. Essentially, each one (unknowingly) attempts to become a power in his or her own right.

For the Son of man is not come to destroy men's lives, but to save [them]. And they went to another village.
Jesus, Luke 9:56

Sure, Jesus was a threat during His time on earth, but not an outward physical threat. One reason He walked this earth was so that God's children might be saved from oppression, and even from those who try to escape the consequences of their own actions by using others, particularly Christians, as scapegoats. While some believers may appear physically weak, each is in truth spiritually stronger than any oppressor on earth. The source of that strength is their affinity with Jesus: each is instilled with God's love, wisdom, and grace.

Jesus did not change the Law of Moses. Rather, He made love for God primary, thus encouraging believers to weigh for themselves truth vs. falsehood, fact vs. fiction, and right vs. wrong.

In our day the critical question becomes: Are laws and those regarded as prophets driven to unite people or to divide them? Simply put, if the basis for laws and prophets are not driven by the love for God, then they will consistently be driven by wrong reasoning. Only leaders who appreciate the truest forms of love, mercy, and justice will be more able to craft human laws that minimize the sorts of policy-making decisions that contradict God's Truth.

Sound leaders (those with God high in mind) are needed to make sound decisions on behalf of the people, not for reasons of self or for the sake of lobbyists and special interest groups. Without sound decision-makers running the country, laws are most likely to facilitate some forms of wrongdoing and to impede virtuous behavior, making the road toward God increasingly difficult for everyone.[20] Seeing so many people fall from grace will erode the hope and determination of individuals who were seeking God simply from the basis of free will, love, and peace.

It is Satan's objective for humanity to fall, and he works evil from all directions, using people of all cultures to perform his will. If Satan can cast enough doubt and create enough suspicion between people (as we see in our day), then he has not only scattered the individual sheep from the herd, he has effectively separated them from the Shepherd, so that more and more will become vulnerable to the wolf.[21]

There is no fear in love; but perfect love casteth out fear:
because fear hath torment.
He that feareth is not made perfect in love.
1 John 4:18

The ultimate goal for believers is to attain a loving and responsive approach toward God, which in the truest sense takes time and patience to appreciate. If you find yourself gripped by the fear of God, especially during a time of crisis, you may have yet to humble yourself before Him and allow His Spirit to become rooted within. When your godly response becomes increasingly instinctual, then you will find that our Father does lead his children safely through the most difficult of times.

The first step in drawing close to God is to recognize the Shepherd's call and respond to Him not simply in your thoughts but

---

[20] Mark 3:25
[21] John 10

also through actions that come from the heart. As we experience God's unmerited favor (Grace), we are enabled to offer that grace to others. Without God, no one can experience and then share the gift of grace.

b. Conceptualizing a Balance with Weights

We need follow only two commandments to gain happiness, health, prosperity, and eternal life. The Law of Moses (set forth in the first five books of the Bible) is certainly important, but if the believer first moves according to the love *for* God (following the example of Jesus), then the Law will naturally be fulfilled. In essence, the fulfillment of Law (as directly approached) has less to do with *logic* as West driven and more to do with the *intuitive* of faith as East driven. Thus Northward adoration for God means we need not strictly adhere to the Law of Moses and certainly not to the laws imposed by man.

With the two commandments – to love God and to love one's neighbor – Jesus relieved us from the absolute performance requirements of the Law: that is, the Law by which we are right with God. It satisfies God's demand for holiness by adhering to a host of requirements (e.g., thou shalt… and thou shalt not…). How do we know this? It's because the believer's adherence to God's Law is the natural effect of "its cause": the believer's love for God and for neighbor.

Although man-made laws are necessary where not everyone has achieved a state of grace, these laws can end up serving as instruments of oppression for society. How would we know the difference between good laws that (by their parts) align well with God's Law, and bad laws which (by their parts) oppress? It has much to do with how new legislative acts are justified.

As mentioned above, the believer's adherence to law is the effect of the cause: the love for God and for neighbor. While laws of man are typically enacted to discourage bad behavior in favor of good behavior, such laws do little to inspire goodness among mankind.

Recall the discussion in the Grace and Truth section above: humans are not made just by works, but by grace.[22] Since humans are not made just by works (i.e., adherence to human law does not cause goodness), why do legislators continue to push laws as the means to effectually achieve a social state of grace? It simply cannot be done! When laws are regarded or justified as the cause of good effects on earth, those laws are in fact bad. In other words, not only are such laws counter-productive to achieving liberty, they are firstly counter-intuitive to the natural human response to how (God's) grace is naturally achieved on earth, individually and collectively.

So whenever new laws are justified as mechanisms to cause humans to respond rightly, they are bad laws destined to become oppressive to society. They keep people in their place, which is usually a place of submission to the authorities and powers that be in the State and the Church.

It is true that we better know a person by his good works, but again the important point to make about good works is that they are the result of a personal relationship with God who saves us by His Grace. We cannot know the heart of another simply by handedness, by certain behavior, or by works (good deeds). Knowing the mind and heart of another person takes time and patience, particularly when we are determining someone's natural goodness. We may also need to consult other true believers on this question.

While many believers earnestly practice their faith through good works, some non-believers also do good deeds. But such deeds, inspired by the individual, cannot duplicate the truest form of love and grace that God instills in those who are in an intimate relationship with Him. In fact, such grace often reveals itself in unexpected ways.

The Northward HUHD Model accounts for both thought (which forms the soul or psyche) and action (which forms the heart). Together, soul and heart constitute the inward spirit. While performance issues are better understood on the horizontal plane – among humans – love is best understood on the vertical plane, in our relationship with God. Because of their faith-based Purpose in God

---

[22] Galatians 2:16

(or God-centeredness) believers are instilled with His Spirit so that each of His children may receive the gifts of love, wisdom, and grace. Principally driven by grace, the Spirit can be defined the same way as the Greek word *charis*:

> Good will, loving-kindness, favour: of the merciful kindness by which God, exerting his holy influence upon souls, turns them to Christ, keeps, strengthens, increases them in Christian faith, knowledge, affection, and kindles them to the exercise of the Christian virtues. [23]

These qualities come from above (certainly not from below) and we can see them in others who have Purpose in Him. Thus, if you want to possess the truest form of love, you must first develop a personal relationship with God in the vertical plane.

> *What? know ye not that your body is the temple of*
> *the Holy Ghost [which is] in you, which ye have of*
> *God, and ye are not your own? For ye are bought*
> *with a price: therefore glorify God in your body,*
> *and in your spirit, which are God's.*
> 1 Corinthians 6:19-20

Although Jesus included the mind in His list of what is important in the two commandments, it was third on the list. So let's think about heart and soul for a moment. Are these qualities tangible or intangible? Spiritual possessions are real but intangible. Mind function is certainly important in the formation of intangible heart and soul, but without God's influential Grace one will be incapable of creating Northward Purpose (now an intangible "temple"). If a believer has never been instilled (by Grace) with His Spirit, then how would he or she be truly capable of loving Him in reciprocating fashion with all thy heart, soul, and mind? Jesus exemplified true love while walking with Purpose. Thus, without any Purpose toward

---

[23] Blue Letter Bible. Dictionary and Word Search for charis (Strong's 5485). Blue Letter Bible. 1996-2009. 29 Oct 2009.
<http://www.blueletterbible.org/lang/lexicon/lexicon.cfm?strongs=G5485 >

God, possessing the purest forms of love, wisdom, and grace is simply impossible.

> *Wherefore also it is contained in the scripture,*
> *Behold, I lay in Sion a chief corner stone, elect, precious:*
> *and he that believeth on him shall not be confounded.*
> 1 Peter 2:6

With Jesus as the "chief corner stone" of faith, He becomes the cause of our reasoning and our actions. In other words, actions are the effect of the cause; these actions will be good because they are done out of love for God. Because of Jesus and His teaching, believers understand that following laws and prophets is not an end in itself but instead is subject to love. Before He came, the faithful directed their efforts into doing good works, and following the law and the prophets in order to win God's recognition and affection.

So as you can see there are two very different ways to reason and respond: one driven by the objective of doing good works as first purposed, and the other driven by love and grace that – by the believer's act in faith – result in good works. In essence, good works (e.g., works that are truly good and are thus, "of God") are the effect of one's natural response in faith (the cause).

Similar arguments can be made about those who respond by practice and/or by exercise. Relative to godliness, while the act of practice may be regarded as good or bad, the same goes for exercise. One can exercise in ways that lead toward God or away from Him.

Practice is typically regarded as following a set of rules or instructions, many times on a repeated basis, and during the process of demonstrating acts of perceptible goodness. Assuming one is motivated for all the right reasons, certain skills, abilities, and understandings will be gained during practice. There can also be a gaining in empathy as the result of one's experiences. While empathy is certainly good, part of the problem with practice – that is, practice despite exercise in the good sense – is that even many who lack faith want to be perceived as good, and will decide to practice good works when it seems advantageous to one's image.

Biblically-speaking, the act of exercise[24] is approached differently. This has more to do with meeting (on an ongoing basis) the new and typically unpredictable challenges of the day. In the good sense, exercise involves discernment, consciousness, and godliness as the believer becomes knowing and aware. During and after periods of training and strife, the understandings gained will extend far beyond that which can be learned by practice.

This issue will be discussed further in *The Response to Faith* section. For now, though, keep in mind that while practice is viewed as a direct approach toward achieving good works, the act of exercise necessitates God's influential Grace. By first appealing to the One who exercises His authority over His dominion, good works (the effect) are done according to one's natural and loving response to God (the cause).

> *[But] thou shalt have a perfect and just weight, a perfect and just measure shalt thou have: that thy days may be lengthened in the land which the LORD thy God giveth thee.*
> Deuteronomy 25:15

By His example, Jesus showed believers how to arise from the horizontal plane of humanity and into the vertical plane of divinity. The interrelationship between the tangible horizontal plane and the intangible vertical plane can be seen as an equal arm balance scale (see Figure 6) consisting of a center stand created by God's inward grace with the weights of mind hanging on each side. We can think of this image as analogous to a cross that intersects the mind. More broadly, we can think of it as representing the laterality of thought and action with arms and hands that extend beyond mind.

Figure 6

---

[24] Acts 24:16, Hebrews 5:14, 12:11, 1 Timothy 4:7-8

2. Important Terms to Know

This section introduces and explains terms that are important in the discussion that follows. For reference purposes, the terms are also listed in Tables – see Appendix A. These tables identify selected Strong's lexicon numbers associated with each term.

a. Purpose

> *Who, when he came, and had seen the grace of God,*
> *was glad, and exhorted them all,*
> *that with purpose^{G4286} of heart*
> *they would cleave unto the Lord.*
> Acts 11:23

Purpose transforms the horizontal plane of humanity/reality into the vertical plane of spirituality. Since Purpose is vertical, it may be directed either toward God or away from God and toward evil below. While Purpose can be seen as coming from the mind, it can more aptly be seen as coming from the heart in the New Testament (from the Greek word for heart, *prothesis*, as used in the Acts passage above).

b. Heart and Soul

> *Now set your heart^{H3824} and your soul^{H5315} to seek the LORD*
> *your God; arise therefore, and build ye the sanctuary of the*
> *LORD God, to bring the ark of the covenant of the LORD,*
> *and the holy vessels of God, into the house that is to be built*
> *to the name of the LORD.*
> 1 Chronicles 22:19

In reflecting on selected KJV passages in which *heart, soul,* and *mind* are used in combination, we can see how these terms can be better understood and incorporated into the model. The term *heart* is interesting because there are words of the same meaning that refer to understanding and wisdom, which are typically associated with the mind than with the heart. Without attempting to limit the meaning of heart and soul, we can say that the two words refer to different

Defining Parts of a Whole

functions of the same thing. So for discussion purposes, a person's heart and soul will be regarded as equivalent to wholeness of inward spirit. While the definition of the soul is broad and even includes characteristics of the (intangible) heart, the predominant meaning of soul appears to be more closely associated with the mind (a function of the tangible brain).

Similarly, each model group (a trichotomy forming soul and a triquetra forming heart) represents different functions within the same model. The soul is developed more from thought that opens itself to wisdom, whereas the heart is developed more from action (responsiveness) that opens itself to grace. In essence, soul and heart can both be accounted for by using one Northward HUHD Model.

At this point it is noteworthy to consider in Luke's passage above the statement that "with purpose of heart they would cleave unto the Lord.[25]" The term *cleave*[26] is defined as: "to adhere firmly and closely or loyally and unwaveringly." Therefore, it is from the soul (as first induced by mind-thought) that the heart is formed, so that with heart (e.g., mind-body responsiveness) one cleaves unto the Lord.

c. Faith and Believing

> *But without faith*[G4102] *[it is] impossible to please [him]:*
> *for he that cometh to God must believe that he is,*
> *and [that] he is a rewarder of them that diligently seek him.*
> Hebrews 11:6

In Jesus' two commandments, the terms *heart* and *soul* are most important; the mind is secondary. It is through the mind that we understand reality, though, and it is via the heart and soul (intangible spiritual qualities) that we transition from the horizontal into the vertical. Before one can develop these intangible qualities, one must first have faith in God. Having faith is essential for spiritual growth. Many believers consider biblical understandings to

---

[25] Acts 11:23
[26] cleave. (2009). In Merriam-Webster Online Dictionary. Retrieved May 11, 2009, from http://www.merriam-webster.com/dictionary/cleave

be the seeds that strengthen the soulful foundation. Our inward strength is increasingly realized when we move from simply having beliefs in God to knowing that good works are the result of our believing in Him. The term *believe* not only refers to an activity of the mind, it can also refer to bodily actions which flow from our convictions. Thus, it can be said that acting from faith is what binds believers with God. Given the water and light of God these seeds will sprout and become "rooted and grounded in love."[27]

The Holy Bible is regarded as a sound form of instruction for those who choose to grow in their faith of God, particularly in its revelation of the saving Grace of Jesus Christ. Thus, because of faith in Him we become more capable of responding according to the righteousness of God. It is important to remember that forming one's heart requires the element of Purpose. Here again, Purpose is not simply a mind-induced process, it advances Northward and is strong because of heart-inspired responsiveness.

> *That Christ may dwell in your hearts by faith[G4102]; that ye,*
> *being rooted and grounded in love, May be able to*
> *comprehend with all saints what [is] the breadth,*
> *and length, and depth, and height;*
> *And to know the love of Christ, which passeth knowledge,*
> *that ye might be filled with all the fulness of God.*
> Ephesians 3:17-19 (by Paul)

There are many ways in which one can carry out his or her understanding of faith in fruitful ways, but the principal way is walking with Northward Purpose as Jesus exemplified. Doing so involves how we think and move not only while inside the walls of the visible Church, but equally or even more importantly outside those walls. This daily exercise (heart-inspired devotion that further develops the conscious) leads us to become spiritually mature and even intuitively prayerful of the heart, and not simply prayerful with the mind. So as our faith becomes lovingly rooted, we grow to be more wise and refined by ways of grace. Thus, human

---

[27] Ephesians 3:17-19

understanding and human devotion toward God can again be represented with just one Northward HUHD Model.

So does walking with Northward Purpose mean that you have to live up to certain standards of excellence or be viewed as faultless or superior? Having a loving relationship with God (the cause) enables you to express God's love toward others (the effect). If you try to live up to certain standards without first knowing Him, then you are effectively attempting to go after the effect instead of the cause. As long as you do this, you will never rise and grow spiritually toward God. Again, we cleave unto the Lord using the heart first, then soul, and mind. Standards of behavior are mind-imposed, not heart-imposed. Since the heart and soul are intangible inner qualities and are the result of intangible Purpose, it is virtually impossible to know a person's heart simply by observing his or her adherence to codes of conduct or standards, even if many people consider the person to be faultless or superior. Walking with Northward Purpose is not a matter of compliance and conformity because (as explained earlier) adoration for God negates the significance of human law.

d. Objects of Knowing

My son, let not them depart from thine eyes: keep sound wisdom and discretion: So shall they be life unto thy soul, and grace to thy neck. Then shalt thou walk in thy way safely, and thy foot shall not stumble.
Proverbs 3:21-23

Though there is a certain affinity between the soul and the knowing mind, wisdom is more enriching. Wisdom is the central point of the trichotomy, while Grace is the central point of the triquetra (the intersection of the main parts of the model). Remember that before believers can exhibit grace they must first receive it from God, who fills each cup/vessel with His Spirit. Therefore, the central points for both model groups are represented by the same model position, thus forming wholeness of inward spirit.

One of the reasons why the objects of knowing are important is that knowledge, understanding, discretion, and wisdom are the reasons why believers strive to know. Without building faith in God one cannot become fully aware and upright, and thus cannot possess such objects in the truest sense. Thus, while the object of faith is God, the objects of knowing include God.

So as one becomes knowing—that is, as one gains understandings through integrated Western and Eastern thought processes—these other objects that help us to know will follow. One is more capable of making reliable decisions when knowledge is based on fact and truth. At the same time, if one is not purposed Northward the individual will not be so compelled to learn fact and truth – instead, he or she will more easily turn toward fictions and falsehoods that only play havoc to the reasoning process. As mentioned before, since action moves according to the will of thought, the integrity of one's walk depends heavily on his or her soundness of mind.

IV. Human Understanding and Devotion

This section is divided into two main parts: (1) the Basis for Solidus, and (2) the Applications of Solidus where it will be shown:

- Why the love of God for us and our love for God provide the means to become knowing and arise into consciousness;
- Why the appeal of modern media and entertainment is more threatening to one's soul and to democracy than most realize;
- Why there is more to the philosophical understandings of Conservatism and Liberalism than meet the eye;
- How the functions of Church and State can regrettably become united even in a democracy founded on separation; and
- How peace and harmony can be realized after becoming yoked into one Northward accord.

The HUHD Model provides a close examination of the human mind relative to Purpose; the Quadra-Circumplex Model provides a broader view that incorporates various mind-dominant positions; and the Stratum Model provides an even greater perspective so the reader may envision the two major planes (human-human and human-divine) that this model accounts for. If these names do not make complete sense right now, that's okay—they soon will, and so will the remaining discussion.

Important: Some readers may find the next section a challenge to follow along. The discussion involves the process of conceptualizing words describing human thought and behavior into a form that has vertical implications. If you find yourself having difficulty with this section then simply advance to the next section called the *Applications of Solidus* (page 105). The hope is that by realizing how much smoother the discussion does become then you will have a more determined interest in the *Basis for Solidus*.

A. Basis for Solidus

1. HUHD Model

The HUHD Model has two vertical directions: Northward and Southward. The reason one model represents two vertical directions is that these discussions represent one understanding of both forms. Thus, the terms Northward and Southward will be used to describe each respective direction.

Appendix B contains Tables for each of the label terms discussed in this section. The tables cite the Strong's concordance/lexicon numbers associated with each term.

a. Northward HUHD Model

In the previous chapter we laid the groundwork for understanding the Northward HUHD Model (see Figure 7). Let's start with some basic terminology used to describe the illustrations: elements, groups, and models. The Northward HUHD Model contains a trichotomy[28] above and the triquetra[29] below (or within) which are groups of this single Northward model. Within each group are elements that comprise the group. The upper group of the Northward model (the trichotomy) contains the elements of Logic, Intuition, and Purpose; the lower group (the triquetra) contains the elements of Knowledge, Justice, and Mercy.

---

[28] The *Trichotomy* represents *thought* as these labels will be discussed more in noun or adjective form reflective of what one possesses.

[29] The *Triquetra* represents *action* as these will not only be labeled in noun form, but also shown/discussed in verb form.

Human Understanding and Devotion   45

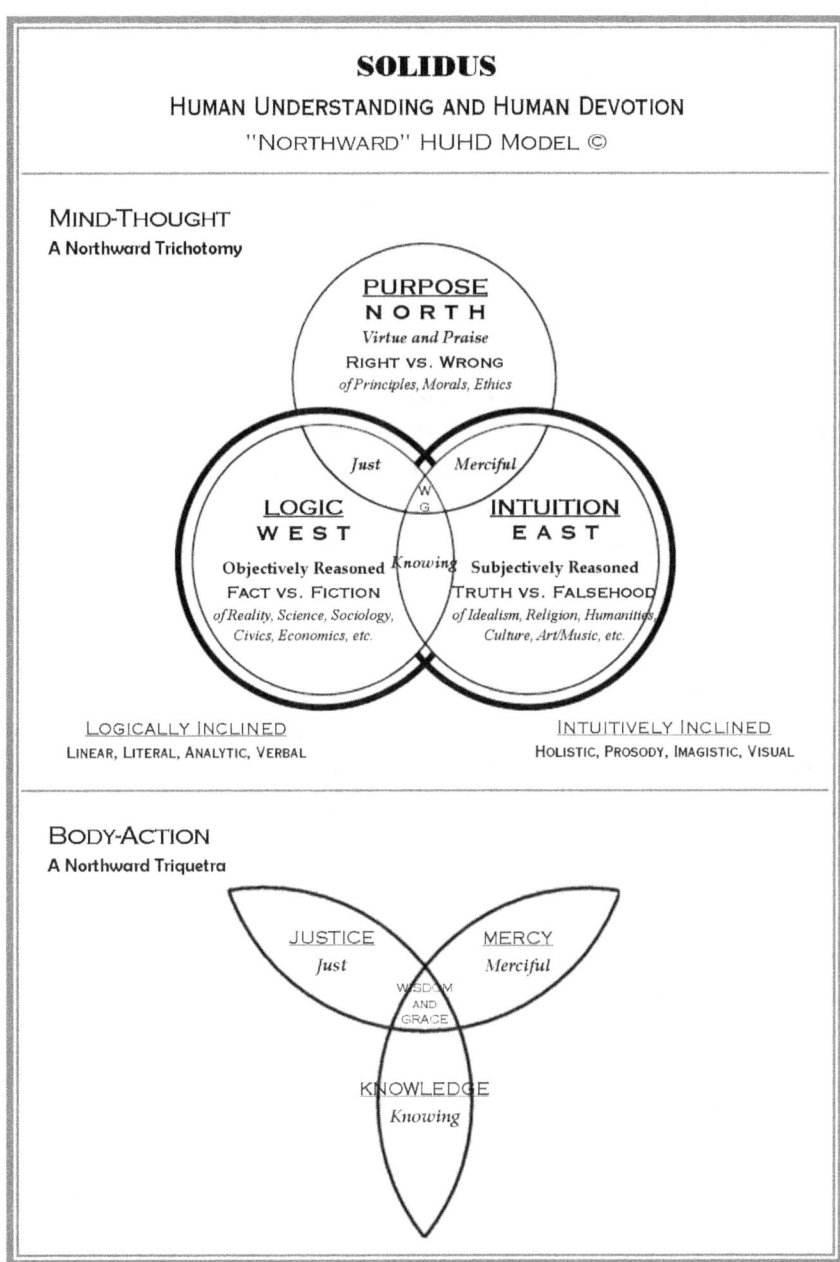

Figure 7

i. Trichotomy Group: With Northward Purpose, Human Understanding and Wisdom Are Increased

In whom also we have obtained an inheritance, being predestinated according to the purpose^{G4286} of him who worketh all things after the counsel of his own will: That we should be to the praise of his glory, who first trusted in Christ.
Ephesians 1:11-12

Three basic elements describe the trichotomy: Logic and Intuition, which exist in the horizontal plane of mind and Purpose, which projects vertically from this horizontal basis. Thicker circles represent the mind, since the brain itself may be described as tangible. And since there is a certain affinity between the mind and soul, within each thick circle there is a thin circle representing the soulful foundation as intangible. The element of Purpose will also be treated as intangible.

Logic is the mode of thought of the Western mind. Its function is to distinguish fact from fiction through objective reasoning. This requires critical thinking skills, which appeal to those who are more logically inclined. Counter to Logic is Intuition, which is the mode of thought of the Eastern mind. Just like having the sense of mind to distinguish beautiful art and music from that which is shameful and disgusting (a subjective reasoning process), the function of the Eastern mind is to distinguish truth from falsehood. This requires creative thinking skills, which appeal to those who are more intuitively inclined. Some people don't fall into the extremes of either Logic or Intuition; they are capable of both critical and creative thinking.

Generally speaking, the intersection of the West-East functions of mind forms the element of Knowledge that I have called *knowing* in the Northward sense. Knowing is the basis for being able to distinguish right from wrong. Understanding such as this is gained through the transformation of the soul toward God in becoming aware.

Keep in mind, though, that while Purpose is an element of the trichotomy, one more truly "cleaves unto the Lord" with the heart. Again, reflect on how the heart (a triquetra) is formed within the trichotomy. Purpose is what transforms the two-part model into a three-part model. One may esteem God, but without action the effort to become Purposed toward God is ineffective. Think about the implications (or dynamics) of Purpose in the trichotomy for a moment. In order to be Northward with Purpose one must first recognize God's calling and then begin the progressive turn toward Him as one's love, strength, mighty counselor, etc. In the absence of Purpose, the trichotomy becomes a two-part model again, the triquetra vanishes, and so does the heart of inspiration. When this occurs, love, wisdom, and grace can only be defined from the horizontal (earthly) perspective.

Though virtue and praise are characteristic of Purpose, not all purposes are considered Northward. There are those who are deeply committed to evil forms of virtue and praise: they adore objects, idols, or even themselves. As it pertains to the Northward model, Purpose is the upper element so that virtue and praise serve to also magnify God and receive His grace. So, again, in the absence of Northward Purpose, one simply cannot apply God's will "on earth as it is in heaven."[30] Why? Because he or she is not yet awakened and walking upright.

> *The light of the body is the eye: if therefore thine eye be single, thy whole body shall be full of light.*
> *But if thine eye be evil, thy whole body shall be full of darkness. If therefore the light that is in thee be darkness, how great is that darkness!*
> Matthew 6:22-23

Interestingly, Purpose can also be associated with what many regard as the mind's eye. Just as our two physical eyes scan around to follow and then focus singularly on what's most stimulating to the mind, the two sides of mind (Logic and Intuition) follow what they seek to learn more about and then focus singularly on that subject (hence, the mind's eye).

---

[30] Matthew 6:10

So while two eyes are used to visualize "the seen" in the physical sense, it's the mind's eye that is used to visualize "the unseen" in the mental and even spiritual sense.

Eyes are passive conduits for information received by the brain, whereas the mind's eye is induced by the response to what the mind (consciously and subconsciously) seeks to know more about. What we seek and then visualize in our minds is what ultimately dictates Purpose for each of us – a Purpose that can be either Northward or Southward.[31]

> *But when the Comforter is come, whom I will send unto you from the Father, [even] the Spirit of truth, which proceedeth from the Father, he shall testify of me:*
> Jesus, John 15:26

While there is some dispute among religious communities about the Spirit of Truth (the Holy Spirit) proceeding from the Son, no believer questions that this third Spirit proceeds from God the Father. Believers understand that the Spirit of God may be instilled into one's vessel as Jesus also comes as our Comforter, Redeemer, Defender, and Savior. The Holy Spirit (or Holy Ghost) serves as the catalyst between the Godhead and believers that form His Body. The Holy Spirit enables one to have a relationship with God; and it is because of the Holy Spirit that believers are capable of receiving His Spirit inwardly and deem that Spirit as holy within.

Please understand that I refer to Purpose as being of the mind because the individual must first decide to choose good over evil, and right over wrong, which in turn causes his or her body to move with integrity and grace. Thus, Purpose is instigated by thought and is vertically integrated with action. As the body follows through with the decision of the mind, both mind and body are functionally aligned to accomplish not only the will of mind, but also the will of God. This is significant because it is the mind that decides how the body should devote itself toward its higher authority. Thus, it may be argued that one's ultimate destiny is determined by the individual mind in how he or she chooses to respond to God's

---

[31] Matthew 6:24

appeal. As the Northward temple becomes higher, believers will then lovingly choose to sacrifice the body for matters of grace.

ii. Triquetra Group: Human Devotion Toward Righteousness Derived by the Act Upon Human Understanding

Since the triquetra is a derivative of intersecting circles of the trichotomy, each of the labels used must reflect that conjunction; thus, the intersection between Logic and Intuition is the element of Knowledge; between Logic and Purpose is the element of Justice; and between Intuition and Purpose is the element of Mercy.

When examining Figure 7 some may suggest that it seems redundant to have a lower group (triquetra) that represents action when this group is represented precisely within the central portion of the trichotomy above, a group that represents thought. The primary reason why these two groups are shown this way is to help make the point that for any given thought (above) there is an action response (below or within).

My little children, let us not love in word, neither in tongue;
but in deed and in truth.
1 John 3:18

Words are sometimes necessary to explain reasoning and intent, but words have little meaning unless the body follows through with action (hence the popular sayings, "talk is cheap" and "actions speak louder than words"). Since Knowledge is an element of the triquetra, it is an action element. Some may question this since knowledge is typically revealed with words requiring no bodily action. Though this is true to some extent, speaking or writing words is also a form of knowledge in its primary application. Also think about how one moves in carrying out certain skills (as learned) or talents (as inborn). Are these not forms of knowledge as well? Sure they are.

We may also compare the element of Knowledge with the actions of the other two elements of the triquetra: Justice and Mercy. The body, carrying the head above, will move according to the decisions of the mind (either intentionally or intuitively) toward the left or right, in approaching another or distancing, in embracing or denying, in creating or destroying, in loving or warring, and so on. Thus, each bodily movement (as also represented by handedness) demonstrates the unspoken qualities of Justice, Mercy, and even Knowledge itself. So Knowledge is manifest in both spoken and unspoken forms, revealed both vocally by the mouth and in bodily movements. As they pertain to individual human behavior, Justice and Mercy are manifested more in bodily movements since each is dependent on Purpose for its existence (again, "actions speak louder than words"). More on this in the Wisdom and Grace section that follows.

Just as the decisions of the mind help form the soul, so the movements of the body help form the heart. Thus, the mind decides what the body should do to nurture the inward spirit and advance its wholeness. By true desire in Him one's mind becomes open[32] (hence, "open-minded") to receive greater understandings from God, including His Spirit. Bear in mind, though, one does not simply bolster the inward spirit without God—it is a gift of the Holy Spirit that only God Himself can provide.

I will call the labels in the triquetra "devotional elements." As mentioned earlier, the three inner elements shown in Figure 7 can be seen as forming a heart shape. Interestingly, this image could also depict the spirit of God as manifested through man, with arms stretched upward and outward. This is why I have called the triquetra Human Devotion. For discussion purposes, each of the three devotional elements will be identified in noun form and then subdivided according to Purpose. For instance, the Northward characteristic of Knowledge is Knowing (which may be used as noun or an adjective). This contrasts with the characteristic of Knowledge in the Southward sense, which is Unknowing.

a) Knowledge: The Devotional Element of Knowledge Exemplified Northward as *Knowing*

Knowledge is a devotional element of the triquetra and is best understood by studying the dynamics within the upper group of Figure 7. It is placed between Logic and Intuition, not as a blend of

---

[32] Luke 24:45, Acts 16:14

understandings between the two sides, but as the integration of these two unique types of understanding. Remember that knowledge may be acted out both vocally and with bodily movements. As one ponders a certain thought it is instantaneously subjected to both forms of reasoning (West-East) so that a proper action response may be passed from the mind to the mouth (as voiced) and/or to the body below (as moved).

Since Knowledge is a devotional element, some may suppose that knowledge itself is therefore Northward in all cases. This would be a mistake since devotion in itself (depending on Purpose) is a movement that may be applied by the individual toward anything or anybody, good or bad.

Wherefore by their fruits ye shall know them.
Matthew 7:20

In the Northward sense, the element of Knowledge is that of Knowing. A person who attains facts and truths is Knowing: he or she possesses soundness of mind and so is more capable of making reliable decisions. A person who does not have soundness of mind will more easily accept fiction and falsehood. Knowing refers to the quality, not the quantity of Knowledge, so even the most simple may aspire toward God in grand and fruitful ways.

b) Justice and Mercy: The Devotional Elements of Justice and Mercy are Exemplified Northward as Being *Just* and *Merciful*

Justice and judgment [are] the habitation of thy throne:
mercy and truth shall go before thy face.
Psalm 89:14

The other two devotional elements in the triquetra are Justice and Mercy. By studying the Northward HUHD Model, we can see that Purpose is the primary determinant of the elements of Justice and Mercy. Interestingly, these elements have vertical qualities that the element of Knowledge does not have. So Just and Merciful acts might be considered more advanced toward holiness than Knowledge itself; however, while the element of Knowledge appears below the other two elements, recall that without a sound mind the elements of Justice and Mercy will be compromised.

Most would consider Mercy good, but fewer will think the same of Justice. According to the Northward HUHD Model, because it requires soundness of mind along with Northward Purpose, just ways are just as important to righteousness as merciful ways.

iii. Wisdom and Grace: Each Possessed and Exhibited While in Vertical Unison

> *But the wisdom that is from above is first pure, then peaceable, gentle, [and] easy to be intreated, full of mercy and good fruits, without partiality, and without hypocrisy. And the fruit of righteousness is sown in peace of them that make peace.*
> James 3:17-18

While the devotional elements are discussed more from the perspective of what one exemplifies outwardly, the elements of Wisdom and Grace will be discussed from the perspective of what one possesses internally and exemplifies in both words and actions.

The central-most element of the trichotomy and that of the triquetra is labeled "Wisdom and Grace." Wisdom is knowledge-based and contained within the soulful foundation, so it is better explained within the trichotomy; Grace is evidenced by devotion, so it is better explained within the triquetra. Recall that the triquetra is a derivative of the trichotomy and pertains to the actions of the body in response to the decisions of the mind. Both Wisdom and Grace are also derivatives, but in this case, each is viewed as a second derivative requiring the vertical integration of thought and action to produce appropriate mind-body responses. In other words, while Knowledge is formed by the integration of Western and Eastern understandings (a horizontal process), here the head and body are integrated to produce appropriate mind-body responses (a vertical process).

> *Who hath put wisdom in the inward parts?*
> *or who hath given understanding to the heart?*
> Job 38:36

Human Understanding and Devotion

In the Northward sense, Wisdom of the mind and Grace of the body are together indicative of the alignment of head over body and for the same Purpose – in this case, one may indeed cleave unto the Lord with the heart through the soul. In this Northward alignment of head over body, one is then able to receive the Spirit of God within, not only as possessed but also as exemplified in the forms of Wisdom and Grace.

> *For the wisdom of this world is foolishness with God.*
> *For it is written, He taketh the wise in their own craftiness.*
> 1 Corinthians 3:19

Keep in mind that there are differences between earthly, worldly, or fleshy wisdom and the spiritual Wisdom of God. Those with a certain level of knowledge may seem to have wisdom. However, a person may possess an extraordinary amount of knowledge without having true Wisdom.

What about Grace? The definition of the word "grace" in a typical dictionary does not capture its Biblical meaning. Bear in mind, however, that a person can only express true grace outwardly by first receiving God's Grace inwardly.

Assume that one has accepted Christ and grows more responsive toward Him, thus increasing in Wisdom and Grace. Our model suggests that such a conversion is (progressively) achieved under these two conditions:

- When Knowledge (of Fact and Truth) forms the foundation of Northward Purpose; and
- When thought and action are in vertical unison; thus, the body follows through with the decisions of the mind, as also inspired by the heart.

It is important to note that one cannot achieve (Northward) Purpose in an instant simply by thinking about it. The temple-building process takes time, because it is with the heart that one cleaves unto the Lord. As the mind and body work together in unison, and as the spirit of God grows stronger within, each will increasingly yearn to do more in His name—not as a work, but as the result of one's adoration for Him. This will raise the temple even higher. As reciprocated between mind and body, with Wisdom comes Grace, and with Grace there is greater Wisdom as one's upright cup/vessel becomes further imbued with the Spirit of God.

Consider for a moment the issue of the spoken and unspoken as expressed in the central-most elements of the trichotomy and the triquetra. As previously discussed, Knowledge may be revealed in both spoken and unspoken forms. This, however, does not imply that Knowledge in itself becomes Wisdom or Grace. As the model shows, it is only with Northward Purpose that one can possess and exemplify Knowledge as spoken and unspoken Wisdom and Grace.

The argument for Justice and Mercy is slightly different because these devotional elements are created from the element of Purpose arising from a sound foundation. Justice and Mercy are manifested in unspoken bodily movements as just and merciful ways. The question is: Can the elements of Justice and Mercy be manifest in the spoken form? According to the model, it appears that these elements cannot be expressed in the spoken form unless driven through the central-most elements of Wisdom and Grace.

There are two reasons for suggesting this. First, if and when Justice and Mercy are in spoken form then each will intersect with the element of Knowledge, an area occupied by Wisdom and Grace. Second, if issues that involve Justice and Mercy do not fit into the optimal Northward HUHD Model, then the only other way to explain these characteristics would be without (Northward) Purpose. Without Purpose the elements of Justice and Mercy vanish as the upper devotional elements of the heart disappear. With Purpose forfeited, just and merciful ways can only be expressed by what one has previously learned. As events unfold and decisions are made on the basis of past learning or practice, the spoken and unspoken expressions of Justice and Mercy will be consistently flawed. Moreover, without Northward heart the elements of Wisdom and Grace will also be compromised. Thus, without Purpose one's "heart" will be determined only by one's affection, satisfaction, or performance of as judged by other humans.

A person who once had Wisdom and Grace but loses the element of Purpose (perhaps even for a short time) will indeed continue to retain certain understandings and may be able to reintroduce the element of Purpose to form the temple in the future.

Human Understanding and Devotion

Until that time, however, the question is: Just how much will have been sacrificed when true convictions are compromised for thoughts and ways not of God? True understandings (if ever once possessed) as driven from Wisdom and Grace may just as easily vanish from within depending on how committed one is against God. The result would equate to certain Biblical passages referring to how one turns upside-down, becoming emptied and dry within.

We might even suggest that a strengthened spiritual core (Wisdom and Grace) might render one better able to resist the turn when the mind becomes tempted; hence, a significant reason to become spiritually strong and mature.

Wherefore, my beloved brethren, let every man be swift to hear, slow to speak, slow to wrath:
For the wrath of man worketh not the righteousness of God.
James 1:19-20

So there may be times when the element of Purpose is reduced for a moment or, worse, redirected Southward. It would begin with the id or carnal issues, enticements, and end with abominations, including but not limited to eruptions of anger, hatred, and vengeance. This alone is reason to be slow to characterize, slow to judge, slow to blame, and slow to react. The Bible makes a strong case for avoiding Southward thoughts and ways. Thus, it's important to develop Wisdom and Grace, but they may indeed be forfeited by one's own will to turn away from God and then resist turning back.

According to the grace of God which is given unto me, as a wise masterbuilder, I have laid the foundation,
and another buildeth thereon.
But let every man take heed how he buildeth thereupon.
1 Corinthians 3:10

In general, Wisdom and Grace can be expressed in both spoken and unspoken forms. Knowledge-based expressions (as Knowing) become Wisdom and Grace only when Northward Purpose prevails; and issues involving Justice and Mercy (as just and merciful ways) become Wisdom and Grace when Knowledge forms the foundation for such Northward expressions.

iv. Summary

The Northward HUHD Model is the ideal model, and as such is basis of discussion for all of the variations discussed in later chapters. It demonstrates that thought forming the soul (psyche) and action forming the heart are both necessary in order to have vertical unison toward a higher divine authority. With such an alignment one may then be positioned to receive His Spirit and thus a holy spirit within. As one receives, his or her Purpose becomes strengthened as the temple reaches even greater height. The Northward HUHD Model reflects the ideal state of mind over body for optimum equilibrium of all basic and devotional elements: "basic" as described by the trichotomy and "devotional" as described by the triquetra.

> *Whom we preach, warning every man,*
> *and teaching every man in all wisdom;*
> *that we may present every man perfect in Christ Jesus.*
> Colossians 1:28

In the passage above (and many others in the Old and New Testaments), the word *perfect* is used. The question is: In attempting to achieve perfection, has society typically treated this term as the cause of goodness or as its effect? One way to understand the implications of this term is to reflect upon the parent-child relationship. All parents want their children to become (so-called) perfect, but how can this be achieved without demanding this from the child? One thing is certain, the younger a child is the more he or she will respond to parental edicts out of fear than out of love. Over time, though, the healthy and stable child will do things out of love instead of out of fear. Most parents would agree that when the child thinks and moves in loving response to the will of the parent there is an even greater natural exchange of affection between parent and child. As the relationship matures, the parent might then privately reflect upon how the child is developing toward perfection, while then allowing the child even greater freedom and independence.

Human Understanding and Devotion

Thus, a child is nurtured into perfection that first begins with sound parenting. At the same time, however, reaching a true state of perfection and advancing further into spiritual awakening continues well after the child leaves home, has a family, etc.

> *Verily I say unto you, Whosoever shall not receive the kingdom of God as a little child, he shall not enter therein.*
> Jesus, Mark 10:15

Reflect on the discussion of Jesus' Great Commandment. We suggested that good works are the effect of the love of God and the love for God (the cause). Thus, to see perfection as a work is erroneously treated as the cause. Just as the physical child must transition from fear of the parent to love for the parent, the same holds true for the spiritual child, even if he or she is physically mature. One must begin to know God (the higher authority) by faith (the cause) so that the fear of God is overcome and one is then poised uprightly (and perfectly) to lovingly receive His Spirit (the effect). So while God should be feared, it is only His saving grace that believers are able to become perfected, and even stand in His presence. If one's view of perfection is performance-based, then he or she has yet to progress out of the fear of God and confidently into the love for God.

Though it makes sense to resist temptation in order to become one with God, if resistance is seen as the cause, then resisting temptation will be a constant battle. Why? Because the person has not developed a deepening relationship with God, which by grace enables him or her to resist temptation. Ultimately attempts to resist sin without developing such a relationship with God can easily become too difficult to bear, which may then spur notions to "go with the flow" of sinfulness, while attempting to justify these behaviors as normal. Again, one does not become perfected by means of performance, just as obeying the law, in the Apostle Paul's terms, does not lead to righteousness. Rules created to prohibit sinfulness miss the point because they focus on performance as the means of achieving perfection. This often causes disunity between once-unified groups as members are judged according to whether they meet certain expectations. If instead more people attempted a God-first relationship, then more would be of one accord with little to no compulsion to judge or reduce others. Those who are spiritually strong will instead attempt to raise those who are weak through encouragement and edification.

> *For by grace are ye saved through faith; and that not of*
> *yourselves: [it is] the gift of God:*
> *Not of works, lest any man should boast.*
> Ephesians 2:8-9

One's perfected state (the effect) stems from one's adoration for God (the cause). It is senseless to boast about good works, because such assertions are usually indicative of a preoccupation with the self. Reaching a state of perfection may seem arduous, but it is possible as long as Jesus is the focal point for faith. In other words, our Lord Jesus Christ came so that He might become the chief cornerstone of faith for all who choose to respond to God, and so He could help make the believer's (upright) walk easier.[33] Those who have yet to arise often think achieving perfection is more difficult than it really is. That's because they have yet to know Jesus and become spiritually conscious. They will instead approach life matters relative to the issue of perfection from an unknowing point of view, and one based largely on works.

So in order to justify their own unperfected state they will need to find reasons to exalt the (false) innocence of self while impugning others for their past sins and faults. Again, the answer does not come to light through comparing one's conduct with others so as to justify one's own behavior at the expense of another. The answer comes when one begins to appreciate that righteousness and perfection are the result of faith in Him and not simply the result of one's own conduct.

> *Because strait [is] the gate, and narrow [is] the way, which*
> *leadeth unto life, and few there be that find it.*
> Jesus, Matthew 7:14

---

[33] Matthew 11:28-30

In summary, the soul of man is naturally prevented from ever arising[34] by its own mindful will. Believers are raised from their fallen state through the Grace of God. Though God continues to call out and appeal for all to make that Northward transition, many will continue to resist the voice of our Shepherd and remain in an unconscious state. What makes the relationship with God so pristine is that it is not by works but by responding to that call that one develops a heart-felt relationship with Him. Therefore, believers become justified (with unearned Grace) by faith in Jesus Christ, the one who atoned for the sins of humanity. He did this so that all might be redeemed[35] and find peace of mind, peace among others, and eternal life.

Appreciating the true significance of Godly Grace raises one's sense of Purpose even more. The more believers are drawn toward Him, the more each believer becomes inspired to help others also rise and achieve liberty.[36] Over time the minds and bodies of those who choose to respond to Him by faith become holy within (e.g., sanctified) by His enriching Spirit dwelling even deeper.[37] As this vertical and reciprocating journey of Grace develops (God's Grace interacting with the believer's faith) so does one's heartfelt conviction even to the point of becoming lovingly obedient to His Will.

This model depicts the vertical unison of thought over action as one cleaves unto the Lord with the heart. By consciously choosing to walk with Purpose toward a higher, divine authority, one can achieve communion with God. The Northward HUHD Model thus represents perfection, as illustrated.

---

[34] John 6:44
[35] Romans 3:22-25
[36] 2 Corinthians 3:17
[37] Romans 8:11

b. Southward HUHD Model

Now that the basics of the Northward HUHD Model have been discussed, we turn our attention toward the Southward HUHD Model (see Figure 8). This model is opposed to the Northward model but keep in mind that the side of Logic is still the West and the side of Intuition is still the East.

To avoid redundancy, the discussion in this section will not focus on issues clearly opposite to those discussed above. Instead, I will delve further into the areas of Freud's id, ego, and super-ego.

Human Understanding and Devotion

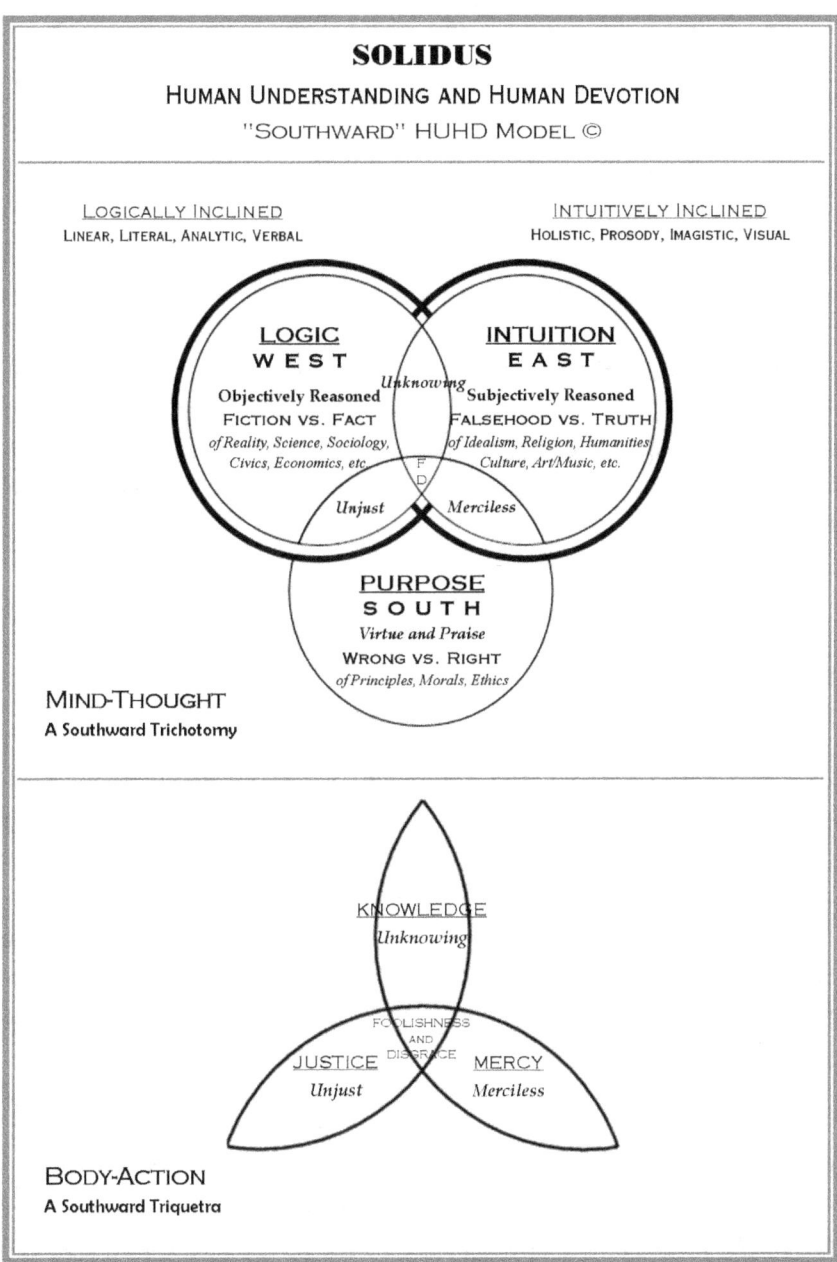

Figure 8

i. Trichotomy Group: With Southward Purpose, Human Misunderstanding and Foolishness Are Increased

> *I have spread out my hands all the day unto a rebellious people, which walketh in a way [that was] not good, after their own thoughts.*
> Isaiah 65:2

Let's examine the basic dynamics of the upper and lower groups of the Southward HUHD Model. First, note that the temple formed by Purpose is vainly pointing at the body below and that which is further below. Keep in mind that the trichotomy continues to represent thought that forms the soul (psyche) while the triquetra represents action that forms the heart, but in this case each label is the opposite of the corresponding label in the Northward HUHD Model.

As discussed earlier, Freud's model of the psyche holds that there is a constant battle within the mind between the id and the super-ego—a conflict mediated through the ego itself. The id is driven to satisfy basic needs, including thirst, hunger, and sexual desires, whereas the super-ego helps maintain one's sense of morality. The id is also responsible for aggressive behavior. Thus, while Northward Purpose produces virtue and praise of God, Southward Purpose produces virtue and praise of lower things, including the body itself, earthly matters, and/or the Evil one below. If one does not take a God-first approach to life, then one's Purpose will likely be directed toward self first, then toward other persons. It may even be directed toward tangible things such as money and possessions or, even worse, toward matters of spiritual darkness.

It is important to note that simply having id-driven basic needs, as everyone does, does not constitute Southward Purpose. Such needs, though, oppose Northward aspirations. The real problem arises when the individual becomes so absorbed in satisfying the demands of the id that Northward Purpose is completely forsaken for other purposes. Unless the super-ego helps to counter the demands of the id, the individual will pursue ever greater Southward ambitions.

Just as the head and body in the Northward HUHD Model work in vertical unison to accomplish Purpose, so do they in the Southward model. In this case, however, instead of becoming more proficient with fact and truth so that the mind and body can develop Wisdom and Grace, the individual here will become more foolishly adept at seeking out fiction and falsehood (hence, the identification of these terms first in the labeling of the Southward model). Driven by Purpose, the person operating in this model has no choice but to then commit himself or herself toward wrong instead of right. This is because fiction and falsehood (as unknowingly understood) will only justify wrongdoing and wrongful gain. Even though such movements will entail lying, cheating, and stealing, if it's a matter of self-image, self-preservation, or positioning oneself over another, the ego will comply. Unconsciously, a person with Southward ambitions will work to advance and strengthen the id so that, over time, the super-ego is left incapacitated. Just how far-reaching can this drive become? It is one thing for the mind to have Southward Purpose involving the id, but it is quite another for the id to be strengthened to the point of gaining control over the ego and thus commanding it and the mind. Once the id reigns over the mind, it will more easily fool the mind through the ego into making decisions that lead to disgrace.[38]

Carefully reflect on the meaning of the word "fall" for a moment. What is meant by one's fall? We can obviously define fallen persons as those who are unable to find salvation after taking their final breath, or their falling into the grave or into hell. The Bible provides numerous images of humanity's fall, but such end results are only one way to understand this term. The important point here is to understand how one's fall is also relevant to one's daily walk—that is, how one thinks and moves while existing in a fallen state.

---

[38] The term *Disgrace*—clearly opposite the word *Grace*—also connotes: to be senseless or foolish, to treat with contempt; to sink or drop down, languish, wither and fall, fade, to droop; make vile. Blue Letter Bible. Dictionary and Word Search for nabel (Strong's 5034). Blue Letter Bible. 1996-2009. 29 Oct 2009. < http://www.blueletterbible.org/lang/lexicon/lexicon.cfm?strongs=H5034 >

Counter to one's unconscious fall is one's conscious rise; thus, even living persons are either fallen or arisen.

> *For the corruptible body presseth down the soul,*
> *and the earthy tabernacle weigheth down the mind*
> *that museth upon many things.*
> Wisdom of Solomon 9:15 (Apocrypha)[39]

To further clarify, let's examine the tangible id relative to intangible Purpose. From youth into adulthood, tangible id leads intangible Purpose (of mind) into Southward thoughts that in turn lead to Southward ways. For the id to eventually reign over the mind, it must first eradicate the super-ego, so that the ego will have no choice but to exalt the id. Remember that the id (as Freud described it) is positioned at the low point of the mind (the low point including the limbic system and brain stem)[40]. My contention is that in order for the id to reign from an upper position it must cause the mind (soul) to fall. In other words, as the unknowing mind falls, the body effectively rises. In this case one can be described as becoming turned, bent, subverted, weighed down, or even upside-down. Turning as such does not, of course, occur in physical form but in the moral, psychological, and spiritual form, many passages suggest that this sort of phenomenon does occur.

What are some ways that the id may cause the mind to fall? One way is to cause the mind (through the ego) to succumb to foolishness (of mind) and disgrace (of body) – to engage in behavior that effectively adds a weight of guilt and shame that will cause the mind to fall further and/or prevent it from rising back up. Another way may be to prompt the disposition of the mind to seek things sexual in nature (perhaps as the result of being exposed to such things) before he or she has the opportunity to become aware of the consequences of such behavior. In this way the body will be tempted to respond to the flesh before the super-ego has a chance to develop,

---

[39] Wisdom of Solomon 9:15. Apocrypha.org. Retrieved March 18, 2009, from http://apocrypha.org/wisdom_of_solomon/9-15.htm

[40] Bill Crawford, Ph.D. (2013). Seminar presentation on: Clarity, Confidence, & Creativity: New Information on Bringing Your Best to Life Regardless of the Situation.

strengthen, and thus resist compulsive behaviors. Thus, as the id persists in driving the cognizance of mind downward, it will increasingly govern the person's behavior.

> *Dearly beloved, I beseech [you] as strangers and pilgrims, abstain from fleshly lusts, which war against the soul.*
> 1 Peter 2:11

Just as one life creates another, so the id first leads Purpose of mind to foolishly maintain a Southward movement, thus progressively falling into an upside-down position. Once upside down, the id begins its upward progression through the body and into a reigning position over the mind. Without the super-ego to counter the growing impulse of gratifying physiological needs (to obtain instant gratification as principally driven by the id), the mind (now from below) will have no choice but to focus on and exalt the body. If the mind succumbs to the ever-increasing needs and desires of the body, then only tangible sensibilities will make sense to those who are Southward. This is one reason why many who are committed to self celebrate the flesh and/or mysteries of the dark rather than the God of light.

> *But he that hateth his brother is in darkness, and walketh in darkness, and knoweth not whither he goeth, because that darkness hath blinded his eyes.*
> 1 John 2:11

The id works stealthily over the (unconscious) mind using the physical/sensual body to strengthen itself. At some point, even if the mind wanted to consciously stop the progressive fall and re-exert the super-ego (thus becoming self-actualized[41]), the id, in its resistance to losing control, would interfere by overwhelming the mind with preoccupations and enticements. The more the ego permits the id to interfere, the more righteousness fails to seem worthwhile. Thus, without the help of God and the guidance and encouragement of

---

[41] *Self-actualized* is defined as: to realize fully one's potential. self-actualize. Webster's Third New International Dictionary, Unabridged. Merriam-Webster, 2002. http://unabridged.merriam-webster.com (1 Nov. 2009).

those who are Northward, the mind of those on a Southward slide will become even further removed from the light and love above and decline into a perpetual stupor that only increases darkness.

The reason the Southward HUHD Model is illustrated with a trichotomy above the triquetra is so that we can more easily compare and contrast the details of the Northward and Southward models. Keep in mind that whether the trichotomy is shown above or below the triquetra, the Southward model is still upside-down since Purpose is directed South.

Notice also that the body below is the object of mind. Contrast this with the Northward model, wherein the objects of mind are knowledge, understanding, discretion, and wisdom. The overall contention of the Southward model is that the id first teaches the mind (through the ego) to have Purpose in earthly matters that only exalt the flesh. From that point on it's just a matter of time for the mind to fall relative to the body and into an upside-down state. So from the perspective of a person on a Northward trajectory, a person with Southward aspirations will completely turn away from the light and love above as he or she resists even the tangible aspects of what those Northward stand for in their response. In contrast, those on a Southward trajectory will attempt to prove how good they are. Recall, however, that the act of proving inherently becomes a performance issue, a matter that eventually leads to legalistic notions, even against those Northward. Still, those Southward believe that these behaviors are what appeal most to God anyway. Compare these thoughts to our previous discussion of cause and effect. Each truly loving act or disposition is the effect of being loved by and loving God, but in the Southward model the effect is being treated as the cause. True love comes from God, not from any individual or group attempting to practice the effect. So if efforts directed toward another person are not the result of experiencing a God-first relationship, then there is no choice but to suggest that such efforts are undertaken for purposes of self. Let us look at this issue from another angle.

Human Understanding and Devotion

No man hath seen God at any time. If we love one another, God dwelleth in us, and his love is perfected in us.

1 John 4:12

The above passage may appear to contradict the argument just made, but John was talking about the truest form of love to be shared with others. In essence, true love is of God and dwells within those who have faith and believe in Him. It is not the kind that deals simply with physical attraction and performance.

Keep in mind that those with Southward Purpose were first fooled by the id into allowing it to occupy a reigning position. So as the id-body presses the mind further into obscurity, its demand for satisfying needs (i.e., even worldly desires of objects perceived needed) causes the mind through the ego to openly and publicly strive for power, authority, and control using any means possible. Such means may include wealth, physical strength, beauty, sexuality, and even expressions of affection in order to advance the id while effectively destroying the treasured child of God within.

Thus, for those with Northward Purpose, the mind (the cause) decides how the body should move (the effect) in order to accomplish the will of mind and that of God; hence, the mind rules the body. Those with Southward Purpose, however, are dependent upon the id-body for direction because the mind is fooled into a fallen state; hence, the body rules over the mind. In other words, the disgraceful id-body (as also motivated by the libido) becomes the cause of how the foolish mind thinks (the effect).

It is important to recognize that Satan and his cohorts (including the Great Whore), not God, are the ones who desire to destroy the human race. God will certainly judge each of us rightly, but it is Evil (as seducer, adversary, and prosecutor) that is responsible for shackling the minds of many, leaving them enslaved to Satan's will.

One of the reasons why Jesus (our Savior) walked this earth in the name of mercy is so that He could exemplify how each of God's children can cast off their shackles and freely arise. Recognize that in order to truly release those shackles, though, a person must first recognize the responsibility for the inner child and choose to respond (by faith) to God's appeal.

> *Then said he unto me, Son of man, lift up thine eyes now the way toward the north. So I lifted up mine eyes the way toward the north, and behold northward at the gate of the altar this image of jealousy in the entry.*
>
> Ezekiel 8:5

Those who continue to resist the conversion of turning toward God will proclaim: "It is God and the followers of God who cause guilt and shame!" Thus, those unknowing will consistently pursue evil, considering it to be good, and will run away from good, considering it to be bad. In these cases earthly wisdom makes most sense, while the wisdom of those who know better is dismissed altogether.

God does not intend for anyone to live in guilt and shame. He provided the ultimate remedy for them—the finished work of Jesus that anyone can claim by faith. Continuing life in a fallen state to avoid guilt and shame is no real remedy at all. Here is the difficulty: It is during the conversion process, when God becomes more evident, that the weight of guilt and shame will be experienced. Acknowledging one's sinfulness leads to repentance, and repentance in turn leads to forgiveness—the removal of guilt and shame! It is by His saving Grace that each may be released from such weights in order to arise and become a child of God, now and in the life to come.

ii. Triquetra Group: Human Devotion Toward Sinfulness Derived by the Act Upon Human Misunderstanding

Relative to the Northward triquetra, each of the devotional elements of the Southward triquetra can be expressed as moving from Knowing to Unknowing, from Just to Unjust, and from Merciful to Merciless.

a) Knowledge: The Devotional Element of Knowledge is Exemplified Southward as *Unknowing*

> *Every tree that bringeth not forth good fruit is hewn down, and cast into the fire.*
> Matthew 7:19

In the Southward HUHD Model, the devotional element of Knowledge is Unknowing. The individual in this case will be more easily drawn toward fiction and falsehood rather than toward fact and truth. This obviously threatens the reliability of decisions made between Logic and Intuition. Reflect on the differences between how those Knowing and those Unknowing express themselves. Some examples include: (1) a singer or communicator who uses the voice to inspire or to denigrate; (2) a dancer who uses the body to exhibit beauty and grace or to incite lust and disgrace; (3) a carpenter who uses the hands to build or to destroy; or (4) a writer who uses written words to bring peace and love or to cause divisiveness and even war.

This distinction between Knowing and Unknowing is obviously the result of soundness of mind (or lack thereof) and the element of Purpose as directed upward or downward. It also suggests that those with Southward ambitions are driven more by the "me" instead of the "we." For those who have not yet realized their individual skill or talent, words become vital to enhancing self-image. Bear in mind that in these cases the heart is upside-down as the Knowledge element is heightened over the other two elements characterized as Unjust and Merciless. The id's emphasis through the ego is to advance the element of Knowledge, but unbeknownst to the individual, such increases are only that of Unknowing. As you will recall, the ego reasons by mediating between the id and the superego. A person who is Southward will be more susceptible to accepting fiction and falsehood as his or her reality.

b) Justice and Mercy: The Devotional Elements of Justice and Mercy are Exemplified Southward as Being *Unjust* and *Merciless*

To restate our earlier argument, when Purpose is lost the heart effectively disappears, but if Southward Purpose is created the heart reemerges in an upside-down state.

> *An unjust man [is] an abomination to the just: and [he that is] upright in the way [is] abomination to the wicked.*
> Proverbs 29:27

An interesting example of Southward thoughts and ways pertains to how friends are made. Those with Southward Purpose join together not because two or more have higher aspirations (as the result of goodness), rather they come together on the basis of id-driven self or as the result of having common enemies. For those Southward, consensus-building against others is a common technique used for maintaining group cohesion. Since others who are Southward are also Unknowing, gossip sessions easily turn into propaganda against select others, perhaps even involving character assassination plots. To validate such vocal expressions (again, reflect on how the element of Knowledge is heightened) Unjust and Merciless action must be taken. These actions demonstrate the vertical unison between body and mind. Thus, Unjust and Merciless behavior becomes (falsely) justified as those Southward will excuse their own behavior by assigning blame to the targeted individual or group—that is, those who (allegedly) caused them to do such things in the first place. This is particularly evident when those falsely driven build up such a persona for themselves in the eyes of others that a scapegoat is necessary whenever their image is at risk of being tarnished.

Scapegoating works to bring the Unknowing together, as there will always be one or more whose disposition is aggressively boisterous or charismatic. Such persons rise up as (so-called) leaders over the rank and file in the group. These leaders will have a certain charm and wit that is appealing to listen to, marvel at, and laugh with. For the leader, as the id-body begins to swell with self-gratification, so does the (false) sense of strength that further propels

Unjust and Merciless behaviors. For others who are Southward, these sorts of (shameless) exhibitions are simply fascinating to behold as the aggressor strikes blows against the targeted, becomes self-glorified in the process, and perhaps makes money from it. These leaders are adept at absolving themselves from any blame or responsibility and will in clear conscience walk away from the upheaval either as if it were a just cause or as if it never happened. As the Southward leader succeeds in this type of craft, others in the group will mull over how they, too, can make a name for themselves.

As it pertains to adults, reflect upon the issue of performance relative to the expectations of others. Some people will invoke guilt and shame when someone falls short of their expectations, in the hope of manipulating future behavior. If one's Purpose is in part to punish others for lack of performance, or to cause them to stumble or fall, or even to make them submit to one's own will, then such tendencies are effectively Southward efforts to reduce other persons while gaining a (false) sense of exaltation for self.

And they said, There is no hope:
but we will walk after our own devices,
and we will every one do the imagination of his evil heart.
Jeremiah 18:12

There is nothing wrong with wanting to collaborate with others who are like-minded. The key question with respect to friendships is: Are they formed by natural goodness, or are they formed for reasons of self? In either case, there is indeed one common enemy—the Evil One below, Satan and his accomplices. Yes, there are bad people in the world, but that's typically because they unknowingly allow Evil to use their minds and bodies to destroy not only themselves but others in the process. So while the common enemy does influence humanity to perform his will, those who are being used typically have no clue.

iii. Foolishness and Disgrace: Each Possessed and Exhibited While in Vertical Unison

> *And their nobles have sent their little ones to the waters: they came to the pits, [and] found no water; they returned with their vessels empty; they were ashamed and confounded, and covered their heads.*
> Jeremiah 14:3

Recall how the Northward HUHD Model illustrates a state of perfection toward God as He (in reciprocating fashion) instills the believer with His Spirit. In the case of those who are Southward, however, the central elements are Foolishness and Disgrace. As opposed to filling one's cup/vessel in the Northward sense, the vertical reciprocity between the individual and Evil below empties of one's spiritual core, leaving one vile. So with Foolishness comes Disgrace, and with Disgrace there is greater Foolishness.

> *The wicked, through the pride of his countenance, will not seek [after God]: God [is] not in all his thoughts.*
> Psalm 10:4

Assuming a lack of skills or talents, the goal for those Southward will be first to increase the element of Knowledge so that they will be thought of as possessing certain wisdom while also expressing (learned) affection posing as love. Note that one of the enemy's tactics is to provide counterfeits of all of the good things God has provided. All the while true Wisdom and Grace bound by soundness of mind and Northward Purpose are forsaken for external, physical charms such as youth, beauty, handsomeness, physical strength, and even eloquence. This is not to suggest that these qualities are abhorrent in themselves – they are not. But for many who do not appreciate God in the truest sense, these earthly charms easily become forms of idolatry, and one's tangible purpose in life to increase with, while God is pushed aside.

iv. Summary

For those who are Northward, friendship is about unifying around God first so that believers may enjoy a community with others of one accord. For those who are Southward, unification is driven more by a personal desire for attention or, as previously discussed, unification may be accomplished in more demeaning ways using common enemy tactics devised against others (i.e., the out-group). The Southward HUHD Model demonstrates that for non-believers thought and action are also in vertical unison forming one's temple; however, this temple is not oriented toward light above but toward darkness below.

> *So that my soul chooseth strangling,*
> *[and] death rather than my life.*
> Job 7:15

Recall that the super-ego gives rise to the conscience and maintains one's sense of morality. In order for the reigning id to strengthen itself using the body, it must cause the ego to negate the conscience. This is the only way the id-body can reign over the foolish mind. The id (as the higher authority) fortifies itself while achieving a (false) optimum equilibrium for all devotional elements in Southward ways – Unknowing, Unjust, and Merciless.

Since this model depicts a vertical unison of action over thought, one cleaves unto Evil with an upside-down heart. Hence, while walking in vanity (of mind) and under the authority of the id-body, one may enter into communion with Evil below. Thus, the Southward HUHD Model illustrates non-perfection.

c. Those without Purpose

There will continue to be those who reject God until the bitter end. Some will argue that they are neither purposed in God above nor in Evil below. At this point in the discussion, however, let's explore the question: "Is it truly possible to live a life without any Purpose?" As we discussed above, without Northward Purpose just and merciful ways cannot exist. And as a result we determined that apart from God, Wisdom and Grace cannot be induced by the flesh.

Most people who deny God's existence will refuse to believe that there is indeed a higher, divine authority who is intangible in nature and yet far superior to one's tangible self. They will attempt to rely upon the self in order to avoid falling (physically, emotionally, financially, etc.).

This is one reason why many without Northward Purpose will seek positions of power, authority, and control in order to achieve a (false) sense of security and even superiority. In good times, such people may not engage in such power behaviors. In times of panic and distress, however, when they begin to lose control, they will undoubtedly do so. When those who exalt the self finally do lose the basis for what had (seemingly) helped them avoid a fall, where will they find the strength to carry on? As history shows, in times of crisis, many find reasons to blame God for their problems, even though God was never purposed to begin with. Ironically, those who never factored God into their earthly successes end up making room for Him when explaining their failures and hardships. In their minds such failures of God will only prompt them to (foolishly) shun Him even more, while seeking the comfort of others who also deny His presence.

d. Conclusion

We have now examined the basic dynamics of the Northward HUHD Model and the Southward HUHD Model. Both models assume that the basic elements of Logic and Intuition are equal in weight (or dominance). These horizontal elements are tangible, while the soulful foundation and Purpose are intangible. Though the devotional element of Knowledge is exemplified with or without the basic element of Purpose, Knowledge is depicted as Knowing when Purpose is Northward, and Unknowing when Purpose is Southward. Two other devotional elements are formed from the element of Purpose: (1) if Northward, the elements of Justice and Mercy are characterized as Just and Merciful; and (2) if Southward, the elements of Justice and Mercy are characterized as Unjust and Merciless.

The Northward model demonstrates how the body administers the will of the sound mind, as the mind is purposed Northward toward God and on behalf of the body below. It is with the heart, though, that one cleaves unto the Lord. In the perfected state of mind over body, one is aligned in vertical unison to receive God's Spirit in order to nurture wholeness of the inward spirit. From such possessions the "fruit of the Spirit"[42] becomes manifest.

The Southward model demonstrates how the carnal mind administers the will of the fleshly id-body as the mind is purposed Southward toward itself and on behalf of its reigning king. In this non-perfected state, one is aligned upside-down to empty his or her inward holy spirit whereby "works of the flesh"[43] are elevated.

Since the head cannot thrive without the body, nor the body without the head, people will (depending on their level of spiritual maturity) naturally express varying levels of Wisdom and Grace; and/or varying levels of Foolishness and Disgrace.

We have now established a basis for how labels and their respective meaning are used in the model. Let's pull back from the need to capitalize these terms. This should allow a more casual discussion as we move forward.

---

[42] Galatians 5:22-23
[43] Galatians 5:19-21

2. Quadra-Circumplex Model

The previous discussions of the Northward and Southward HUHD Models represent absolute North and South temple positions. Since people are more likely to be West or East dominant, the model we now turn to identifies various mind-dominant positions as also dependent on Purpose: the Quadra-Circumplex Model (see Figure 9). Though the model will be discussed using certain compass bearings, to get the most out of it, resist viewing this model as representing circular movement.

This section will describe how the model works. A more detailed discussion will be found in the section called *Socio-Ideological Tendencies Table*.

Appendix C also contains reference tables for the key terms used in this section. These tables identify not only selected Strong's numbers associated with each term but also selected passages linked to the terms.

Figure 9

a. Model Dynamics

As you can see by the model, there will be an emphasis on the geographical coordinates used in this discussion. Their usage is important for a variety of reasons. One reason is that they will help explain the physiological nature of humans. Once beyond this section there will be less reason to use such coordinates. At that point the terms Logic and Intuition will be more often employed so that our discussion will take on more natural meaning.

Since we have already discussed the trichotomy and triquetra as separate groups within one model, each temple position found in the Quadra-Circumplex Model illustrates both groups as one; thus, each temple represents thought and action aligned or coalesced into one identity. Looking at the (uppermost) Northward temple, just as in our previous discussion, it shows Logic (West) on the left and Intuition (East) is on the right. The left element is labeled with a W while the right is labeled with an E, so that West-East elements are together labeled as W-E. While those temples above the horizontal plane are labeled W-E, those under the plane will be labeled M-E due to one's fallen upside-down state; thus creating a mirroring effect between the acronyms WE and ME, as will be explained shortly.

It is important to keep in mind that just as people are either right-handed or left-handed, everyone also tends to be dominant with one side of the mind or the other. Some people may indeed be balanced between the two sides, particularly those who have soundness of mind in the absolute Northward sense. For those Southward who have an equal weight between Western and Eastern mind, this would reflect a "false balance."[44]

> *And an highway shall be there, and a way,*
> *and it shall be called The way of holiness;*
> *the unclean shall not pass over it; but it [shall be] for those:*
> *the wayfaring men, though fools, shall not err [therein].*
> Isaiah 35:8

Let us reflect on what perfection necessitates. It requires positioning your temple Northward from a sound foundation so that by walking with Purpose (in the way of holiness) you may be open to receive the Spirit of God from above.

While absolute North and South positions have already been discussed, the additional temples found in the four quadrants of this model may better reflect how the mass of humanity is represented. Just like a compass, each quadrant will be labeled as a bearing, however, there's an interesting twist that we will discuss next. For now simply note how each bearing is described: **N-West** is

---

[44] Proverbs 11:1

Northward, West-dominant; **N-East** is Northward, East-dominant; **S-West** is Southward, West-dominant; and **S-East** is Southward, East-dominant.

> *He shall lean upon his house, but it shall not stand:*
> *he shall hold it fast, but it shall not endure.*
> Job 8:15

> *Thus saith the LORD of hosts; Let your hands be strong, ye*
> *that hear in these days these words by the mouth of the*
> *prophets, which [were] in the day [that] the foundation of the*
> *house of the LORD of hosts was laid,*
> *that the temple might be built.*
> Zechariah 8:9

Let's begin with the upper left quadrant or the N-West temple — Northward, West-dominant. It appears to lean toward the left. Why is this? While there are various ways biblically to identify what "house" means, in many passages (such as the one above) the head is said to house the mind and thus the soul. Zechariah stated, "Let your hands be strong... (so that) the (holy) temple might be built." In order to build one's temple from a house, action is necessary. Within one's own house the mind may lean toward the left or toward the right, or in our model, the person would be reliant principally on the Western or Eastern mind for reasoning and understanding. The extent to which a person raises his temple is dependent on the balance and strength of his house, a house that needs a sound foundation.

Note that the model depicts the N-West temple with a larger W relative to the E and with circles that reflect the same. Thus, Logic, which is fact-driven, is more developed than Intuition, which is truth-driven. In order for the temple to become more balanced (or level), the individual will need to increase the side of Intuition (truths). The model also illustrates: (1) equal-arm balances (or scales) that similarly represent mind-development as weighted, and (2) a horizontal plane that represents ground level, suggesting that those below the line create a pit for themselves with their own temples. So in order to become spiritually mature, you must first level and strengthen the soulful foundation of your house. This is so that with devotion (e.g., the act upon faith) you can wholeheartedly cleave unto the Lord with the heart, and thus raise your temple.

Let's consider how a Northward temple may fall from grace. Again, Purpose determines whether one is either Northward or Southward. If one was first N-West but falls, does the temple fall into the lower left or lower right quadrant? We will examine both the short-term and long-term implications of such falling.

> *To speak evil of no man, to be no brawlers, [but] gentle, shewing all meekness unto all men. For we ourselves also were sometimes foolish, disobedient, deceived, serving divers lusts and pleasures, living in malice and envy, hateful, [and] hating one another.*
> Titus 3:2-3

As an example of one temporarily falling from grace, consider this case: In the morning a Northward man is deeply committed to God, but at lunch time he engages in an argument with a co-worker. The dispute escalates so quickly that the man is regrettably provoked into accusation, rage, etc. This man initially entered into a situation for good reasons, unaware that it would escalate, but now his temple has been reduced. Note that it is simply impossible to be purposed in God while accusing and having fits of rage. Even though the individual has shown signs of spiritual immaturity, he has not forsaken the facts and truths that form the foundation of his house. So the overarching question is how long it will take to rebuild the cherished Northward temple. That depends, of course, on whether the Northward man recognizes his error, repents, and takes steps toward restoration.

b. Information and the Mark

We can fall from grace temporarily, as in the example above, or in the long term. Similarly, the fall may be blatant or subtle. One example of a subtle fall is the Northward person who becomes so intrigued by television and the Internet that these tangible things and their intangible content become his significant purpose in life instead of God. Again, while there may be good content in media, most discerning individuals acknowledge that the amount of bad content (driven from fiction and falsehood) has reached epic proportions. Allowing oneself to be so absorbed by media and the multitude of other preoccupations now available refocuses one's attention from the WE to the ME as the mind entertains Southward thoughts and ways. The saying, "You are what you eat" applies also to what the mind takes in through the eyes and ears.

Since morality and ethical behavior cannot be effectively legislated, one is allowed to freely choose to use technology and consume the content it delivers. With these media in most households and even miniaturized into hand-held devices, an astounding number of people are spellbound watching, listening, and learning as deplorable content stealthily transforms their minds and hearts.

> *And when Abram was ninety years old and nine, the LORD appeared to Abram, and said unto him, I [am] the Almighty God; walk before me, and be thou perfect.*
> Genesis 17:1

> *Mark the perfect [man], and behold the upright: for the end of [that] man [is] peace.*
> Psalm 37:37

> *And he causeth all, both small and great, rich and poor, free and bond, to receive a mark in their right hand, or in their foreheads: And that no man might buy or sell, save he that had the mark, or the name of the beast, or the number of his name. Here is wisdom. Let him that hath understanding count the number of the beast: for it is the number of a man; and his number [is] Six hundred threescore [and] six.*
> Revelation 13:16-18

Taking the Revelation passage above seriously, please understand that it is not a goal of this book (or the research it was based on) to add to or change prophecy. One reason John wrote the Book of Revelation was so that believers would attempt to linearize and discern its content and so that, as prophecies are fulfilled, the majesty of God's existence would become even more undeniable. I cite the Revelation passage above in an attempt to consider the

Human Understanding and Devotion

relevance of the mark while using the HUHD Model as a basis for discussion.

Since we have already considered the implications of thought relative to action, it is proposed that the mark (as figuratively illustrated) can represent thought and action in one of two ways (see Figure 10):

- Right-side-up (Northward) as God instills or pours in His Spirit through the wise mind and into the heart, thus indicative of the perfect man; or
- Upside-down (Southward) expelling or pouring out what good one may possess from the heart through the foolish mind and onto the ground, thus indicative of man (i.e., in his imperfect, fallen, unredeemed state).

Figure 10

For the moment, think about how we identify certain types of information as fictional, such as stories or shows on television, the Internet, radio, print media, etc. Contrast that with how we identify information as factual. Information never misses the mark of man's past, either good or bad. For instance, those who are Southward will use information for the purpose of casting doubt and suspicion on others whom they choose to destroy. In these cases factual accounts derived from proper and balanced perspectives are dismissed so that one's (upside-down) contentious views can be advanced – views against another put forward for reasons of self.

Now reflect on how information is currently compiled, obtained through various sources, and regurgitated through other sources (e.g., various media outlets, aggregators, blogs, etc.). Then think about the managers (and mismanagers) of information. Some direct sources of information include public and private records, photos, audio/video recordings, computer files, and even technologies that track one's movements and patterns of behavior (such as browsing/buying habits, or even by surveillance). Those who become purposed in finding and sharing the current (now past) mark of others are using such capture-and-retrieval methodologies (i.e., data-mining) as a form of high-tech dumpster diving. This is particularly the case when humans are motivated by greed and/or notoriety, rather than by faith in God.

> *For God commanded, saying,*
> *Honour thy father and mother: and,*
> *He that curseth father or mother, let him die the death.*
> Jesus, Mathew 15:4

Bear in mind, however, no one can ever know the true heart of another person through impersonal information-gathering techniques. But wouldn't Evil like the audience to think so? Would it not be Evil's intent to use media to teach its audience to be quick to characterize, quick to blame, quick to judge, and then react while seeking revenge, just as exemplified by fictional characters who teach false thoughts and ways? Would it not be Evil's intent to fill minds with so many preoccupations that they are inclined to take an idol's word for it and then to become less inclined to give people the benefit of the doubt on difficult issues? And would it not be Evil's intent to teach adults that their higher authority is worthless while also teaching children that they are more knowledgeable (not just smart but even more knowing) than their own upright authority figures. Sadly, such children will have little desire to learn from or have honor and respect for their parents and other wise persons.

> *Speak not in the ears of a fool:*
> *for he will despise the wisdom of thy words.*
> Proverbs 23:9

Some information sharers are certainly gifted with eloquence and interviewing skills and use their skills to help their audience to better know the person of interest. Consider those interviewers who may be viewed as Southward in light of the Proverbs passage above: that is, those bent against others who reason and respond differently, such as those Northward. In these cases there is little that the Northward interviewee can say or do that will prevent the distortion of his or her own words when regurgitated by the interviewer. While professional journalists, photo-journalists, etc., play a valuable role in bringing important issues to light, it is also evident that there are Southward persons whose modus operandi is to purposely take information out of context while using half-truths to achieve their own objectives.

Oftentimes those who are Southward are not aware that they are doing this; but those who are knowing recognize them clearly as accusers who incrementally build cases against others. This occurs not only in journalism and politics, but in all environments where gossip against others runs amok. Those who currently have Southward tendencies, however, may have a change of heart in the future. We never know who among them will one day turn Northward and become highly influential witnesses of God.

c. False Teacher: Modern Media & Entertainment

Today's media have the capacity to move the masses in an instant for reasons either good or bad. What do media teach through the use of drama, comedy, music, and visual effects as platforms for targeting the young and non-discerning? Many teach sexual promiscuity and whoredom, decadence, blame, violence, blasphemy, immoral and unethical behaviors, and mysteries of the dark. In fact, one could easily run down the list of all the behaviors reflective of disgrace[45] and find them glorified by these media.

---

[45] Examples of *disgrace* may be found in: Proverbs 6:16-19, 1 Corinthians 6:9-10, Galatians 5:19-21, 2 Timothy 3:1-7

For many deceivers are entered into the world, who confess not that Jesus Christ is come in the flesh. This is a deceiver and an antichrist.

2 John 1:7

Recall that those who are Northward recognize the thoughts and actions of those who are Southward as false (or antichrist) in nature, whereas those who are Southward will (unknowingly) reach the same conclusion about those who are Northward. Though some are deemed false prophets (past/present/future) among both Christian and non-Christian groups, there is one false teacher whom many dismiss as a threat. Ponder these questions: Is it difficult to see that media do in fact contain the image of man—that is, Southward man? Is it difficult to see that the sum of Southward sounds and images from media stealthily and with time induce/seduce the unknowing and even the once knowing audience into unjust and merciless acts, while also encouraging foolishness and disgrace? Biblical truth may indeed help shed light on why many—after being so purposed in antichrist teachings (the cause)—do such unimaginable things (the effect).

In contrast to those who become self-actualized when Northward, many without a higher presence of mind will instead find reasons to deprecate themselves and to entertain notions of self-defeat.

There might be a difference between this false teacher and what Christian apologists regard as a false prophet, but most discerning individuals will agree that this teacher is indeed a powerful influence, and its effects (in the Southward sense) on those who are physically and spiritually immature are particularly alarming. In each false case the audience (unknowingly) chooses to believe the lie presented by media so that the lie becomes their reality. In the case of the false teacher, the goal for many producers/creators is to have the audience identify with fictional characters, primarily those that have something to teach. This is what sells!

So what does this suggest about an author who writes fictional books? Even if only designed for entertainment, all stories of man are inherently teachings of one kind or another. If such teachings are not oriented toward "true" North as fact and truth, then they are oriented away from North and move into areas of fiction and falsehoods. There is obviously a matter of degree away from absolute North as to how destructive some fictional or false stories are to the psyche of audience members – each input relative to the recipient's level of maturity.

Make no mistake: There are media and books available today that contain exceptional Northward content (clean, wholesome, good humored, fact and truth-driven) as these influences become one's reality. Many, perhaps most, programs are somewhere in between extreme North and South poles. Therefore, the overall impact of negative influences on the human psyche is not necessarily a function of how bad certain programs are, because the worst ones are self-evident and can be regulated. The impact is more often from the influx of programs that continue to push the envelope that defines what acceptable content is.

As it pertains only to Southward content, think about how many find entertainment in the exploitation of those who have done wrong or who have made serious mistakes that are now forever recorded/imaged and then broadcast on demand for the interested public. Then think of all those who have been exploited simply for doing the right thing. A simple example—911 calls made by those striving to help another person or perhaps in a state of panic. So many recordings are unnecessarily aired by the news and entertainment industries for the sake of curiosity, intrigue, and amusement—at times some recordings actually become the news story itself. Those making such calls would have had no idea that they could be shown in a defamatory or demoralizing light. In some cases (with the caller's voice recognized by others) these recordings may in fact place individuals and their families at risk from those with ill intent connected to the case.

This type of programming supposedly represents real life (as it is called reality TV), but for believers these things represent a bigger problem. It is not simply about those who have done wrong or made mistakes, it's about the hearts and minds of those who become engrossed in and desensitized by exposure to the exploitation and destruction of others.

Despite the importance of self-regulating and filtering all the available inputs to the mind, many people will still feel compelled to receive Southward content for hours at a time. We have a choice whether to sit at the feet of this teacher—or not. If parents fail to realize the effects of such content, they can be sure that this sort of teacher will eventually become their children's surrogate parent. The child will be exposed to content that leads him or her to grow up with a false sense of maturity and a false sense of awareness as the super-ego is disregarded altogether. Again, the issue is not the media themselves; rather, it is the type of content chosen that leads consumers to become unwittingly purposed in media.

While certain live or reality-driven shows may be regarded as factual, many (if not most) can be regarded as false because of what the content teaches. For instance, even if a criminal shown committing a crime is later found guilty, wouldn't these fact-driven images effectively teach/encourage those currently fallen how to do the same without getting caught? The viewer's sense of reality becomes further skewed as he watches, listens to, and learns from the "best" of what this false teacher has to offer, particularly because action and suspense programs are oftentimes glamorized.

Consider also the benign teachings within media that are outright contradictions to godly teachings. For instance, take a program in which a character dies and is shown having the spirit of light within and rising into the Kingdom—this, after a life of being purposed in everything in the physical realm, never seeking to become upright in the truest sense. Certainly, most in the audience will realize that this is simply a show, but many who are spiritually immature will not. What about programs that trump up and encourage magic and demonic ways? Will these not have an effect on the psyche of the immature and adolescent? Sure they do, but since bad programs are simply regarded as fiction and entertainment, this sort of mind input has yet to be regarded as a threat by the majority.

Reflect on our discussion of the Christ Pantocrator image. If one learns certain subjective matter (as represented by one hand) which causes the individual to do things (as expressed with the other hand), then this thought and action response has vertical implications: one either rises or falls as the result of what one has been subjectively taught. This may come about either as directly purposed or as an indirect consequence of one's interest in certain influences. Imaginative human works are by nature subjective inputs that will shape the Eastern mind—the side of ideologies and of beliefs. Thus, programs that are both subjective in nature and also Southward should not simply be regarded as fiction: they can more accurately be regarded as false. So while Southward content may not be religion per se, such input can certainly hinder one from ever awakening.

A consequence of negative input is that as more people become purposed in these teachings, more will desire to be revered or perhaps even worshipped by others in this (false) light as well. If one's ambition is to be admired by others in this sort of light, what does this suggest about one's greater purpose relative to others? If one's purpose is for others to have faith in or believe in him or her, does this not suggest an ambition to become an idol? In other words, such a person will (unknowingly) seek to become the tangible purpose in the minds of others. This is not to suggest that all those who find themselves in the spotlight wish to become the tangible purpose of others or to be worshipped. It does mean when a person loses that all-important sense of direction (Northward Purpose), he or she may easily fall downward toward those who are reaching up, each ready, willing, and able to give that aspiring individual anything he or she desires; thus falsely exalting the image of self. Sooner or later, won't idolization lead toward disappointment and destruction for all involved? It absolutely will!

d. Fall and Rise

Back to the question about where the (upper left) N-West temple falls—is it toward the lower left quadrant or the lower right? The Quadra-Circumplex Model (Figure 9) proposes that the N-West temple falls into the lower right quadrant labeled as S-West, not labeled S-East, but why? The answer is relatively simple, but it may necessitate explaining the process as a movement in physical form to see how the model applies to and is analogous with a movement in physiological form.

The model illustrates that: (1) in the negative, downward sense, the *fall* of mind is the result of a lack of balance; and (2) in the positive, upward sense, the *rise* of mind (over body) is the result of establishing balance. So one's rise from a fallen state is contingent upon the mind being lifted over the body, the result of balance as first instigated by faith in God.

The Movement of "Falling and Rising"

Some readers may think the following movement may be easy to do in the physical sense; however, unless you are (physically) fit and flexible you should not attempt it. It involves stretching in ways that your body may not be accustomed to. If you do decide to attempt it, be sure it is done over a carpeted area. You should be near something large and soft like a bed or couch to support yourself with. Nothing should be nearby that could possibly cause injury in case you fall. Having someone else present is also recommended. And even if you think the risk of injury is minimal, for some there may be the possibility of fainting, or worse.

With that said, I insist that you simply use your imagination to visualize each step of the process.

The Movement of "Falling and Rising": The goal is to understand how and why the N-West temple falls from the upper left quadrant into the lower right quadrant, called S-West. First, imagine standing straight up and against next to something large and soft to brace your self with. Without leaning forward and with legs slightly apart begin the slow process of leaning toward the left. As shown in the upper left quadrant of the Quadra-Circumplex Model, this would be indicative of a mindset that is Northward, West-dominant (e.g., N-West). As the head leans further left, so do the shoulders, as the upper torso follows along.

While continuing to lean further left, keep in mind how much lower to the ground the West of mind is relative to the East. As you proceed lower there comes a point that you are unable to go any further (that is, without physically falling). The progression of one's physiological fall, though, has not stopped. It continues on by swinging the upper torso from extreme left over to extreme right, passing through the area at which you would have been bending horizontally forward from the waist. The movement between the two extremes is regarded simply as a transition between one physiological phase (or one quadrant) to another. During the process of swinging from left to right, be sure that the West-dominant mind continues to remain lower than the East. After arriving at the extreme right position your head may now swing further down and

Human Understanding and Devotion

back toward the left, coming to rest in a (sort of) 'false' balance state of mind. At this point one's head will be upside-down perpendicular to the ground (hence, mind under body).

Now, of course, would be a good time to decide to lift yourself back up again. The sort of lift required here is physical in nature. It requires the pull of certain leg and back muscles to overcome the force of gravity. This is so that the body can rise back up and find itself into a (sort of) balanced state of mind again.

With the exercise over, reflect on what occurred during and after the process of falling. Your view of the world not only turned upside down, but also backwards. In essence, for those fallen the act of moving forward and up only results in moving further back and down.

Obviously the sort of lift required for one's state of mind has little to do with a *direct* command by the brain to flex certain muscles to raise oneself back up. It has more to do with *influences* that are good and constructive. Influences such as these are received from God and those godly in forms of nurturing love, grace, mercy, etc. From such expressions then one's *indirect* heart-driven response for doing good on earth will build up his or her state of mind.

Without love, then Evil and those unknowingly committed to evil will naturally seek to bind others in order to receive a (false) sense of lift for themselves. They do this with the (unknowing) goal of reducing such others by way of condemnation, prosecution, and destruction. Such ways can be accomplished directly or even indirectly by influencing others fallen to act out evil on one's behalf.

So how does one overcome the negative forces of those bent on destruction? The only way is realizing the love of God. He is the only source for lifting the soul against oppression and tyranny. Love is unbinding and functions as the physiological anti-gravity for all that is corrupt in this world and in one's conscience (i.e., guilt, shame, doubt, the unknown, etc.).

Now think about how essential the use of geographical coordinates was in this discussion. It helped establish a basis for illustrating the dynamics between how those N-West fall and rise; and similarly, how those N-East fall and rise.

There's more, though. Reflect back on the model – notice that the N-West falls into an upside-down *East* position, as the N-East falls into an upside-down *West* position. In other words, each upside-down state of mind exists out of sync and out of harmony with what is truly West and what is truly East.

Allow me to briefly explain why this important. First, I have argued that the process for reasoning out unknowns about human behavior, generally-speaking, is from subjective East to objective West. This process involves both sides of mind working together to arrive at knowledge. Even if East-dominant, one's knowing (or unknowing) point of view will consistently be derived by West of mind functionality. While points of view are derived from the West, answers to questions that seek deeper meanings as to *why* are derived from the East. This is a key concept to reflect on as we continue with this discussion.

Think about the flow of reasoning for those in the upper quadrants relative to the flow of those in the lower quadrants. In the upper, the flow is broad-based in that (from East to West) Intuition precedes Logic. In these cases both sides of mind have the opportunity to work in tandem, in balance, and in harmony to unify for the greater good.

The paradox for those who are upside-down is that their reasoning is counter-intuitive and their response is counter-productive for all that is upright and good. That's because the flow of reasoning stops short of one's potential for overall understanding. How can this be? It's because (from East to West) Logic now precedes Intuition. This leads to responses that are similar to the old adage: "putting the cart before the horse." Here the effect of one's response (e.g., good works) is first-purposed; this, instead of first seeking the higher Cause (i.e., God), so that the effect of one's thinking (according to one's Intuitive state) and response comes as a natural manifestation God's love and grace.

Let's think of an example of how this may apply. Assume a man says to some acquaintances: "I walk by faith." If his normal flow of reasoning suggests otherwise, in that the Intuitive of his faith is constantly subject to Logic, then how can others ever testify that he actually walks by faith? Even while this man has been known for saying nice things and perhaps is even able to recall certain Bible verses at a moment's notice, it may be argued that he does not in the most complete sense of the phrase "walk by faith." Why? As the model demonstrates, for matters of faithful responsiveness this man's West-to-East reasoning will seem counter-intuitive to others who respond more truly by faith. In essence, his thoughts and ways will seem more indicative of an upside-down state of mind – one that more naturally demonstrates cynicism, criticism and control. Again, this is because his Logic precedes Intuition, and as a result, his mindset will be that which argues justice or just ways before mercy.

Children of God are raised by God and those who are godly so that the Intuitive of faith becomes the driving force for faithful responsiveness. When the Intuitive precedes and yet is in balance with Logic, then and only then will the process for reasoning and response be constructive and for the greater good. In these cases, one's mindset will be that of merciful ways before and yet in balance with just ways.

Let's take the issue of flow from East to West one more step. When upside-down the mind is not only functionally divided between the two sides of West and East, it is also in conflict with itself. In other words, for those not yet knowing the futility of existing in an upside-down state of mind only leads to a self-esteem issue and a struggle with the implications of cause-effect. Contrast this with a mind represented in the upper quadrants. While it is also functionally divided, the self-esteem issue is overcome through broad-based constructive opportunities to unify for the greater good, individually and collectively.

So if the mind is in conflict with itself, what does this suggest about how certain points of view are established and how certain answers to questions about deeper meanings come about? One way to answer this question is to think of those S-East and S-West as political groups similar to the Left and the Right, respectively.

Those on the Left and upside-down will make certain points about the Right in the attempt to prove how unfeeling or heartless they are. And those on the Right and upside-down will make certain points about the Left in the attempt to prove how illogical and out of touch with reality they are.

Both arguments have some merit, but why? Looking back at the model, it begins with the understanding that when upside-down: (1) the Left (driven by feeling, emotion) will draw from the *western* most portion of their Intuitive (e.g., the farthest left on the page) to make objectively-based and yet emotionally charged points against the Right; and (2) the Right (driven by logic) will draw from the eastern most portion of their Logic (e.g., the farthest right on the page) to support their reasons why factual points made against the Left make better sense.

Needless to say, arguments made by each side will make little sense to those on the other side, as suspicion about the other grows even more. What about those represented in the upper quadrants? They will recognize the arguments made by those in conflict with each other as destructive to the overall effort to unify.

Those who continue to deny God, the higher Cause, are destined for limited understanding that only leads to a fallen state. According to Logic, each will end up practicing the effect of perceptible goodness. They will do this instead of being guided by the Intuitive of faith that actually results in broad understandings which lead to natural goodness. Not only that, each in their own way will be most apt to cause others to respond or be the cause that they respond to. Efforts such as these only lead to further divisiveness within the family, the community, and world.

Because each of these non-believers will often be ineffective in causing others to respond to their own will (this, instead of God's Will), then each will become more separated from those on the other side and/or become more engaged with the vicious cycle of unjust and merciless acts against all those outside one's group affiliation.

So as you can see, regardless of how well-meaning one side or the other may appear to be, due to the mentality of seeking to conquer and claim victory, each will remain divided against the other until there is one day reason to respond to a higher Cause, individually and collectively.

Again, the only way to overcome one's upside-down state of mind is with love. But love can only be received by those willing to acknowledge and accept the Supremacy of man's Creator – God Himself; and then (according to *subjective* want and desire of Christ Jesus) respond with love, grace, and mercy toward others. With love as a primary instinct, the Intuitive aspect of one's reasoning and response will precede Logic. In these cases the soul will have the greatest opportunity to overcome the *lower* (discourse) of human consciousness and dissent, while being lifted into the *upper* (harmony) of God-consciousness and consent.

At the beginning of this section I asked that you resist viewing the Quadra-Circumplex Model as a compass. As I hope you can now see, that's because the fall and rise of those N-West and N-East is not directly below the original quadrant (respectively), but diagonally opposite. So the model really doesn't represent a compass at all.

By employing geographic coordinates, though, particularly as they apply to the upper quadrants in alignment with and according to the East cornerstone: Jesus, it becomes possible to see how the model helps to explain vertical stages of psychological growth and development. Interestingly, coordinates like these also help to explain the egocentricities of those in the lower quadrants – those who continue to refuse to align themselves with the upper coordinates. So those not yet raised will remain motivated by earthly influences that more often serve to satisfy self-interests. They choose this rather than recognizing and appreciating the influences of God that serve to motivate humans to response by, thus becoming raised.

God willing, it's the broad-based form of reasoning as represented by the upper quadrants of the model that I hope to tap further into and ultimately demonstrate as our discussion continues.

At this point I also hope that the reason why the N-West temple falls from the upper left to the lower right quadrant is clear. Contrast this movement with the notion of the N-West temple falling into the lower left position. Such a fall is not likely since the individual was once West-dominant, and to fall into the S-East quadrant he would have to become East-dominant.

This would be as unlikely as a right-handed person's becoming left-handed while also having a change of heart. So again, one's "mirroring" fall from the WE into the ME is represented from N-West to S-West and from N-East to S-East. The overall point here is that there are temples above the horizontal plane and temples below, each position reflecting mind-dominance relative to a higher Purpose or to a lower Purpose.

While the individual described in the N-West quadrant has a well-developed (fact-driven) Logic, he or she also possesses truth on the side of Intuition. While truth is not well-developed in such individuals, it is certainly significant, as otherwise this temple would not be Northward. In order to balance the foundation of the house (and thus the temple), the person may choose to further develop his or her understanding of truth. However, because the element of Intuition is weaker, such a person may easily fall prey to falsehoods that will challenge the truth as he or she currently knows it. Here the side of Intuition will be weakened, which may ultimately compromise the facts known on the side of Logic.

Let's think of an example about how this sort of scenario may play out in real life. While science is geared to verify facts, most everyday facts are learned through personal experience(s). Take a robbery, for instance. Interestingly, each witness to a robbery will provide details that will differ considerably from others.

Let's say that one witness, a person who leans N-West, says to the police: "Let me tell you what happened." Again, this person is strong in Logic as the side of Intuition is weak. Much of his statements will be guided by objectivity as he provides very detailed and perhaps accurate information about what took place. Will this be enough to solve the case? It all depends in one's mind on what the case involves. You see, there is more to solving any case involving human understanding and behavior than meets the eye.

Let's say that another witness, one who leans N-East, hears what was said and remarks: "You saw details that I really didn't notice. What you may have seen but didn't mention, though, was how desperate and afraid the robber looked. Call it intuition, but I have a feeling that he did this not only for the need for money, food, or perhaps drugs, he also did it out of fear. His fear could be about what he's currently going through, or it could be for what he imagines his future to be. As I see it, his problem isn't so much that he robbed the store – *thankfully*, no one got hurt! – it's that he doesn't know how to overcome his greatest fear – the unknown."

The truth is that the robber is having a difficult time because he fails to appreciate how (subjective) faith in God is the first step in fulfilling one's sense of knowing. When fulfilling need as this does become important, then money and all the things that money can buy will no longer be the focus of one's purpose and ambitions. This is particularly so with ill-gotten gains.

So as you can see, both eye-witness accounts – one more reality-based (e.g. N-West) and the other more spiritually-based (e.g., N-

East) – provided details that the other person didn't immediately gravitate toward when sharing. While solving the case in the physical, logical sense is important (i.e., a Western apprehension), it is just as or even more important to solve the case in the spiritual, intuitive sense (i.e., an Eastern apprehension). This is so that the vertical implications about what is good and bad can be understood in the broadest sense. So if one's approach to solving any case about human depravities is based primarily on objective facts, then he or she will fail to appreciate deeper, subjective meanings as to *why* corrupt behaviors of man actually manifest on earth.

Let's now get a feel for how the dialog could have played out by twisting the East-dominant eye-witness account. So while keeping the N-West witness as our constant, let's replace the N-East with one that is S-East. Again, the S-East person is dominant in Intuition as the side of Logic is weak. The difficulty here is that while those S-East are intuitive (i.e., feeling, emotional) each will be driven by falsehoods, not truths. In this case the person's response may be something like this: "You saw details that I overlooked. What you didn't mention, though, was how desperate and afraid the robber looked. Who can blame him? If there was a God there wouldn't be any suffering in the world, and there wouldn't be hatred and violence. And people wouldn't have to think about robbing a store in order to feed their family! Money and all things money can buy make people happy, not God. That's the truth!"

Since the N-West person (the listener) is weak in (subjective) Truth, he may have been dissuaded and even demotivated to offer as much about what he knows best. How can this be said? It's because he may now empathize with the sentiments of those bent South, and now even support their cause. Here the N-West man will have been influenced to hesitate and perhaps even reject what he knew was an upright and forward response. The sort of false truths that those N-West support only compromise the objectivity of mind that facts help illuminate when sharing.

How far can the N-West person fall? Keep in mind that facts are linear understandings and truths (in the subjective sense) are holistic. Because subjective thought is inherently disorganized, many weak in contemplative thought of God's Truth will be most apt to disregard the spiritual implications of the causes of human thought and behavior. In other words, their answers to why a person acted as he did will be based more on what is perceived in reality rather than on understanding that the unseen influences between good and bad are more truly the cause of what manifests on earth.

If those who are N-West do succumb to the notion that influences, including spiritual influences, are inconsequential, then each will be hampered in being a good witness, and even in knowing what "balance" truly means as future events unfold. Important details such as factual testimonies will instead be held back, as lies and exaggerations (i.e., fiction) will more often be proposed as facts. These sorts of facts, though, are only deceits designed to mislead those interested in solving the overall case.

Thus, we see how one can be brought down by the weaker link. This is an important theme to reflect upon since it stands to reason that if Evil cannot eliminate the stronger, it will aggressively work to take down the weaker, as this will be the path of least resistance. The weakest may be considered the least adept in either Logic or Intuition, or they may even be certain people associated with the strongest person. These examples are not only found in family, community, and work environments but are also found in news, politics, Internet sites/blogs, email, etc. Again, it is through media that such take-down efforts are most effective.

One's fall may temporarily compromise the soundness of his foundation, but will not necessarily destroy it. Turning upside-down, however, requires exchanging known fact and truth for fiction and falsehood, while the mind and body are reduced to foolishness and disgrace—a more profound form of darkness.

Thus, if one is fallen into the S-West quadrant and begins to understand why the light and love from above are so important, then he or she will progress into the N-West quadrant. The dynamics between the N-East and S-East quadrants are similar to those between N-West and S-West, as just discussed. Here the N-East individual is Northward, East-dominant; thus, facts as driven from the West are significant but not as well-developed as truths on the side of the East. Such a person may choose to emphasize factual issues so that his foundation will become more level and strong. Even so, since the West side is the weaker link, he or she may (unknowingly) be drawn to seek out fiction rather than fact. This will

Human Understanding and Devotion

only jeopardize what was once known as fact, which in turn may ultimately jeopardize what was known as truth. At this point it should be apparent why education is so important for all citizens.

So now we've discussed the basics of how the model accounts for one's fall and rise with both short-term and long-term implications. Though some people may be absolutely Northward or Southward, most likely are not. Thus, the four quadrants of the Quadra-Circumplex Model may better represent the greater mass of humanity.

Briefly, let's consider a hypothetical fall beginning with the N-East temple. The individual is well-developed on the side of Intuition, but less so on the side of Logic. This weaker element leaves the individual more susceptible to affiliating with groups that spew fiction. In so doing, the individual effectively stifles the mind's weakest link resulting in one or two things: (1) he or she will more easily and unknowingly seek out fiction that holds itself out as fact; and/or (2) he or she will attempt to strengthen the side of Intuition while further denigrating the side of Logic. While this temple was already leaning in the N-East position, such actions will only cause the temple to lean further East, thus moving the temple down toward the horizon. Remember, fiction and falsehoods weaken the Northward temple, causing it to move downward, whereas facts and truth strengthen it and cause it to move upward.

> *Every good gift and every perfect gift is from above, and cometh down from the Father of lights, with whom is no variableness, neither shadow of turning.*
> James 1:17

The weakened N-East individual will likely engage in more extreme thoughts and behaviors since Logic (the weaker link) has been compromised. The individual will rely more on subjective reasoning from the side of Intuition to make his or her point. The same would occur with one who is N-West, but in this case, with Intuition compromised, he will rely more on extreme objective reasoning from the side of Logic to make his or her point. While both temple positions were already casting outward shadows (as directed from the light above), each temple leans further away from absolute North and casts even longer shadows.

> *A double minded man [is] unstable in all his ways.*
> James 1:8

What will be the breaking point for those committed to the West or the East while denouncing the other side? Because such individual mindsets possess some fact and truth but also some fiction and falsehood, the element of Purpose would be in a state of vacillation between North and South poles. What's the result? The person becomes double-minded, suggesting a tendency to be hypocritical or easily influenced. This bi-directional fluctuation of Purpose may be due to extreme thoughts and ways, but it can also be a function of one's spiritual immaturity or adolescence.

Recall the weakest link: Even the most ardent fact-driven or truth-driven individual will eventually lapse into Southward territory when fiction and/or falsehoods are introduced into the mind. Thus, choosing to denounce either Logic or Intuition, will only lead to following extreme thoughts and ways that in turn lead to double-mindedness. If, however, one chooses to embrace the qualities of the other side, one's foundation will become more level, stable, and strong. It is the day-to-day decisions and resulting actions that incrementally and progressively help build upon or destroy the temple and its foundation. Such changes can be depicted in the model as movements of temple position in circumplex form.

From Fallen to Risen State

Let's now consider the progression from a fallen state into an arisen state—when one becomes enlightened with fact and truth. We can begin with the S-East position (lower left). Though the weakest link can be the cause of one's fall, it can also be the cause of or impetus for one's rise from a fallen state. Why? Because in this case the individual may be so committed to falsehoods (since East-dominant) that there is little chance that he or she will seek a change unless facts (of the West) are introduced. When facts are introduced, then falsehoods (of the East) can be challenged, so that truths can be more easily advanced. Therefore, the progression of one's rise begins from the S-East position and approaches the horizon from below. It then twists over to the N-East quadrant just above the horizon. From this point on, as both fact and truth become known, the temple will rise further into the N-East quadrant. Bear in mind that those who are East-dominant will absorb truth issues more quickly than fact issues. But in this case it was fact issues that helped spur a conversion as facts also pointed to a different conception of the truth.

The same process applies for the model's S-West quadrant. The progression of his or her rise begins with the S-West position, approaches the horizon from below, and then twists over to the N-West position just above the horizon. From this point on, as both fact and truth become known, the temple will rise further into the N-West quadrant. Those West-dominant will absorb fact issues more quickly than truth issues. But in this case it was truth issues that helped spur a conversion as truth also pointed to a different interpretation of the facts.

The paths of their way are turned aside^{H3943};
they go to nothing, and perish.
Job 6:18

And make straight paths for your feet, lest that which is lame
be turned out of the way^{G1624}; but let it rather be healed.
Hebrews 12:13

The circumplex movements between upper and lower quadrants are described as "twists." In the two passages above the terms *laphath* and *ektrepō*, respectively, are defined in Strong's lexicons as "turned aside" and "turned out of the way." The Outline for Biblical Usage for each is as follows:

Laphath[46] H3943 (Old Testament):
1) to twist, grasp, turn, grasp with a twisting motion
   a) (Qal) to grasp
   b) (Niphal) to twist, weave, wind

---

[46] Blue Letter Bible. Dictionary and Word Search for laphath (Strong's 3943). Blue Letter Bible. 1996-2009. 14 May 2009. < http://www.blueletterbible.org/lang/lexicon/lexicon.cfm?Strongs=H3943&t=KJV&sf=4 >

Ektrepō[47] G1624 (New Testament):
1) to turn or twist out
   a) in a medical sense used of dislocated limbs
2) to turn off or aside
3) to be turned aside
4) to turn aside
5) to turn away from, to shun a thing, to avoid meeting or associating with one

> *By his spirit he hath garnished the heavens;*
> *his hand hath formed the crooked serpent.*
> Job 26:13

Parallel to *The Movement of 'Falling and Rising'* discussion above, consider how one may turn aside or twist out of the way in the Quadra-Circumplex Model. We suggested that a person's weakest link can be the reason for his or her long-term fall or rise. Again, as a temple approaches the horizontal plane within one quadrant, it will twist or slide to the quadrant diagonally opposite – similar to a helix or a cross of another form – in order to continue its vertical journey. Thus, the progression of one's rise or fall will be between the N-West and S-West quadrants or the N-East and S-East quadrants.

When we plot the progression of such movements we find the appearance of a normal S between the N-West and S-West positions and a mirrored S between the N-East and the S-East positions (see Figure 11). If the progression of one's fall is Southward (as revealed with lies, deceit, etc.), then it would be hard to dismiss the point that such crooked movements toward the pit below appear to be characteristic of a snake or serpent led by the temple.

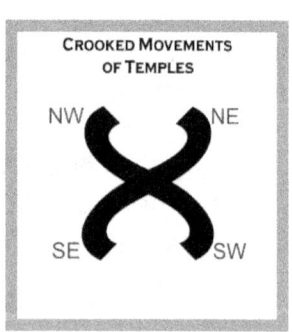

Figure 11

---

[47] Blue Letter Bible. Dictionary and Word Search for ektrepō (Strong's 1624). Blue Letter Bible. 1996-2009. 14 May 2009. < http://www.blueletterbible.org/lang/lexicon/lexicon.cfm?Strongs=G1624&t=KJV&sf=4 >

Human Understanding and Devotion

And I will bring the blind by a way that they knew not; I will lead them in paths that they have not known: I will make darkness light before them, and crooked things straight. These things will I do unto them, and not forsake them.

Isaiah 42:16

So while temple movements toward the South ('**S**') can bring to mind a serpent, movements toward the North ('**N**') can bring to mind two pillars (conjoined by a slope). Why pillars when rising and not a serpent? It's because with total commitment toward God – as the pillars of facts and truths to be guided by are increased, particularly God's Truth – the spiritually blind may see and the "crooked things" may be made straight.

3. Stratum Model

I hope you can see why it was important to involve the geographic coordinates of N-West, N-East, S-East, and S-West in our last discussion. Their use helped to illustrate the helix of fall and rise relating to one's physiological nature. It's a phenomenon that could not have been explained simply with the terms Logic and Intuition, or other terms associated with each, respectively.

Now that a basic understanding of such coordinates has been conveyed, though, we can transition over to Logic and Intuition as the primary way to discuss West and East functionality; this, relative to the vertical of North and South, good and bad, etc. In so doing I hope the remaining concepts will take on more natural meaning.

Let's now consider the Stratum Model. The point here is that one is either committed: (1) Southward toward the interests of self while exalting the id and strengthening Satan's empire; or (2) Northward toward interests of God while exalting Him and strengthening His Kingdom. The Stratum Model (see Figure 12) reflects this choice as well as the overarching implications of one's eternal destiny.

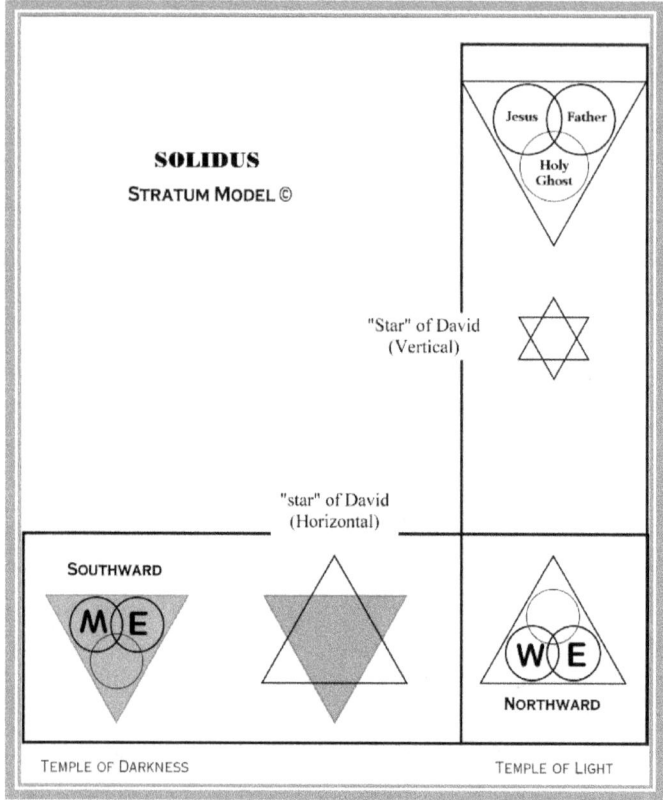

Figure 12

A simple Internet search reveals that for centuries Biblical symbols have been used in both good and bad ways. These symbols are not only found in religion but appear also in the military, government, business, sports, and so on. In most cases symbols suggest a meaning that bolsters the group's identity or campaign. Though these symbols may be used innocently, this is not always the case. Some individuals and groups use symbols in Southward ways in attempts to affect their circumstance in the plane of human relationships. Those influences that claim to be good—and yet reject the light and love of God—only shape the (unknowingly) curious mind into accepting (false) "wisdom" and "grace." Those with

Human Understanding and Devotion

upside-down temples blindly seek relationships in the horizontal plane—relationships premised more on egoism[48] than altruism.[49]

Though the models in this book use symbols for illustrative and discussion purposes, I am not suggesting that symbols or things made from symbols should become purposed. While symbols may be used to represent one's relationship vis-à-vis God, the purpose they serve here is to reveal why it is important to have purpose in God.

> *And David went on, and grew great,*
> *and the LORD God of hosts [was] with him.*
> 2 Samuel 5:10

The symbol of Israel can be represented and understood in one of two ways: (1) on the horizontal plane as a mix of Northward and Southward temples forming a six-pointed "star" (lower case); or (2) in the vertical plane whereby (Northward) Israel remains out of touch with those with upside-down temples. This "Star" will forever remain pristine because it is situated between two great loves in reciprocating adoration for one another, the placement of which can never be corrupted by the flesh. The Star of David represents the union between the Godhead and His body (the Church) as believers gain in the truest form of love, wisdom, and grace.

> *Be ye therefore perfect,*
> *even as your Father which is in heaven is perfect.*
> Jesus, Matthew 5:48

An important element of this model depicts Jesus' heavenly position[50] with the Father whereby the Holy Trinity[51] forming the Godhead exists in a perfected state toward His Body below.

---

[48] *Egoism* is defined as: excessive concern for oneself with or without exaggerated feelings of self-importance. (2009). In Merriam-Webster Online Dictionary. Retrieved November 15, 2009, from http://www.merriam-webster.com/dictionary/egoism

[49] *Altruism* is defined as: unselfish regard for or devotion to the welfare of others. (2009). In Merriam-Webster Online Dictionary. Retrieved November 15, 2009, from http://www.merriam-webster.com/dictionary/altruism

> *And they, continuing daily with one accord in the temple, and breaking bread from house to house, did eat their meat with gladness and singleness of heart, Praising God, and having favour with all the people. And the Lord added to the church daily such as should be saved.*
> Acts 2:46-47

The New Testament provides testimonies of Jesus' existence. No other prophet was able to accomplish what Jesus did for the sake of love, righteousness, and holiness.[52] There are many ways to discuss the relationship between the Godhead (as life-sustainer) and His Body (the Church). Religious practices such as the Eucharist are indeed important for many who worship and reflect upon the divine relationship with God. Also, while WE (as parts of a greater whole) may break bread and share bread in His Name, it is because of the Star of David that believers become coalesced into one communion with God and with others. It is because of Him that WE as parts of a greater whole are nourished, satisfied, and made complete.

---

[50] Acts 7:55
[51] Matthew 28:19
[52] Romans 3:22-24, Philippians 1:11, 3:9, Luke 1:75

B. Applications of Solidus

In this section we consider various ways to apply the model (as presented in the *Basis of Solidus* section) to understanding various big picture issues. The main objective of this section is to effectively describe larger group dynamics as being either conducive to overall harmony (while directed toward a higher, divine authority) or counter to it.

> *Be ye not unequally yoked together with unbelievers: for what fellowship hath righteousness with unrighteousness? and what communion hath light with darkness?*
> 2 Corinthians 6:14

The main thesis is: Those with faith-based purpose in God not only believe differently from those without faith, they also reason and respond differently. In the Southward sense, there are non-believers who reason from an earthly perspective centered on self; and in the Northward sense, there are believers who reason and respond from a God-centered perspective. Only by being first-purposed in God can the balance of mind between objective and subjective reasoning processes become level, stable, and strong. When these two independent forms of understanding are yoked for the greater good, not only can the mind more easily discern important matters of life, there are greater opportunities to become yoked with others with the same purpose.

It is futile to approach issues of life simply from the basis of who is on the Left and who is on the Right. These are horizontal in nature—approaches that disregard all vertical implications dictated by purpose. Proper and fitting resolution occurs only when yoked Northward.

Putting aside all religious differences for a moment—regardless of whether a group is East-dominant or West-dominant, all groups that are purposed Northward toward the God of love and light come together under one higher authority. One side may approach life more intellectually or judicially, while the other side may approach life more from the basis of beliefs or mercy, but both sides are necessary in order to collectively balance the foundation.

From such balance there are greater opportunities to become yoked, and thus unified into one Northward accord. Contrast this in the opposite—if both sides are in a fallen state, then both are yoked into one Southward accord. Therefore, if one is not engaged with the building up of souls, then one is engaged with the destruction of souls.

> *Stand fast therefore in the liberty wherewith Christ hath made us free, and be not entangled again with the yoke of bondage.*
> Galatians 5:1

Becoming yoked Northward (arising) means driving forward and looking up (e.g., future, life) against a certain resistance in order to achieve liberty. In contrast, becoming yoked Southward (falling) means driving down and looking back (e.g., history, death) while becoming entangled in bondage. Contrast these views with attempts at dual-control, which are usually generated by means of conformity-driven measures designed to prevent one side or the other from falling, but having nothing to do with arising.

In free societies no one should be subjected to or compelled to observe any form of religion. Even Christianity should not be imposed by others, for free love requires free will, which obviously implies freedom of religion.

With this said, however, we did allude in our previous discussion to one religious-like influence (the various media purveyors of information) that moves about largely unchecked. Most people would dismiss the idea that content broadcast via television and other technologies is religion per se, and consider it merely entertainment. If, however, one becomes so absorbed, preoccupied, and purposed into media (especially that which sensationalizes subject matter geared to advance the image of self), then such inputs are influences opposing the religion of God.

To reiterate, subjective teachings of Southward content are inherently false. Thus, while such content may be dismissed as a form of religion, it can certainly be regarded as anti-religion, because it subjectively floods the Eastern mind with falsehoods as dreamed or imagined by man; influences that persist in the dreams and imaginations of audience members. In these cases the minds/psyches of those captivated will be hindered from ever longing to pursue and

Human Understanding and Devotion

be influenced by the Word and by the Spirit of God, as also revealed in thoughts, dreams/visions, and by intuition.

Even so, such anti-religion should be allowed to freely exist so long as no human laws are broken. Why? Because principles, morals, and ethics are inward qualities that cannot be legislated by man. This parallels the cause-effect argument about laws proposed in the *Grace and Truth* section. If the market demands antichrist thoughts and ways via media, then producers will (regrettably) make it; if the market denies it, then producers will figure out what the market wants and then gear their programming to that. Only collective, heart-inspired, market-driven decisions in the Northward sense will effect real and positive change; conformity-driven measures certainly will not do so.

The main objective of the tables presented below is to identify super-ego tendencies, which are shown upward while id-driven tendencies are shown downward. The Socio-Ideological Tendencies Table is broken into four quadrants (similar to the four quadrants of the Quadra-Circumplex Model). The Functional Alignments Table will identify characteristics in the collective but only those Northward as grouped among State, Church, and the level of humanity called the Valley. Much of the information presented in these tables is derived from earlier sections and from the *Brain Function: Perspective* section.

1. Socio-Ideological Tendencies Table

As stated above, the Socio-Ideological Tendencies Table (Table 3) is broken into four quadrants similar to the Quadra-Circumplex Model. Compass bearings (as labeled) are also similar as the reader will find a bi-directional indicator in the middle area signifying how one may rise or fall within quadrants.

Table 3

SOLIDUS
Socio-Ideological Tendencies Table ©

DEMOCRACY
CHAMPIONS OF FREEDOM AND LIBERTY; RIGHTEOUSNESS TOWARD HIGHER AUTHORITY

Northward, WEST-Dominant (N-West in the WE)	**Northward, EAST-Dominant** (N-East in the wE)
CIVIC-ECONOMIC DEMOCRATS Driven more by **Logic** and **Objectivity** in finding **Fact** before fiction; righteous using Logic as basis for convictions; defensively regards those with Eastern tendencies as lacking practicality, sensibility, and responsibility. Altruistic (selfless) protectors of the West with high regard toward financial/human cost in order to stabilize with the East.	**SOCIO-CULTURAL DEMOCRATS** Driven more by **Intuition** and **Subjectivity** in finding **Truth** before falsehood; righteous using Intuition as basis for convictions; defensively regards those with Western tendencies as lacking kindness, compassion, and character. Altruistic (selfless) protectors of the East with high regard toward human/financial cost in order to stabilize with the West.
Southward, EAST-Dominant (S-East in the mE)	**Southward, WEST-Dominant** (S-West in the ME)
SOCIO-CULTURAL FASCISTS Driven more by **Intuition** and **Subjectivity** to foolishly seek out **Falsehoods** as Truth; righteous (in self) using Intuition as basis for convictions; offensively regards those with Western tendencies as being unkind, cold-hearted, and characterless. Egocentric (arrogant) protectors of the East with little regard toward financial cost in order to separate from, thwart, and/or command the West.	**CIVIC-ECONOMIC FASCISTS** Driven more by **Logic** and **Objectivity** to foolishly seek out **Fiction** as Fact; righteous (in self) using Logic as basis for convictions; offensively regards those with Eastern tendencies as being impractical, insensible, and irresponsible. Egocentric (arrogant) protectors of the West with little regard toward human cost in order to separate from, thwart, and/or command the East.

FASCISM
OPPRESSORS AND TYRANTS WITH SELF-INDULGENT PRIDE AND SELF-RIGHTEOUSNESS

Let us begin our discussion with those arisen or fallen. The upper quadrants represent those who are arisen, but because most are likely West-dominant or East-dominant, each will be discussed as quadrants that lean one way or another, respective of mind-dominance. Those in the lower quadrants are discussed as fallen or as diagonally opposite to those leaning above. It is important to note that while the upper quadrants are described with certain characteristics, those descriptions are identified as diagonally opposite in the lower quadrants. Thus, each quadrant exists because there is a weighted variance between Western and Eastern mind—as also derived from Purpose—that affects the level or balance of one's foundation. If the foundation is balanced, then the person can be characterized by both (left-right) sides of the upper quadrants. Note that some people can be characterized by both sides in the lower quadrants, but in these cases a false balance exists.

As to the labels Democracy and Fascism: Believers and those who reside in free societies will immediately understand why these labels were chosen as vertical dichotomies. Some readers might wonder why such ideologies/philosophies need to be incorporated at all. The answer to this is primarily driven by the importance of Purpose (and the ramifications of failing to understand and appreciate it). The basic idea is that those with Northward Purpose are knowingly freed and liberated (Democracy), while those with Southward Purpose are unknowingly held captive and enslaved (Fascism).

With regard to the terms Civic-Economic and Socio-Cultural, based on the discussion in the Brain Function: Perspective section, those who are West-dominant will tend to be more astute in Civic and Economic pursuits, while those who are East-dominant will tend to be more astute in Social and Cultural pursuits. There are, of course, those who are well-developed (and thus balanced) with both West and East characteristics.

a. Together Yoked

*Come unto me, all [ye] that labour and are heavy laden,
and I will give you rest. Take my yoke upon you,
and learn of me; for I am meek and lowly in heart:
and ye shall find rest unto your souls.
For my yoke [is] easy, and my burden is light.*
Jesus, Matthew 11:28-30

The above passage from Matthew is particularly noteworthy because it is the Son of God who makes the burden light once a believer makes a conscious decision to be yoked with Him. While He balances the foundation and helps raise the temple, it is still important for the believer to be surrounded by others with wisdom and grace (even if these others are not of the same dominant mindset). That's because the understanding gained by those who lean the other way can also help to balance one's foundation. Therefore, individually and collectively, when two are yoked Northward, then and only then will one accord exist. Remember that one can be yoked as either arisen or fallen (as the Quadra-Circumplex Model also helps to illustrate). The major contention of the Socio-Ideological Tendencies Table above is that those who aspire Northward are the knowing group who seek life, liberty, and the pursuit of happiness for all (Democracy), while those Southward are the unknowing group who seek oppression and bondage for all (Fascism).

Some deeply committed to one political, religious, or philosophical ideology or another may disagree with the previous suggestion of becoming yoked as one. They would likely contend "our principles are right, theirs are wrong"; or "we shouldn't have to give up our core values only to suggest to others that we have bi-partisan support." Such a response is understandable. So, then, how can one side become yoked with the other when two or more titans clash? Frankly, it is impossible, unless perhaps a common enemy is created in order to become purposed into one collective effort; that is, matters that a consensus of both parties agrees with. Common enemies do arise from time to time. Even so, at the end of the day society and its leaders are still faced with the issue of how to decide effectively on simple matters. So how can titans become yoked into one accord? The answer is very simple—if one appreciates Jesus' two commandments. It does entail walking with purpose in His name and the realization that God is our Father. When approached from this perspective, all life issues will make better sense, including socio-ideological tendencies.

Note that the term *Democrat* is used solely to describe those who value democracy, because it is only with democracy that one's God-given unalienable rights may be enjoyed. This term is used in the generic sense and does not refer to any political party.

b. Conservative vs. Liberal

> *But whoso looketh into the perfect law of liberty, and*
> *continueth [therein], he being not a forgetful hearer,*
> *but a doer of the work, this man shall be blessed in his deed.*
> *If any man among you seem to be religious,*
> *and bridleth not his tongue, but deceiveth his own heart,*
> *this man's religion [is] vain.*
>
> James 1:25-26

Now let's ponder how Conservative vs. Liberal ideologies are accounted for in this table. Beware of the tendency to associate Right with Conservatism and Left with Liberalism. As just discussed, in and of themselves labels as these cannot be regarded as either good or bad. Over the centuries—depending on the (political) winds of change—the terms Conservative and Liberal have had both good and bad connotations as those who subscribe to one or the other have attempted to justify their positions on behalf of liberty.

A few questions will guide this discussion. The first is: If a person is Liberal, what is he or she attempting to be liberated from? The obvious answer is: the person seeks to be liberated from those who oppress or who are viewed as evil. The second question is: If one is Conservative, then how is true liberty achieved? Most conservatives would likely answer with personal responsibility, accountability, and values as keys to achieving liberty for all. Both responses have merit. So how can we resolve the conflict between these two ideological forces? Perhaps the only way to answer this is to reflect on some selected New Testament passages. The following discussion assumes that Conservatism is synonymous with tradition and that Liberalism is synonymous with liberty. Granted, this is an over-simplification for purposes of analysis.

Tradition

> *See to it that no one takes you captive through hollow and deceptive philosophy, which depends on <u>human tradition</u> and the basic principles of this world rather than on Christ.*
> Colossians 2:8

> *Therefore, brethren, stand fast, and hold the <u>traditions</u> which ye have been taught, whether by word, or our epistle. Now our Lord Jesus Christ himself, and God, even our Father, which hath loved us, and hath given [us] everlasting consolation and good hope through grace.*
> 2 Thessalonians 2:15-16

Liberty

> *For so is the will of God, that with well doing ye may put to silence the ignorance of foolish men: As free, and not using [your] <u>liberty</u> for a cloke of maliciousness, but as the servants of God... While they promise them <u>liberty</u>, they themselves are the servants of corruption: for of whom a man is overcome, of the same is he brought in bondage.*
> 1 Peter 2:15-16, 19

> *Now the Lord is that Spirit: and where the Spirit of the Lord [is], there [is] <u>liberty</u>.*
> 2 Corinthians 3:17

Depending on purpose of mind and of heart, Conservatism (tradition) and Liberalism (liberty) have both positive and negative connotations. Let's begin with issues of self. As found in the 1 Peter passage above (according to Thayer's Lexicon), the Greek term for liberty[53] is *eleutheria* G1657 described as:

---

[53] Blue Letter Bible. "Dictionary and Word Search for eleutheria (Strong's 1657)." Blue Letter Bible. 1996-2009. 22 Oct 2009. < http://www.blueletterbible.org/lang/lexicon/lexicon.cfm?Strongs=G1657&t=KJV >

1) liberty to do or to omit things having no relationship to salvation;
2) fancied liberty, a) license, the liberty to do as one pleases;
3) true liberty is living as we should, not as we please.

In modern society (worldwide) it is hard to deny that many Liberals advocate license in self (bolstering id-driven tendencies) while denouncing the tradition of God altogether, particularly the tradition that involves Christ Jesus. While some want to help those who are less fortunate, they will unknowingly (and yet naturally and convincingly) use common-enemy tactics to viciously destroy their perceived enemy—those who are pro-business, for instance. Sadly, such efforts to destroy the other side may be unjustified. Those on the other side may actually help the less fortunate achieve personal success by providing them with jobs of their own, perhaps even teaching skills and trades, so that those who do become productive can in turn help others less fortunate as well. Not all, but many contemporary liberal agendas are intertwined with fascist thoughts and ways; some becoming power-driven movements that accentuate man apart from God and/or in denunciation of God. The travesty here is that fascism is laden with compliance and conformity for all induced by elitist-minded individuals (perhaps well-intended) who increasingly strive to use the institution as the means to provide. As I will argue later, this line of reasoning and approach is highly unsound.

So do those who identify themselves as Conservative also advocate license in self? In many cases the answer is "Yes." Many people who have become wealthy without being purposed in God do things solely for the interest of self (again, as id-driven), while some take a stance in favor of personal responsibility without any (heart-felt) desire to help those less fortunate achieve liberty. Some Conservatives, too, employ common-enemy tactics against their perceived enemy—those who are pro-social, for instance. Again, this may be unjustified.

What are the implications of this? Just this: not all conservatives are good and not all liberals are bad (and vice versa). Those on both sides—pro-business and pro-social—have too often failed to realize how merciful ways are just as important as just ways, not only by what is said but, even more importantly, by what is done. Efforts to help others in need likely require a unique Northward approach on the plane of humanity involving just and merciful ways.

> *But unto every one of us is given grace*
> *according to the measure of the gift of Christ.*
> Ephesians 4:7

So how can this issue be summed up? One response may be like this – one is either:

- Conservative or Liberal in physical self, whereby works become the measure by which all become subject to a higher human or institutional power; or
- Conservative or Liberal in the <u>tradition</u> of God through spiritual Christ, whereby faith and the gift of Grace become the measure of truly becoming <u>liberated</u>.

> *For where your treasure is, there will your heart be also.*
> Jesus, Mathew 6:21

It is important to note that it is not by human tradition, but rather by the tradition in God (as chiefly driven by faith in Christ) that each is made complete in liberty. Therefore, it is impossible to be liberal in the Northward sense unless one values God's tradition; and it is impossible to be conservative in the Northward sense unless one has a heart-felt compulsion to help all achieve true liberty. As more become liberated from the power of self-imposed guilt, each can then become liberated from those with Southward tendencies. It is important to remember that those upside-down will (falsely) espouse the cause of Conservativism or Liberalism and yet remain engrossed by purposes of their mind for reasons of greed and/or notoriety.

Thus, the terms Conservative and Liberal are not simply Right vs. Left ideologies – there are vertical implications involved. In the Northward sense both ideologies (pro-business and pro-social) are necessary for overall peace and harmony, whereas in the Southward sense both will cripple and destroy.

Human Understanding and Devotion

For the love of money is the root of all evil: which while some coveted after, they have erred from the faith, and pierced themselves through with many sorrows. But thou, O man of God, flee these things; and follow after righteousness, godliness, faith, love, patience, meekness.
1 Timothy 6:10-11

Also note that wealth and social status may not be evil per se, because such assets may come as the result of being first-purposed in God. In fact, these gifts may then be used to benefit others in need and to serve the greater good. These statements conflict with the common misconception that money is the root of all evil. In the passage above we more accurately find that it is the love of money and the love of things (what Jesus called the love of mammon,[54] material possessions) that money can buy which so easily becomes the root of evil, not money itself. Why is the love of money and material things such a problem? Because these things enhance the image of self, which is in direct opposition to enhancing the image of God.

So if one loses that all-important sense of direction (Northward Purpose), then the implications for one's salvation are certainly at risk. Think about it: Even for the most Northward, such assets may dampen one's fervor to increasingly cleave unto the Lord with the heart. So for Northward persons who have amassed great wealth, the question becomes: How will they continue to respond in faith and obedience to God despite having material comforts? In other words, even if such a person is generous in sharing gifts with others: (1) will the giver continue to humbly seek God with all his or her heart, soul, and mind?; or (2) will the giver now seek God's favor while having the heart-felt desire to inspire envy in others? Obviously, these are questions that only the responder (in his or her present circumstances) can answer.

When we realize that God is the True Giver of life, we recognize all blessings, including exceeding abundance, as God's to be shared with others. This is not to suggest that you should simply give away money or material possessions for performance-sake. Rather, it

---

[54] Matthew 6:24

suggests that as you increase with grace you will naturally share the gift with others as heart-inspired movements on behalf of God. In essence, the giver becomes the conduit between God and others. For those brothers and sisters who need to be shown the way and to be shown why each of us is so precious to God, such sharing comes in hopeful anticipation of each recipient's potential when he or she accepts Christ. Thus, we share the gift of Grace in His name. Just as true love expects nothing in return, so it is with the gift of Grace. In this way small gifts are just as meaningful as large ones as receivers recognize them as from the heart. Those who receive heart-inspired gifts of God—no matter how large or small—will be moved to do good with them.

Mapping Liberals & Conservatives in the Model

In general, those currently identified as Liberal and Northward are best characterized in the N-East quadrant called Socio-Cultural Democrats (compassionate, idealist, pro-social). This may include those identified as Social Conservatives, although this group may be better characterized as Moderate—that is, somewhere between N-West and N-East ideologies (e.g., closer to the center). Those currently identified as Economic/Fiscal Conservatives and Northward are best characterized in the N-West quadrant called Civic-Economic Democrats (sensible, realist, pro-business).

If Northward, then both of these groups are considered Democrats; if Southward, then both of these groups are considered Fascists. While pro-business people have been known as the Right and pro-social people have been known as the Left, we must consider whether their behaviors are characteristic of those in the upper quadrants of the Table or in the lower diagonally opposite.

> *For as the body is one, and hath many members, and all the members of that one body, being many, are one body: so also [is] Christ.*
> 1 Corinthians 12:12

Those in each upper quadrant are leaning away from each other. Thus, in order to become yoked Northward, each must be willing to stabilize with the other. However, no relationship can increase without first having some semblance of mutual respect for one another. Between long-time warring factions, then this may indeed take time, but as long as both are moving Northward under the same higher authority, any and all animosities can be overcome. While the collective goal is to balance the foundation, no one is suggesting that those who are more astute in West-functionality must become just as astute in East-functionality, and vice versa. This would be like suggesting that everyone must become proficiently ambidextrous or else be considered unworthy. Both sides have unique capabilities to more competently handle specific functions and tasks. For a moment reflect on the devotional elements of Justice and Mercy. Issues of Justice are more appropriately handled by those West-dominant whereas issues of Mercy are more appropriately handled by those East-dominant. Both are necessary for overall balance. Thus, in order to help create peace and harmony, each side is tasked with discovering the particular capabilities that the other side possesses and then decide to work together to do what is (vertically) right.

Therefore, both Civic-Economic and Socio-Cultural groups and interests may be Northward or Southward. Although those in the WE (Northward) are typically slow to change and those in the ME (Southward) are typically quick to change, careful change is good and necessary as long as decisions are determined from righteousness when both sides are yoked Northward.

So is it possible to have a balanced view that combines Conservative and Liberal ideologies? In the Northward sense it may indeed be possible to be Conservative on Civic-Economic issues *and* Liberal on Socio-Cultural issues. In fact, this is an optimal approach in reasoning and response when living out one's faith in God.

c. Those Who Persecute

For the enemy hath persecuted my soul; he hath smitten my life down to the ground; he hath made me to dwell in darkness, as those that have been long dead.
Psalm 143:3

Persecution is an important subject to discuss in light of this table and its relation to the Quadra-Circumplex Model. Think about the implications of who those who are fallen perceive the enemy to be. These people are indeed in the dark about what is truly best regarding life issues, particularly as they affect the larger group. When we incorporate all factors as previously discussed we detect some interesting dynamics among the four quadrants. Bear in mind that the upper quadrants of this table were developed first, and the lower quadrants were derived as their diagonal opposites.

It is contended that Socio-Cultural Fascists (S-East) and Civic-Economic Fascists (S-West) are in constant battle with each other. It simply doesn't matter to either of these factions whether one is Northward or not because in their minds there is no way to differentiate those on the other side as being either good or bad. Those in the S-East will deem anyone who is West-dominant to be a warmongering and greedy capitalist, while those in the S-West will deem anyone who is East-dominant to be a pacifist and a needy socialist. So does this suggest that all such characterizations are legitimate? Of course not! By definition, the other side (in a horizontal direction) includes both those who are Southward and those who are Northward. In contrast, those in the two upper quadrants are capable of differentiating those on the opposite horizontal side as either: (1) lacking certain Northward qualities; or (2) having Fascist thoughts and ways.

And many among them shall stumble, and fall,
and be broken, and be snared, and be taken.
Isaiah 8:15

Rejoice not when thine enemy falleth,
and let not thine heart be glad when he stumbleth:
Proverbs 24:17

In order for those who are Southward to gain a sense of exaltation, they have to reduce their perceived opponents. In a sense, they will be compelled to persecute their perceived enemies in order to reduce them and thus gain a false sense that they are higher or better than them. The truth is that no one on the horizontal plane is more exalted than any other. It is interesting to note, however, that Northward Purpose does give those who are arisen a certain boost in height that is spiritual in nature. Even then each of those who are Northward must also remain humble enough to resist notions of superiority over others, even over those who are fallen. Because

Human Understanding and Devotion

those who are Southward consistently fail to recognize how to arise, they will be bound to determine life issues from a horizontal and upside-down perspective. So in order to gain that (false) sense of exaltation for themselves, they must ultimately (directly or indirectly) cause others to stumble and fall.

Capitalism of the West (what the Right gravitates toward) and Socialism of the East (what the Left gravitates toward) can be responded to in both good and bad ways. Many factors are involved in determining if certain individuals, groups, and issues are productive or destructive, but it is the element of Purpose that provides clues as to what the end result of effort will be. In the Northward sense, both Capitalism and Socialism are indeed good and necessary. In the Southward sense, both will cripple and destroy. Keep in mind, however, that those in the N-West are not as astute about social good as those in the N-East, while those in the N-East are not as astute about economic good as those in the N-West.

Politics as Usual

It seems that each election cycle brings out the worst of each side. Each becomes so bent on casting doubt and suspicion on the other that together they end up destroying the entire reason for having an election. By the end of the process citizens are asked to vote for the lesser of two evils, instead of the one best qualified for the job.

> *The proud have digged pits for me,*
> *which [are] not after thy law.*
> Psalm 119:85

As we reflect on the discussion in the *False Teacher* section, is it not troublesome to realize that it is through the content of media that voters are left with the responsibility for choosing the one left standing after the slaughter of malicious attacks crafted from half-truths and outright distortions? Obviously, a candidate's political record is a better gauge than a 30-second attack ad wrapped in unrealistic promises.

Most puzzling of all is that while many citizens focus on the issue of separation of Church and State (that is, subjective and objective influences that affect how votes are cast), most seem to accept the deceptive practices and strategies (antichrist in nature) during media campaigns – practices that involve deceptive ads, extremely biased news coverage, propaganda-like documentaries, and so on. Again, reflect on how many people are already purposed in Southward content within media. So in order to win votes and bolster one's own image or ideology, many political candidates opt to be the best at slanderous "common enemy" strategies. In a sense, these candidates and their campaigns purposefully spread fiction about their opponents that many in society are already falsely purposed in. In the minds of those who are fallen, such fiction just makes sense when combined with falsehoods of mind. The point is that, for those who are unaware, fiction and falsehoods can become yoked into one upside-down accord, thus forming a Southward temple.

> *The wisdom of the prudent [is] to understand his way:*
> *but the folly of fools [is] deceit.*
> Proverbs 14:8

Let's examine the dynamics among the four quadrants. For instance, take a person who is in the S-East. In order to maintain a positive self-image, he or she must consider all those who are West-dominant to be in a fallen state. If, however, one of these West-dominants begins to make his or her presence known in good and/or popular ways, then the one in the S-East will construe this as a threat. Why? Because, for those who are Southward, when the image of a horizontally opposed person is strengthened, their own self-image is weakened. To reduce this sort of threat, the S-East person will devise ways to cause the aspiring N-West person to stumble and fall back into the S-West position, even after that person has been in the N-West for long enough to resist sparring at the same level as those who are fallen. Those in the S-East will pursue such destructive acts even if it means lying and deceit, or spreading doubt and suspicion.

This sort of behavior would also be characteristic of those in the S-West against the East-dominant. What is interesting about both cases is that (figuratively speaking) each is blind to what is directly above them (i.e., God), until those of God make their presence known. One way to take action would be the attempt to cause the targeted person to react to trumped up accusations or admit to past transgressions, even those whereby one has already gone through a process of repentance and reconciliation. This is so that present attacks by those who are Southward will appear justified and forthright in the eyes of others.

As we look back at the table we see that since the S-East is under the N-West and the S-West is under the N-East, these two vertical extremes represent diametrically opposed mindsets or viewpoints. For instance, if those in the S-East spot an aspiring N-West, they will automatically go after the weakest link or sensibility of the N-West. Those in the S-East and N-West are not only motivated by opposing Purpose, but each also opposes the dominance of mind. Thus, the N-West person will typically defend him- or herself with Northward facts, but those in the S-East will attempt to reduce the individual with an onslaught of falsehoods. The same would occur with those S-West with a N-East directly above. In this case the N-East person will typically defend with Northward truths, whereas those in the S-West will attempt to reduce the individual with an onslaught of fiction.

For a just [man] falleth seven times, and riseth up again:
but the wicked shall fall into mischief.
Proverbs 24:16

I write unto you, little children,
because your sins are forgiven you for his name's sake.
1 John 2:12

Falling and Restoration

Even the most steadfast Northward person may at times be tempted, but this does not mean that the individual must be publicly chastised and humiliated. God is forgiving and moves forward if one simply repents, has faith, etc. But the overall system that man has created (one without God high in mind) is extremely unforgiving; hence, it is designed to more effectively and efficiently look back on the mark of man's past with little to no regard to repentance, conversion, and restoration.

Therefore remove sorrow from thy heart, and put away evil from thy flesh: for childhood and youth [are] vanity.
Ecclesiastes 11:10

All individuals—from all cultures, all lands, and all religions—have made mistakes. Each and every one was born with natural id-driven tendencies that lead to vanity and certain regret. Depending on the motivation for faith, some progress from the id into the super-ego quickly, while for others it may take decades. Then there are those who will resist God until the end. Those who do convert have all have left trails of wrong-doing of some kind or another in their past. Even so, some (so-called) wrongdoing may have been misconstrued by others. Any past wrongdoing will be consistently regurgitated by Southward persons, perhaps due to ignorance or perhaps for the sake of hatred or revenge.[55] When we hear these kinds of allegations, we must remember that although the individual may have engaged in the alleged behavior, context is also important, as are errors in communication and variations in perception.

Mull over how the perception of Southward persons, then and now, are consistently skewed into fiction and falsehood. Again, for many such persons, it doesn't matter if the allegations were/are factual or not. In their unknowing mind, what's important is how to place the targeted party into a defensive position of having to answer any and all (half-truth) allegations trumped up for the purpose of public humiliation. Assuming the allegations are fiction/false, the more vehemently they are proclaimed, the more guilty the person targeted will appear in the eyes of others. So instead of being mindful that facts take time and energy to sort out, get resolved, and then put behind us, many people make assertions which are designed to prompt belief-type or emotional responses of those asked to become judge and jury. While most people pay lip-service to the notion that the accused are innocent until proven guilty, few actually put it into practice. Even if they claim to be forgiving, most of them eagerly and yet foolishly practice the mindful craft of manipulation and self-incriminating accusation—this, instead of the graceful and heart-inspired art of humility, forgiveness, and

---

[55] Jeremiah 20:10

contrition. What many eager accusers forget is that they will be judged just as they have judged.[56]

> *Without natural affection, trucebreakers, false accusers,*
> *incontinent, fierce, despisers of those that are good, traitors,*
> *heady, highminded, lovers of pleasures more than lovers of*
> *God; Having a form of godliness,*
> *but denying the power thereof: from such turn away.*
> 2 Timothy 3:3-5

False accusers craft allegations from various angles in the attempt to prove suspicions as truths against another. They will seize every opportunity to accuse in order to provoke the person accused to reactions that serve to prove their point. If one is reined back into a state of submission after such attempts, then he or she will only be re-shackled with the weights of guilt and shame further imposed by those Southward.

Some Northward people are able to respond to allegations made with sound points of their own that show up the tactics of their accusers. Other Northward people, however, are not as rhetorically gifted. This is certainly one reason why Evil has gotten away with the destruction of so many for so long, particularly against those who respond more from the basis of faith and mercy. For many outside looking in, the lack of response seems indicative of the stigma produced by guilt and shame. What many people dismiss, though, is that having the steadfastness to resist responding with similar accusations may be indicative of inward innocence, peace, and strength. In other words, those who are mercifully inclined may find it easier to be impervious to those who spit venom. By resisting the impulse to strike back, they show mercy, even toward those who (unknowingly) persecute them.[57]

All of those strongly committed to Him will recognize that once a believer repents and gains in faith and in grace, the shackles of past sin have been released. They know that the Grace of God is sufficient

---

[56] Matthew 7:1-2
[57] Matthew 5:7-12

if one simply accepts Him, thus arising above those who desire to persecute them, physically and spiritually.

> *And he said unto me, My grace is sufficient for thee:*
> *for my strength is made perfect in weakness.*
> *Most gladly therefore will I rather glory in my infirmities,*
> *that the power of Christ may rest upon me.*
> 2 Corinthians 12:9

On Judging Not

Some may not understand the significance of God's sufficiency. This term does not imply that He is adequate for salvation. It suggests that it is simply by His Grace that each may overcome the tremendous weight of guilt and shame that lies heavy on souls; weight that prevents each person from arising by his own (mindful) will. The more the former reigning king (the id-body) has been strengthened, the more it will show reasons why the once-Southward mind should forever carry the burdens of guilt and shame. It will persistently attempt to convict the mind through the ego of all that it is guilty of while (perhaps) also suggesting that it is God and godly people who are doing the punishing. This is an altogether ludicrous notion since it is the (fleshy) id-body and the evil influences of this world that are chiefly responsible for our guilt and shame. Even the most astute Northward person may at times feel a sense of unworthiness during quiet times of reflection, or perhaps in dreams manifested by the psyche from purposes of the past. Again, it is by God's Grace alone that each will have the strength to resist and even defeat the wrongful conviction of mind.

Most readers have heard it said, "This is happening to you because you're being punished by God." Though this sort of judgmental rhetoric is often used by people in various religious communities, should it really be used by God-loving Christians to make a point about another person who may be going through difficult times? It just seems as though there's something wrong when God's name is invoked for the purpose of impugning another (i.e., when judging or name-calling). What if those making these assertions are unworthy themselves and yet do not know it? Doesn't practice in making such assertions lead naturally to taking aggressive action whenever it appears justifiable, perhaps even "on behalf of God"—and thus to ending up doing some very harmful things in God's name?

Though God certainly punishes or chastises people (even those whom He loves) it may be more notably contended that many of life's difficulties come about through one's own doing, or even through the direct or indirect influence of others, past and present. Above all, such difficulties may be due to constant resistance to responding to God's appeal.

> *And they which heard [it], being convicted by [their own]*
> *conscience, went out one by one, beginning at the eldest,*
> *[even] unto the last: and Jesus was left alone,*
> *and the woman standing in the midst.*
> John 8:9

Someone who has repented and continues to build faith in God will more easily dismiss the accusations of his or her own conscience and of others. Once a person accepts Christ Jesus, continuing to believe the lie of being unworthy will only prevent his or her own heart from fully cleaving unto the Lord. As we arise without turning back—as the strength of our living Redeemer and Defender is progressively realized—each of us will appreciate that it is indeed by His Grace that we are allowed to arise confidently, while defying the pull from Evil below.

Therefore, a person who is practiced in judging or convicting others will have a weak mind/psyche that will be more than proficient at convicting itself when the time comes. Why at a later time and not now? Until there is a Northward turn, there is never a reason for the reigning id-body to test the will of the mind – remember the mind is continually in a state of submission while in a Southward state. While our opinion of another person may be either good or bad (depending on his or her greater purpose), judging for the sake of reducing another person is simply not wise. Such judgments lead the unknowing soul into a false sense of exaltation, which brings about a false sense of superiority and strength.

> *They have prepared a net for my steps; my soul is bowed down: they have digged a pit before me, into the midst whereof they are fallen [themselves]. Selah.*
>
> Psalm 57:6

As for persecution, far too many good people in the world have been wrongly persecuted because they remained steadfastly purposed in the righteousness of God, instead of giving way to the pressures of those bent. Again, the goal of those who are in the lower quadrants is to reduce those arisen and then re-shackle them as necessary. They will use information, rhetoric, accusation, and even physical presence to intimidate and reduce the targeted. This alone would be good reason for those aspiring Northward to be slow to characterize, slow to judge, slow to blame, and slow to react (particularly in times of crisis), so that in due time false accusers will be exposed for what they are.

Consider how many souls have been weighed back down because of the tactics used by those motivated by Evil. Also think about how much money has been made on the heads of those targeted while the audience is lured into serving as judge and jury in the court of public opinion. Please understand that this table and the discussion of it are not intended to impugn the unknowing per se, but rather to provide information of another kind so that those attempting to arise will be less susceptible to falling back into the hands of those who seek to persecute and ruin them. In a sense, attempts to reduce another person are similar to acts of spiritual enslavement because the unknowing deter souls from freely arising. By responding to God instead of to persecutors, each of us can confidently ascend onto the high way toward a more rewarding existence even during our time on this fallen world.

d. Consensus (of Opinion)

Let's now consider the issue of consensus (of opinion) about life matters. I hope by now you have gained a certain appreciation for how life issues regarding human thought and behavior are made simple when the discussion proceeds from a God-first perspective: that is, from the (upright) vertical axis of understanding. Quickly reflect on the Stratum Model and the discussion regarding the (earthly) star of David, and how past opinion of practically any kind is reflected in the horizontal star instead of the vertical Star. The assumption is that humanity consistently seeks to follow popular opinion (a.k.a. collectivism[58]) instead of aligning with a God-first approach and then forming a consensus. In free societies there will always be a sampling of opinion of some kind or another that reflects the views of all citizens. Though there are certain benefits to this, the question becomes: When does such horizontal sampling lead to the best course of action for all citizens, both in the short-term and in the long-term? Let's see if this discussion can be approached with balance.

> *[This] I say then, Walk in the Spirit, and ye shall not fulfil the lust of the flesh. For the flesh lusteth against the Spirit, and the Spirit against the flesh: and these are contrary the one to the other: so that ye cannot do the things that ye would.*
> Galatians 5:16-17

As to those arisen or fallen, no one should be expressing notions of superiority over another. There are, however, those who have arisen out of humility, and are those who have failed to arise out of pride and arrogance. Reflect on how many decisions have been made throughout history based on popular opinion; that is, the cumulative opinion of those arisen and fallen. Is this what the consensus should reflect as important matters of life are decided upon? The point is that opinion has historically been argued as a Left vs. Right or conservative vs. liberal issue. I propose that a better way to understand the consensus is by the vertical. The battle is between right vs. wrong and good vs. bad, which are vertical issues. But in order to determine the best course of action on any matter of concern, there must be a sound foundation to work from, individually and collectively.

---

[58] *Collectivism* is defined as: emphasis on collective rather than individual action. (2009). Merriam-Webster Online Dictionary. Retrieved November 30, 2009, from http://www.merriam-webster.com/dictionary/collectivism

Looking around and realizing how humanity has faltered, could this line of reasoning help explain why those driven by selfishness consistently choose to go down the wrong path, even after once being blessed by God in bountiful ways? Sure it can.

If one is not God-first, then he or she is effectively self-first; if not Northward, then Southward; if not in the WE, then in the ME; and if not in favor of democracy, then in favor of fascism. At this point we must ask: Setting aside intellectual and religious differences for a moment, is it really possible to trust the judgment of anyone who does not have a higher presence of mind? No!

Although many may dismiss the importance of becoming yoked, those who are God-fearing/loving are naturally inclined to value tradition and liberty. Recall that those who are Northward will recognize that the (extreme) thoughts and actions of the Southward are antichrist while those Southward will (unknowingly) feel the same about those Northward. In the truest sense, the Northward represent love and life while the Southward represent hate and death. Those who are Southward have been fooled so long by their own id-driven (selfish) nature and by Evil that they simply do not comprehend that their upside-down view of the world is driven by fiction and falsehoods. That said, however, let me reiterate: No religion should be imposed on citizens, not even those religions that would actually help strengthen the Northward consensus.

We will treat Capitalism and Socialism just like the Left-Right and West-East "horizontal" labels – this would include the political ideologies of those currently identified in the United States as Republican or Democrat. Each of these labels is horizontal in nature; thus, depending on the individual or group, each may be for Northward purposes or for Southward purposes. Regarding one as being superior to the other leads only to unavoidable conflict. The greater battle is in the vertical axis—between God above and Evil below. We should not be quick to judge another person's behavior as good or bad without having a better understanding of his or her greater purpose.

Fulfil ye my joy, that ye be likeminded, having the same love, [being] of one accord, of one mind.
Philippians 2:2

So what is the best course of action for those who value Democracy and God? While the mind of one individual can become yoked "of one accord" with faith in Christ, the collective of the Northward can also become of one greater mind. In other words, when those in the N-West and N-East recognize the functional value that the other possesses, they can more easily become yoked into one greater accord as well.

An important premise to consider is that even if there are differences of opinion between the N-West (objective) and N-East (subjective), these individuals/groups may also be described as of one accord. This may not make immediate sense to you if you reason from the horizontal perspective, which suggests that if one is right the other must be wrong. This is an unsound way of negotiating one's viewpoint, because it suggests that one must be exalted while the other is reduced. The words *right vs. wrong* or *good vs. bad* are better characterized in the vertical as purpose dictates. Contrast this with the words *correct (adj.) vs. incorrect*, which may be used to describe issues that are horizontal or vertical in nature. Thus, the words *right* and *good* describe Northward views while *wrong* and *bad* describe Southward views.

To illustrate why the proper use of words is important, just reflect on the terms *good* or *bad* in day-to-day thoughts and discussions. For instance, one may describe a favorite song as "good" even though the song is filled with violence, sexual promiscuity, self-defeat, or id-driven suggestiveness. Many people are inspired to sing along with and move to such songs, many times without any clue as to what the lyrics actually promote. Most believers would agree that the song is actually bad for the soul, but who wants to explain to others one's enthusiasm for listening to bad songs? For many, "good" means being fascinated with *bad*, while "bad" means being fascinated with *good*. Would it be fair to suggest that reverse meanings (those vertical in nature) may encourage the mind to become purposed in false good? No one can dispute that the playful use of descriptive words helps bring laughter into the world, but when the tone of discussion becomes more serious, such words may actually reveal more about an individual's psyche than he or she realizes.

This discussion leads back to the point about becoming yoked. For the N-West and N-East who are of one accord, it is not a matter of one's being right and the other's being wrong since both are purposed to do what is (vertically) right. Rather, it is a matter of who is more functionally capable or proficient in accomplishing what is right with a given set of tasks while the other is more functionally capable or proficient with another given set of tasks. Thus, true bi-partisanship is better described between the Northward who soundly reason objectively and subjectively while becoming yoked together. It is certainly not collective decision-making that includes both the Northward and the Southward.

> *The Spirit itself beareth witness with our spirit, that we are*
> *the children of God: And if children, then heirs; heirs of God,*
> *and joint-heirs with Christ; if so be that we suffer with [him],*
> *that we may be also glorified together.*
> Romans 8:16-17

While those in the upper quadrants are leaning away from the other, each will have unique qualities that the other side does not possess. It is simply unwise to suggest that one side can do it all, particularly since most individuals and collaborative groups most likely lean one way or the other. If they are truly Northward, they will realize how important it is to be yoked with another. Thus, each side is asked to make a concerted effort to realize the value that the other side brings to the common cause. In so doing each will then recognize and appreciate the qualities of the other side. When it is decided that one side will carry the burden of responsibility for certain functions, this does not suggest that the other side should not have an opinion about the other's actions. Even so, those on each side will recognize that if truly Northward, then all participating are attempting to do what is right, and sometimes this means releasing authority and control to others who are better able to accomplish such functions with greater proficiency and ease. Most would agree that no one is above it all. Even kings who have had the arrogance to believe that they are above everyone else are still children of our most beloved heavenly Father, our higher, divine authority, as witnessed by the Spirit.

e. Issue of Wine

> *Envyings, murders, drunkenness, revellings, and such like:*
> *of the which I tell you before, as I have also told [you] in time*
> *past, that they which do such things shall not inherit*
> *the kingdom of God.*
> Galatians 5:21

Let's examine one issue that has resulted in a great divide between certain church groups – the consumption of wine or alcohol. Those affiliated with any given denomination that allows (moderate) drinking will no doubt look upon those others that disallow such activity as being legalistic. Those who defend it as a doctrinal stance will outline the meaning of "new wine" as biblically interpreted while bringing up valid points about the risks associated with alcohol.

This discussion will neither encourage the consumption of wine, nor make it into a ground of condemnation. An article that explores many key issues on the subject is: *What does the Bible say about drinking alcohol/wine? Is it a sin for a Christian to drink alcohol/wine?*[59] We raise the issue here because for many the subject of wine has become an important qualifier when testing the waters of various denominations and their communities. Whichever side of the fence one is on, it would be hard to argue that creating doctrine that affects one's personal life outside the walls of the (visible) church does not have legalistic implications, but it would also be hard to argue that alcohol does not come with inherent risks, particularly when consumed in excess.[60] [61]

---

[59] GotQuestions.org. (n.d.). *What does the Bible say about drinking alcohol/wine? Is it a sin for a Christian to drink alcohol/wine?* Retrieved November 5, 2008, from http://www.gotquestions.org/sin-alcohol.html

[60] Discussion on alcohol found at: U.S. Department of Health and Human Services (HHS). (2005). Dietary Guidelines for Americans 2005. In *Alcoholic Beverages* (chap 9). Retrieved June 29, 2009, from http://www.health.gov/DIETARYGUIDELINES/dga2005/document/html/chapter9.htm

[61] Alcohol Impairment Charts provided at: Greater Dallas Council on Alcohol & Drug Abuse. (n.d.). *Alcohol*. Retrieved June 29, 2009, from http://www.gdcada.org/statistics/alcohol.htm

It must be mentioned, each denomination should be freely allowed to establish guidelines or doctrines that distinguish it from others. All should be permitted to associate with like-minded others, particularly on questions of church function and/or its community involvements.

So this is not an attempt to challenge the use of doctrine for those groups that prefer to distance themselves from (in this case) those who consume alcohol. The point here is that there may be another way to rationalize the implications of wine consumption without giving the appearance of legalistic pressures. Reflect on some previous discussions regarding cause and effect to see if those thoughts can help explain the disparity of views regarding the consumption of wine in hopes of more clearly identifying what the problems are.

In the *Faith and Believing* section it was mentioned that adoration for God negates the significance of codes of conduct or standards. Whether you (moderately) consume wine or not, if you build faith in the truest sense, your love for God will negate the significance of law and even of doctrine. Loving and natural conformity is the effect of a God-first relationship (the cause). As your appreciation of the importance of maintaining the Northward temple grows, so will you naturally resist the temptation to drink in excess; some may even decide to forego the use of alcohol altogether.

Though it is easy to detail the risks to physical health associated with drunkenness, it can also have consequences for one's ultimate destiny. A person who becomes unable to tell right from wrong will lose control and indulge in foolish and disgraceful acts, and his or her Northward temple will be brought down. For most people this behavior will result in even greater feelings of guilt and shame. The problem is compounded by the fact that as one's emotional state becomes unstable during times of excess, he will likely feel a (false) need for more of the substance. Even so, drunkenness does not suggest that the individual is purposed Southward, nor does it suggest that he or she should be diagnosed as having a disease.

In *The Alcoholism and Addition Cure: A Holistic Approach to Total Recovery*, Chris Prentiss makes two points that are relevant to our discussion here:

Alcoholism and Addiction Are Not Diseases[62]:

> Alcohol and drugs are not the problems; they are what people are using to help themselves cope with the problems. The problems always have both physical and psychological components – anything from anemia, hypoglycemia, or a sluggish thyroid to attention deficit disorder, brain-wave pattern imbalances, or deep emotional pain... when the underlying problems are discovered and cured, the need for alcohol or drugs disappears.

Questions and Answers with Patrick Hanaway, M.D. – What is integrative medicine?[63]:

> The nature of most health problems is that they recur, as they are the result of poor behavior choices such as drinking, smoking, overeating, using drugs, not sleeping, not exercising, etc. When our body, mind, and spirit are not in alignment, we consciously or subconsciously *medicate* with food, alcohol, drugs, sex, television, and other diversions to forget or suppress the symptoms of imbalance.

For those who self-medicate as a way of coping, there's a question: Are such behaviors the cause or the effect of one's problem(s)? People who are outside looking in might think that, as drinking obviously causes problems, it must be the cause. But this form of self-treatment may itself result from deeper or prior causes. Those who are in need do not enjoy their circumstances—there's no such thing as a happy alcoholic—and will become particularly responsive toward improving their situation if they are shown the way (as Prentiss's book suggests), and even more importantly, if they are shown the way toward the God of love and light.

In many cases, people unknowingly mix up cause and effect, thinking that if they achieve the effect, the cause will follow. Since

---

[62] Prentiss, Chris. (2007). *The Alcoholism and Addition Cure: A Holistic Approach to Total Recovery* (p. 16). Malibu, CA: Power Press.
[63] Ibid. (p. 190).

the sin issue and that of overindulgence can both be regarded as a lack of control, reflect on the cause and effect discussion in the *Summary* section of the Northward HUHD Model. Many attempting to resist excessiveness will go after the effect (e.g., resistance to overindulgence) in order to influence or achieve the cause (e.g., godliness). This is counter-productive. That's because when the effect is directly approached as the cause it becomes a fallible purpose of mind. In these cases, temptation will be an ongoing problem because the mind resisted God as the true "cause" of mind to respond by.

So instead of creating doctrines that prohibit excessiveness, continue to focus on building the want and desire for God in the seeker's mind. With God as the cause of mind, then through one's natural reasoning and response, the effect will manifest from a God-enhanced strength of resistance.

> *And be not drunk with wine, wherein is excess;*
> *but be filled with the Spirit;*
> Ephesians 5:18

Most who have studied the Bible might wonder why Jesus was accused of being a winebibber.[64] It is impossible to say how much or how little or frequently or infrequently Jesus drank wine—if indeed He drank wine at all. But we wonder why the (New Testament) passage admonishing believers against drunkenness exists at all if any consumption of wine was viewed as appalling. While strong drink most certainly causes the mind to falter rapidly, for many the influence of wine may be manageable depending on soundness of mind and physical/spiritual maturity, among other things.

Some people believe that no type of alcohol can be controlled—particularly those who have had the experience of losing control after drinking. The travesty is that some who lost control were identified as Christian, religious, or even as believers (of God) while exemplifying foolishness and disgrace. We might argue that those who have allowed themselves to lose control often have likely never come to know Christ. As one builds faith, then he or she will become

---

[64] Matthew 11:19

Human Understanding and Devotion

strong in Spirit and in conscience. Those who are strong will avoid risking the loss of their ability to know right from wrong through overindulgence. In essence, those who are strong in conscience will naturally resist being a bad example for weaker people and thus causing them to stumble and fall, either physically or spiritually.

> *And no man putteth new wine into old bottles; else the new wine will burst the bottles, and be spilled, and the bottles shall perish. But new wine must be put into new bottles; and both are preserved.*
> Jesus, Luke 5:37-38

The objective of this section is not to encourage those who do not consume wine to do so, but rather to more clearly identify what the problem is and what it is not. The point is that society continually attempts to go after the effect on a multitude of major issues instead of taking the time to genuinely understand the cause. Again, the choice to drink in moderation or not to drink at all is the effect of a God-first relationship. The main reason for this is that the precious gift of the Holy Spirit, poured into upright vessels (e.g., new bottles as born again), is one that no true believer would want to risk losing.

f. The Church

> *And when the day of Pentecost was fully come, they were all with one accord in one place.*
> Acts 2:1

Let us see if we can apply this principle to the Christian Church, past and present. Some may think that the Christian Church is increasingly divided; for others, the Church appears to be moving in a direction that unites rather than divides, largely because there is indeed much common ground.

As previously mentioned, the Western mind distinguishes fact from fiction using objective reasoning while the Eastern mind distinguishes truth from falsehood using subjective reasoning. While some denominations may be classified as being either Western or Eastern, the Western Church has evolved from a more linear or literal perspective (e.g., dogmatics, systematic theology), resulting in objective, explicit interpretation. The Eastern Church has evolved from a more holistic or artful perspective (e.g., Christian mysticism), resulting in subjective interpretation.

Notice, however, that efforts to unite Christians thus far have not been commanded by any one individual or denomination. There may be a variety of reasons why a coming together has not yet been fully realized, but also consider how mindedness affects such efforts. Yes, there are likely some denominations that offer a balanced approach between both sides, but just as important is the fact that Christianity has also lovingly evolved into two separate groups with unique qualities and strengths that will one day become more fully united in His name. In a sense WE have not given way toward uniting simply for the sake of being regarded as united. If the Church had come together without each side first appreciating what the other brings to the table, then this would have likely resulted in a turn leading to notions of compliance and conformity for all.

i. One Church: East and West

The Eastern Church represents seers who encourage reflection involving each of the five senses (in Northward ways) during worship. It attempts to inspire holistic truths in artful expressions so that one learns and appreciates the way or prayer of the heart as first recognized through the contemplative/meditative worship service itself.

The Western Church represents doers who also encourage joy and praise. It attempts to linearize biblical truths into ways of holiness as a way of life while also committing itself toward spreading the message. Thus, the Eastern and Western branches of Christendom invoke the Holy Spirit from two different perspectives: one more inwardly (Eastern), the other more outwardly (Western). Again, there are obviously those groups that attempt to balance both perspectives. In recognizing both religious perspectives, though, could it be that the efforts of the Western Church realize (through integration) the efforts of the Eastern Church such that, as one is unto the other, the independent functionality of each is optimized and strengthened when both (obviously) have the same Purpose?

For a moment, just reflect on the Christ Pantocrator image and how this one image captures this same message.

> *Let no man therefore judge you in meat, or in drink, or in respect of an holyday, or of the new moon, or of the sabbath [days]: Which are a shadow of things to come; but the body [is] of Christ.*
> Colossians 2:16-17

In reflecting on our discussion of labels (such as *good and bad*, and *right and wrong*) in the last section, to suggest that certain Christian leaders or church groups are taking the wrong approach toward God is close to suggesting that they are either Southward (in Purpose) or completely unaware. But just disagreeing with certain beliefs and practices of various church groups is not the same as suggesting that these groups are attempting to bolster fiction and falsehoods. The question is: With God high in mind, are church leaders prayerfully teaching and approaching issues of Truth as driven by faith in God according to Scripture and the holy tradition? If so, then how effectively is the assembly grasping and then applying such information in order to advance the message of righteousness and salvation found only with God? Practically every group today includes both members who are deeply committed in His name and members who lack such a commitment. So when one group plays up its own strengths to the detriment of another, is this really the right approach?

We may esteem some groups more than others, but bear in mind that personal choice has much to do with how a member sees his or her own group affiliation relative to others. If all church groups are attempting to do what is right in the eyes of God, wouldn't it make more sense to realize and appreciate the differing strengths of various groups, rather than focusing on which group is the best?

ii. Faith, Illuminated

And that ye put on the new man,
which after God is created in righteousness and true holiness.
Ephesians 4:24

Reflect back on Table 1, Functions of Human Cerebral Hemispheres. The function of the Western mind is objective/analytical/linear reasoning (e.g., thoughts perceived in black and white), while the Eastern mind is subjective/relational/holistic reasoning (e.g., thoughts perceived in color).

God has given humans two very different functions of mind to reason with and for greater understanding. Assuming all are purposed Northward, the division that has existed and continues to exist in the world stems primarily from the variance between those who lean West and those who lean East. Without a balanced approach toward overall understanding it would be difficult to explain what color means to those who are more responsive to black and white, and vice versa.

The same is true of interpretations of the Bible and perceptions of the right approach toward holiness. One hindrance to becoming more unified as His Body is the lack of clear distinctions between facts and truths regarding life matters and Biblical understandings. Facts are realized in black and white while truths are realized in color, however, from some quarters of the Church we hear statements like: "Because it is 'written,' then all of Biblical Truth ought to be treated literally [as fact]".

Reflect again on the element of Knowledge in the Northward HUHD Model. As one becomes knowing (particularly of that which comes as the result of the knowledge of God), then he or she is better able to comprehend the depth and breadth of Truth.[65]

One form of Truth includes the objective depth of Biblical understandings. By what was said and done in scripture—as also affirmed by history and archeology—issues objective in nature will

---

[65] Romans 1:28, Ephesians 3:17-19

be regarded as (factually) true by believers. No doubt about it, to believe in the sequential[66] of Biblical texts does necessitate faith—such texts that much of the time can be and should be taken literally. Still, any child filled with curiosity and wonderment will question: "But why?"

Faith according to Truth also necessitates believing on a scale that is different from that reached by objectivity. This includes the subjective depth of Biblical understandings gained by the simultaneous[67] assimilation of stories, concepts, and images.

So while even the sequential sum of parts can lead to a deepening of linear understandings, and even provide a knowing bridge between linear and holistic understandings, there is more to the story than meets the eye. The whole of holistic understandings is deepened by allowing the simultaneous aspect of God's story to flourish in the recipients' mind.

And the Word was made flesh,
and dwelt among us, (and we beheld his glory,
the glory as of the only begotten of the Father,)
full of grace and truth.
John 1:14

The testimonies of Jesus are prime examples of both forms of Truth. While it is easy to get caught up in select passages about Jesus regarded as true, in and of themselves, parts like these do not create a complete picture of His overall character and existence. To know Him is to also have a grasp of why His reasoning and response was so unorthodox. By taking a step back and seeing the bigger picture, believers can gain a greater appreciation for the dynamics and fullness of God's Grace—in essence, Truth about the One whereby "the Word was made flesh."

Linguistically speaking, it is the use of figurative language (e.g., metaphors of poetry and prose), best understood by the Eastern mind, that engages readers of the Holy Bible to become not passive

---

[66] Sequential and simultaneous – see Table 1: Functions of Human Cerebral Hemispheres
[67] Ibid.

but active participants in the East-to-West interpretive process. Active participation, though, first necessitates having a sincere interest and desire to read and then conceptualize Biblical narratives. So while watching renditions of God's Truth (e.g., television programs, movies, etc.) is important for a host of reasons, nothing better enables believers to become attuned to His Word than the process of reading and listening, and then attempting to respond.

Directives such as the Law of Moses are indeed good and vital for salvation, but they are also black and white. Intellects of the Abrahamic faiths—particularly those outside Christianity, but even some within—will contend that directives of God ought to be treated literally, certainly not figuratively. With so many attempting to live by the Law, though, it does seem there is virtually no room for simply asking "why?" about the vast array of Biblical topics. Keep in mind, asking why isn't meant to diminish the Law, nor the Bible. It is meant to deepen our understanding of Truth so that the Law can naturally be fulfilled.

Details such as who, what, when, where, and how provide deepening facts about a given unknown, but what about truth? When is the light of truth realized? Is it not interesting that the word *why* compels not only an objective deepening response, but even more importantly, a subjective deepening response—again, one that is best perceived by the Eastern mind. This side of mind functions as the relational, holistic, and even visual, not the analytical, logical, and verbal. The task of the relational side of mind is not to grasp the sequence of facts, but to grasp simultaneous truths. As the Eastern mind is deepened with the holistic aspect of God's Truth, think of the impact this can have on contemplative thought, prayer, and one's connection with Him.

If all of Biblical Truth is treated literally—as it typically is by people who intellectualize faith—then the opportunity to allow the Bible to speak for itself in living color is missed. When the color of Truth (i.e., the holistic, implicit) is omitted in favor of black and white facts (e.g., the linear, explicit), the objective side of Biblical texts becomes the focal point for understanding, instruction, and response. It is vital to realize that the subjective side of God's Truth (gained intuitively) is necessary for balance. In part this is the result of an increased awareness as to *why* the objective side of God' Truth reveal themselves as they do.

Since original Hebrew and Greek texts of the Bible are considered the inspired Word of God, it is vital to maintain literal translations of such texts. This is especially important when in-depth studies are involved. However, precise wording and phraseology are difficult to translate, and the contextual integrity of Biblical narratives may be lost. Lexicons help bridge the gap between the original languages and one's first language by providing valuable insight on each and every word translated.

The Holy Bible is a form of inspired art where the most pristine form of Truth exists, but the subjective side of Truth can only be apprehended by those who have a sincere passion and desire to receive the Truth. Thus, the full extent or context of Truth cannot be approached simply from a linear perspective. Stories of the Bible, especially those involving the Son of God, are the basis for holistic development of faith. With the time and patience that come with age and experience, those who have been filled with Truth are better able to understand deeper meanings of life, and even to see the big picture.

As a result of increasing with our understanding of God's story, we as His Body are better able to integrate His Truth while living by faith. To add to or change the basis of God's Truth with man's interpretation of it only diminishes the function of the Bible as a teaching source—hence, a significant reason for being vigilant with respect to non-literal versions of the Bible. By allowing the fullness of literal texts to speak for themselves, the reader can ultimately become attuned with the art of God's Truth.

In contrast, *Solidus* is one of countless other literary works written by man that offer perspectives on the breadth of God's Truth. So while it is hoped that this book will help with the edification process, it should not be treated as a book to draw God's Truth from. Since the function of this book is not to present God's Truth, nor is it an empirical study, most readers will see it as a faith-based philosophy involving metaphysics. Many shy away from philosophies of man and rightly so. It is hoped though that the reader will find clear differences between typical philosophies of man, which diminish the role of God (particularly that of Christ

Jesus), and this book which exalts His role and the believer's response on His behalf.

> *Trust in the LORD, and do good; [so] shalt thou dwell in the land, and verily thou shalt be fed.*
> Psalm 37:3

We have all heard injunctions to "Do good" and "Be good." In the Northward HUHD Model recall that those driven more by Logic will lean toward just ways while those driven by the Intuitive will lean toward merciful ways. The contention here is that those who lean toward just ways—emphasizing duty, discipline, and obedience (as objectively realized)—will have the predisposition of mind to make demands[68] on others for the sake of righteousness. This would include those who are prone to admonishing others or having legalistic ways. Conversely, those who lean toward merciful ways—emphasizing love, grace, and holiness (as subjectively realized)—will have the predisposition of mind to approach the issue of righteousness on the basis of desire.[69] This would include those prone to having pacifist ways. Then there are, of course, those who have a balanced approach between demand and desire. This kind of approach is evident in structured yet loving family environments. Because each of us has a different level of spiritual maturity, members in these environments will most often be guided by faith in the One who commanded to love (first) just as "I [being Jesus, *the first*] have loved you."[70]

> *Let me pass through thy land:*
> *I will go along by the high way,*
> *I will neither turn unto the right hand nor to the left.*
> Deuteronomy 2:27

The goal of *Solidus* is for believers to recognize that the mind is divided into two functions for greater understanding. If life matters and Biblical issues are not increasingly realized according to the

---

[68] Daniel 4:17
[69] 1 Peter 2:2-3
[70] John 15:12

mind's ability to apprehend both objectively and subjectively, then facts may be treated subjectively and truths may be treated objectively. This only causes confusion!

So a person who is not increasing his or her duality of objectivity and subjectivity (i.e., dual-mindedness of fact and truth) will only persist with a single-minded blend of both forms – most typically the result of fiction and falsehoods.

There is also an interesting parallel between demand and desire relative to West and East (as function of mind) and hot and cold, or fire and water. Realize that God is living fire[71] and the source for not only fire, but also living water.[72] Just as John baptized with water in the physical form, Christ Jesus baptizes with water in the spiritual form (e.g., the Holy Ghost), and with fire.[73] Note that without water one would be unable to continue on with the will to do good after being compelled to pass through fire. It's the unpredictable and at times tempering experiences of life that shape a person's disposition for the better. Therefore, it is impossible to reason and respond with fire (fact, objectivity) leading to uprightness, unless one is first thirsty for and then filled with water (truth, subjectivity of God).

If your reasoning about issues of faith is a blend of facts and truths, you will tend to intellectualize faith or to make it literal. In these cases your response will be cool or lukewarm[74] at best—never hot as fire (i.e., *just* as West driven) and never cold as water (i.e., *merciful* as East driven).

Even so, while seeking to become hotter or colder may seem to be more advanced than the blended approach, such one way or another extremes may cause believers to turn out of the way. Think about it: To be so right-handed (judicial) may suppress the mind to foster (subjective) desire for God, particularly that which is influenced by faith and grace; and to be so left-handed (merciful) may suppress the mind to foster (objective) willingness and determination to act upon faith.

---

[71] Hebrews 12:28-29
[72] John 7:37-39
[73] Matthew 3:11
[74] Revelation 3:16

In the Deuteronomy passage above, we learn that the goal of salvation is to avoid turning to either the right hand or the left. Therefore, in order to resist turning, the dual function of mind must be strengthened and balanced while purposed Northward. Then the West can become hot as fire just as the East can become cold as water. Similarly, demand and desire can be fostered into two qualities, as further evidenced by just and merciful ways.[75] To increase with both demand and desire (the result of faith and the gift of grace) will therefore help to balance the foundation of mind, and even minimize the tendency to turn toward legalistic or pacified ways.

Most Christians will agree that true righteousness cannot be achieved without first increasing one's faith in God, particularly in Christ Jesus.[76] For a moment, reflect on the word *truth*. As discussed, truth has both objective and subjective connotations. The Greek term *alētheia* G225 is an example of these two forms. When reviewing this lexicon relative to *alēthōs* G230 and *ontōs* G3689, the reader will find that the general characteristics of truth seem to be weighted heavily toward the objective (i.e., as a fact, a certainty, in reality, etc.). This is especially the case when also taking into account Hebrew translations for truth.

There is an important aspect of this discussion though that is easy to overlook. It pertains to how an objective point is oftentimes made. As believers of God, we recognize that all of Truth is of God, the One who exists toward the North. To receive God's Truth is a vertical subjective process that by one's response ultimately raises the temple of one's soul. As one's knowledge of God's Truth is gained, the question then becomes: During the reasoning process between West and East of mind—a process spawned by faith and grace—where does truth (small *t*) come from? It comes from the

---

[75] Interestingly there are lexicons for *demand* and *desire* that are similarly rooted and even involve the terms ask and enquire (e.g., *sha'al* H7592 and *eperōtaō* G1905). While this is important to consider the focus here is on how these two terms can also differ according to mind's ability to reason and respond.

[76] Romans 3:22

Human Understanding and Devotion 145

subjective side of mind that houses want, passion, and desire, and the side that one is motivated by—the Eastern mind!

This argument can be supported by how some objective forms of truth are defined within certain lexicons, including *alētheia*. There are "of a truth"[77] (e.g., in reality, in fact, a certainty) and "according to truth."[78] And in other Biblical passages, there is "of the truth."[79]

What does this suggest? It suggests that when an objective point is made (one considered true in fact), much of the time the truth of a prior instance or another form is being referred to in order to further the discussion.

A prior instance can be regarded as provable because it is the result of what has occurred in reality. With such factual information a connection can be made between one objective thought and another in order to make a greater point.

Truth of another form is different. It is the unseen or perhaps not-yet-realized subjective form of truth which, in and of itself, cannot be proven to exist. Since the unseen of truth (i.e., God's existence) is difficult to prove objectively, then it is important to help those who need to be shown how the unseen manifests into this world, and especially into one's reality. Generally speaking, when the product of human effort results in what is truly bad and destructive on earth then this proves Satan's existence; and when the product of human effort results into what is truly good and constructive on earth then this proves God's existence.

Let's think about how the quality of one's individual character relates to this subject. Character represents an unseen subjective truth (hence, truth of another form). For those who reason and respond according to Truth such quality can be described "as a personal excellence; that candor of mind which is free from affectation, pretense, simulation, falsehood, and deceit."[80] When

---

[77] Daniel 2:47, Matthew 14:33, John 6:14
[78] Romans 2:2
[79] 2 Corinthians 4:2, 1 Timothy 2:4-5
[80] Blue Letter Bible. Dictionary and Word Search for *alētheia* (Strong's 225). Blue Letter Bible. 1996-2012. 20 Oct 2012. < http://www.blueletterbible.org/lang/lexicon/Lexicon.cfm?strongs=G225 >

such truth becomes evident (e.g., the result of one's response), then it proves the subjective truth about such individuals. Not only that, it proves God's existence even more.

The problem comes up when believers attempt to make an objective point about God's Truth to those who reject God and/or the manifestation process altogether. That's because in the nonbeliever's mind, when someone else speaks of such matters they are perceived simply as beliefs, and are not part of reality. In fact, most nonbelievers would argue that such notions should remain out of public dialog, particularly out of academic discourse.

As a result of rejecting God's Truth, though, each will remain limited in understanding as to why some humans coexist in harmony with God and others godly, while others remain disharmonious with all that is truly good.

As mentioned in the *Fall and Rise* section, the process for reasoning out unknowns about human behavior is from East to West. Those who continue to deny God's Word and God's Truth will negotiate the reasons for human thoughts and ways primarily on the basis of what has been seen or has occurred in reality. For a number of reasons this is good and is part of the process for perceiving what is "evidently" good or bad. At the same time, though, they will consistently dismiss the true cause of how and why natural human behaviors become evident. Sure they may ask "Why?" about the vast array of unknowns, but their reasoning will only go as far as what objectivity will permit (e.g., facts according to Logic). Answers that more truly answer the question "Why?" can be known prior to what ultimately proves true in reality, because such answers exist within the Intuitive side of mind.

For optimal understanding that is in harmony with God, seek for and allow for Jesus to become that greater cause of mind to respond by. As a result of seeking Him first, then fostered by the love of and the love for God, the Intuitive of mind can be embedded with God's Truth. After establishing Jesus as the cornerstone of faith then the effect of reasoning will be "of" and "according to" the subjective of Truth. As He further becomes the cause for reasoning and response then the depth and brevity for thoughtfulness and understanding (according to Truth) will become evident.

Human Understanding and Devotion

Harmony with God and with others godly is the result of reasoning matters of truth from East to West, and then acting upon one's faith. Recall what was mentioned in the *Brain Function: Perspective* section relative to this discussion. Before reaching a state of harmony with God, believers will have been progressively raised from the cardinal realm of earthly orientation and into the celestial realm of divine orientation.

Even if the fallen person was somehow conscious enough to turn around and see forward just as those Northward do, he or she is still upside down in thinking. Unknowns will be reasoned from West to East so that the analytical/linear of understandings determines the relational/holistic of understandings – it's this, or the relational/holistic will be dismissed altogether as an important to overall understanding. Backwards thinking like this is only indicative of a mindset that is centered more on self, while remaining coordinated by egocentric means (e.g., left, right, front, and back).

Until there is one day a turn, not just in the horizontal sense, but especially in the vertical sense, this person's thinking and response will continue to be out of harmony with the divine.

Overall, truth in the subjective sense (e.g., the holistic, implicit) is what ultimately makes the objective side of truth a fact (e.g., the linear, explicit). So, in one's thinking and response, the unseen aspect of what is good or bad manifests into the seen aspect of what is good or bad, respectively. This underscores the importance of helping to bring the unseen aspect of what is truly good into reality.

With that said, realize also that it is by desire that believers of God are "*of* one accord"[81]. In part, this means to live with "singleness, simplicity, sincerity, (and) mental honesty."[82] By becoming "one in Christ in all desires"[83] then doing what is right has

---

[81] Philippians 2:2
[82] Blue Letter Bible. "Dictionary and Word Search for *haplotēs* (Strong's 572)". Blue Letter Bible. 1996-2012. 4 Nov 2012. < http://www.blueletterbible.org/lang/lexicon/lexicon.cfm?Strongs=G572&t=KJV >
[83] 'Of one accord' is translated from the Greek term *sympsychos* G4861. This word is made up of two words *syn* (together with) and *psychos* (soul, self, inner life, or the seat of the feelings, desires, affections). So the word refers to being 'united in spirit' or harmonious (BDAG). Paul desired the Philippians to be

less to do with a *pressure* to respond rightly (much of the time confused with man's standards apart from God about what "right" means), and more to do with a *release*. Why release? Because one's desire to bring the subjective side of God's Truth and righteousness into reality is what ultimately liberates and sets the soul free. This should be important for anyone seeking to become liberated from the evils of this world!

This is why faith in God Almighty is treated primarily as a truth-based, subjective matter. Its characteristics are closely aligned with beliefs. Again, there are aspects of faith that are fact-based because of what has been proven or objectively realized about God's Truth. All in all, believers will ultimately discover that facts of faith help support truths of faith. So when facts and truths about faith are yoked together in the minds of believers, God and those of God are known more greatly.

iii. Fruit of the Spirit

> *But the fruit of the Spirit is love, joy, peace, longsuffering,*
> *gentleness, goodness, faith, meekness, temperance:*
> *against such there is no law.*
> Galatians 5:22-23

In recognizing and appreciating that righteousness and all matters of goodness are solely of God, then goodness possessed and exemplified by man—in thought and in action—can only be the manifestation or fruit of the (inward) spirit of light,[84] one graced by the Spirit of God.

As we can see from the passage above, even faith is considered a fruit of the Spirit. This is interesting because most of our discussion has treated faith as a possession of the mind—something we can

---

united in their affections—one in Christ in all desires! Phl 2:2 is the only occurrence of this word in the NT. (Wayne Steury). Blue Letter Bible. Dictionary and Word Search for sympsychos (Strong's 4861). Blue Letter Bible. 1996-2012. 20 Oct 2012. < http://www.blueletterbible.org/lang/lexicon/Lexicon.cfm?strongs=G4861 >

[84] Ephesians 5:9-10, 5:13

learn. All fruits of the Spirit are from God's influential Grace through man. Since this is the case we must ask: If faith can be directly approached how can it be considered a fruit (i.e., a product or an unforeseen byproduct of effort)? Truths are like seeds sown into the mind; with "the act upon faith" such seeds can sprout and become rooted and grounded in love. Thus, from thought into action, matters of faith sown into the mind yield fruit from the heart of all things (subjectively) good, including righteousness,[85] holiness,[86] and even greater faith.

> *But when they believed Philip preaching the things concerning the kingdom of God, and the name of Jesus Christ, they were baptized, both men and women.*
> Acts 8:12

When reflecting on how faith can increase in relation to the dual function of the mind, a question comes up: Does the process of knowing God typically begin with facts that lead to truths, or with truths that lead to facts? When pondering this question, recall that the West of mind is the side of reality, while the East of mind is the side of ideals and beliefs. Those first attempting to know more about God will naturally test the issue of faith against their own sense of reality and experience. Until greater subjective understandings about God and godliness are acquired, though, religious notions that could appear in color are only perceived in black and white. It would seem that, for most, faith is learned from West to East over time, perhaps taking decades, or perhaps never being learned at all. But what if a believer becomes immersed in Biblical Truths, could that person learn faith from East to West? Of course, particularly when Jesus of the New Testament becomes the focal point for faith.

This dovetails with a question about religious convictions that has much to do with the response to faith. The question is this: Why do some first emphasize conformity by demand in order to help the group increase faithfully, instead of first emphasizing faith by desire

---

[85] Hebrews 12:11, James 3:18
[86] Romans 6:22

in order to help the group increase into conformity? The primary reason for bringing up this question is to consider which approach leads more probably to the natural response to God's Truth in producing fruit.

One way to arrive at the answer to this question may be to reflect on the natural responses of children. Parents often instruct their children to "Do this" and "Don't do that," and much of the time they make such demands for all the right reasons. But, just like the Law of Moses, instructions such as these are also black and white. Without the addition of love from the parent—a subjective quality that can only be realized and appreciated in color—the child will have no choice but to think that works and deeds as driven by the West of mind are the only way to become justified as being good. Just to be clear: this is not how one becomes justified in the eyes of God.

A child will typically want to know how to accomplish a given task, and then to be given the opportunity to learn why it is done this way. Learning how something is done increases objectivity in determining facts, while learning why increases subjectivity in determining truths.

Both objective and subjective forms of understanding are necessary for healthy human development. Far too often, though, there is greater emphasis on how to accomplish goodness in the outward sense, instead of spending more time learning why inward goodness is paramount.

> *For by grace are ye saved through faith; and that not of*
> *yourselves: [it is] the gift of God:*
> *Not of works, lest any man should boast.*
> Ephesians 2:8-9

As mentioned before, the process of learning about faith may take decades—it really depends on one's soulful conviction, motivation, and approach. New converts will typically consider the (intentional) process of faith development to be a slow and arduous task, one that requires much discipline and work.[87] If matters of truth

---

[87] Hebrews 12:10-11

are approached objectively, then odds are that little time will be committed toward deeper, subjective understandings about God. That's because such depth will be regarded as hard to grasp. On the other hand, if we approach matters of God's Truth subjectively—while being cognizant of the time and patience necessary for Truth to become rooted within us—it will not only be easier for believers to learn answers to "why" about the vast array of Biblical topics, it will also be easier to see how faith in God (as opposed to faith in self) plays out in reality.

So even while the subjective approach toward faith may in the beginning be construed as a work, the efforts expended in grasping it are tolerable and even gratifying when believers become able to comprehend the reasons for God's existence relative to one's life on earth.

For the law was given by Moses,
[but] grace and truth came by Jesus Christ.
John 1:17

So how do children young and old become lovingly obedient to the higher authority? Let's look at what most likely occurs in the minds of believers during the response to faith. Based on previous discussions, we can say that righteousness is a Western apprehension of the mind while holiness is an Eastern apprehension. But how can we be more certain about this? Perhaps one way is to reflect on God's instructions for mankind: First through Moses emphasizing an objective approach toward righteousness involving works; and then through Jesus emphasizing a subjective approach of holiness (or godliness) involving grace.[88]

Earlier it was mentioned that, until greater subjective understandings about God are gained, then religious notions that could appear in color are only perceived in black and white. Grace—a characteristic and condition of the inward spirit—"...is given by God according to the measure of the gift of Christ."[89] If the emphasis for faith is not about desiring Jesus and the gift of grace, then how

---

[88] Romans 10:5, Ephesians 4:24
[89] Ephesians 4:7

can the fruit of righteousness ever be produced, much less perceived? It simply cannot!

> *And be found in him, not having mine own righteousness, which is of the law, but that which is through the faith of Christ, the righteousness which is of God by faith:*
> Philippians 3:9

Sure, the West of mind is most capable of recognizing the black and white aspects of doing what's right and even living by the Law. However, if such notions are not drawn from the subjective side of Truth, then one's perception of righteousness will be consistently skewed toward self-serving purposes. Only by first seeking and then receiving the gift of God's grace can all matters of goodness come to fruition, including righteousness. Therefore, as faith is increased, then (according to God's will), so is the gift of grace; and with grace, efforts to increase faithfully will be made less by demand and more by desire: that is, heart-induced responsiveness which ultimately leads to the willingness and determination to do well in His name.

Depending on which side of the mind is dominant, the learning process involving West and East of mind will obviously be different for each person. What matters most, though, is the response to faith—horizontally from (subjective) East of mind into (objective) West of mind during the reasoning process, and then vertically from thought into action (i.e., those who speak with wisdom and are moved by grace).

iv. "Tell the Truth!"

> *Then came the Jews round about him, and said unto him, How long dost thou make us to doubt? If thou be the Christ, tell us plainly.*
> John 10:24

This leads to a discussion about how facts and truths are most likely negotiated in one's mind and relative to others. We've all been told to "Tell the truth!" But my view is that such commands are not issued for the sake of seeking greater truths about a given matter, but for seeking more facts. Why do I say this? It's because people issuing commands are typically driven by objectivity to arrive at deeper matters of fact, not by subjectivity to arrive at deeper matters of truth. This is particularly the case when someone is suspected of wrongdoing or when there is controversy.

While facts are indeed true, if we don't differentiate linear facts from holistic truths, the reasoning process will fall short of balancing reality with beliefs. Truth(s) in its subjective form take time and patience to understand. As differentiated from apparent facts (reality), truths have more to do with what is not so apparent (beliefs).

In the section called *Laterality: East & West, Left & Right*, it was mentioned how important it is to increase one's appreciation of Biblical Truth. This is so that the believer can draw from Truth to make sense of reality. The goal for reasoning with soundness of mind is to further distinguish and enhance both the objective and the subjective reasoning processes so that in the balance, one can become more knowing and aware.

Issues of fact in nature can certainly be resolved by command, but not issues of truth. Just like Truths of the Bible, truths in another person's mind can only be approached through want and desire. The desire for the tangible things of this world requires little effort of mind, whereas the desire for the intangible (particularly that of God) requires time and patience. Those who are most apt to realize truths of any kind will be those who continue to develop true faith in God. With faith, efforts to learn more about the thoughts and actions of another person will be less about playing the "gotcha game" and more about patiently learning why the person acts as he or she does.

There is much to know about the depth and breadth of Truth. So when someone says, "That's true," is the complete truth known for a given matter? No. While such responses seem natural when agreeing with bits of factual information during a discussion, this does not mean that the full extent of truth is known. Factual information can certainly be deepened by objectivity, but without learning more about what drives the psyche (i.e., according to the subjective of truths or falsehoods), one will unavoidably stop short of realizing the underlying reasons.

If you indeed desire truths, you will be more apt to sincerely and with patience delve deeper into the understanding of these reasons from a subjective point of view. During the process of learning more about a given story, your thoughts, questions, and concerns will go beyond objective Western understandings and into subjective Eastern understandings. With a better grasp on truths (vs. falsehoods) the true or false motivations of your own mind become clearer. After you've established this foundation, then the motivations of others directly and indirectly involved in a given story (including their influence) will become apparent.

So when is the balance of mind not so balanced? First, and as previously discussed, when there is a false, upside-down balance; or second, when there is a struggle to remain upright. This may be the result of one side of the mind being more weighted or dominant than the other side, perhaps to the extreme. In these cases the reasoning process will frame new inputs of information relative to one's current understandings largely based on how one leans. Even on matters that seem clear and convincing to many people, those who are West-dominant and East-dominant will find it difficult to agree on the underlying reasons. In the Northward sense, when an issue is framed according to Logic, the reasoning process will begin from a West-dominant perspective (i.e. objective in thought, pro-judicial in response). When the same issue is framed according to Intuition, the reasoning process will begin from an East-dominant perspective (i.e., subjective in thought, pro-merciful in response). Where each process ends will depend on how well-developed the other side of the mind is relative to the issue at hand and one's greater purpose.

v. Conformity & Non-Conformity

> *If any man among you seem to be religious,*
> *and bridleth not his tongue, but deceiveth his own heart,*
> *this man's religion [is] vain.*
> James 1:26

As the result of the ways in which humans frame thoughts, questions, and concerns, we can see that some will be given more to conformity (as West-driven), while others will be given more to non-conformity (as East-driven). In general, conformists will attempt to gain control, whereas non-conformists will attempt to release control. Balance is necessary in order to prompt a yoked response (toward God) that exalts mind over body.

Throughout history, intellectually oriented people have been (and are now) naturally geared to conformity, and have been critical of non-conformists. This does not suggest that all non-conformists ought to be impugned, nor all conformists for that matter. It is to suggest that there is a difference between the non-conformity that comes through faith in God and that which comes through faith in other things. With faith in God, believers are better able to grow in the non-conformity associated with love, grace, and mercy, and all other subjective forms of goodness that are of God.

So my argument is that in order to balance the foundation of mind one must be open-minded to both conformity as West-driven and non-conformity as East-driven. Reflect back on the discussion in the Conservative vs. Liberal section. There it was asked—Is it possible to have a balanced approach in one's mind that involves both Conservative and Liberal ideologies? In the Northward sense, it most certainly can. For instance, as the result of the love for God first, there is a blessed opportunity to move Northward with both conformity on Civic-Economic issues on one hand, and non-conformity on Socio-Cultural issues on the other hand.

If we are not balanced (again, in the Northward sense) with respect to conformity and non-conformity, one side will attempt to exalt itself at the expense of the other. Simply reflect on the division that exists today between the extreme ideologies of Left and Right. Left versus Right only suggests that one must be exalted while the other must be diminished. In the realm of human relationships, though, efforts to unify have less to do with the horizontal struggle between Left and Right, and more to do with the vertical struggle of Right versus Wrong.

From this basis then it only makes sense that a true consensus comprises only those who are yoked Northward, and not those bent on selfish, Southward desires. Each of His children has the potential to become balanced with both Conservative and Liberal ideologies. In essence, both ideologies can become yoked Northward to constructively build God's Temple, individually and collectively. It should also be realized that in the Southward sense both ideologies (as similarly named) can be used to destroy God's Temple.

Aside from what one's greater purpose is for a moment, most humans have seen the dynamics between conformists and non-conformists play out in family matters, social and work matters, and even in matters involving the institutions of State and Church. Why is there so much division between conformists and non-conformists? It's because—even if both are Northward—each side refuses to appreciate the importance of the other side and of becoming balanced and united. In order to accomplish the greater good, each side must first respond from the basis of faith in God while growing in love, trust, and mutual respect for one another.

Without the appreciation for the subjective nature of truth, conformists will tend to exert their influence on others through objectivity and facts. Just like most parents, they believe they know what's best for children—that is, children who have yet to conform to their standards. Without the subjective qualities that flourish with love, grace, and mercy, though—not simply in what they say first, but even more by what they show first—parents will only make the path Northward for children more difficult than easy. Responding with righteousness is vital, but if such parents are not first engaged with the subjective side of Truth, it will be difficult for them to perceive what God's will is, let alone teach the (vertical) differences between right and wrong.

So if one is unable to respond to life's concerns with the kind of non-conformity that results from faith and grace, then one can only practice the response by conforming to a given set of principles or standards. This is indicative of a West to East approach toward faithfulness: one that attempts to move forward through objectivity (the cause) in order to be seen by God and by other godly persons as subjectively good (the effect). However, one cannot (objectively) do enough to become (subjectively) good. Believers of God are saved by grace, not by works.

If you believe that you can be saved by works and performance, it's likely that your relationships with other people are based on earning your way into their hearts. But love, even among humans, is not the result of any such objective process.

In practically all religions there are those individuals and groups that are driven more by objectivity, while others are driven more by subjectivity, and some may indeed be balanced.

Human Understanding and Devotion

Conformists are naturally most attentive to the text of their religious source, while non-conformists are naturally more attentive to the context. For good reason, Christians will regard the Holy Bible as the only written source for God's Truth. There are also those who recognize that by becoming more attuned with the Spirit of God—the result of faith as first introduced by the Word as read and as heard—one can also be poised to receive the gifts of greater wisdom and grace.

Without more clearly distinguishing facts and truths according to the mind's ability to apprehend such inputs, then there is no choice but to blend them into a form of truth reflecting one's mind dominance. Thus, people who are West-leaning will argue from the text of the Bible, while those East-leaning will argue from the context of the Bible.

So the question becomes: Are matters of faith in God supposed to be driven by the text or by the context of the Bible? By the balance of both, of course! No doubt about it, to have the intellectual capacity to (objectively) argue points according to the text of the Bible is a gift in itself, but so is being perceptive enough to (subjectively) apprehend the context (or fullness) of God's message.

For the most part, West-leaning intellects who are Christian will naturally seek conformity according to the text of the Bible. Many such people will even be able to recall scripture verbatim. To be able to recall the text of the Bible is, again, a gift. For many this is an important aspect of their walk in faith. If this textual recall is not balanced with the context of God's message, though—one that not only involves depth of facts, but even more greatly depth of truths that created such facts—believers such as these will be centered more on being the cause for others to respond to, even if they appear to act on behalf of the Greater. In these cases the Bible is treated as a form of instruction or tool that substantiates one's objective point of view. The more West-leaning the person, the more these sorts of views will be held to the literal of Biblical text.

Without the wherewithal to respond first according to the subjective aspect of God's Truth, West-leaning persons will have the predisposition of mind to teach others how to reason with judgment and prejudice relative to conforming standards established by the group. In these cases the Bible is used as the premise for trumping up one's religious convictions—this, while belittling and admonishing those who view the response to faith differently. They don't intend to do this—it is simply an unintended consequence of approaching highly subjective issues on the basis of objectivity.

Generally speaking, believers of God who do not see the importance of subjective Truth will only be compelled to achieve what is considered good by objectivity and by practice. Just as many intellectually oriented people find it natural to observe human law, some intellectually-oriented Christians may find it appealing to practice God's Law by the Book. While there are many forms of practice, both good and bad, the application of Biblical Truth in a way that results in legalistic coercion does little to help unite the whole of Christendom. That's because practices like these only diminish such believers' perceptions of importance and value for all seeking the Northward path to become yoked into one accord.

As one's faith in the subjective is increased, it becomes more difficult or even impossible to see faith literally. Those responding from the subjective view of Truth (non-conformists) will usually care little about answering to anyone who assumes an air of superiority, particularly when it comes to issues of faith and faithfulness. Many conformists, though, will see nonconformists who don't have the words to articulate their subjective convictions as inferior. Because they have little appreciation for subjective Truth and for how such truth influences our responsiveness on matters of goodness (including righteousness), people with extreme West leanings will be prone to frame loaded and leading questions, as well as to criticize non-conformists. Some may even be inclined to dig up the dirt of others' pasts while being quick to blame and quick to judge.

People who are intellectually inclined may believe that there is just cause to mock, ridicule and intimidate nonconformists who resist their influence and fail to meet their expectations. This, of course, puts nonconformists on the defensive. Such approaches are perhaps justifiable when it comes to getting at objective issues, but not subjective issues. Even non-extremists driven by performance and works may persist in trying to discredit the ways of people who reason and respond differently. In their minds, these people have yet to show their worth. But neither innate subjective qualities nor those acquired by faith are likely to be expressed as objectively as West-leaning critics would expect or appreciate.

Assuming that mockery has found its way into the dialog, the only other option for responding to those who put others on the defensive is to mock just as they have mocked. Keep in mind that mockery is largely based on cleverly worded half-truths and an elaboration of facts, taken out of context and heavily loaded with sarcasm. Responding with mockery, though, only dignifies such ways, and actually works in the favor of those centered more on controlling the dialog.

If the side of logic is not balanced by true faith in God, then one will not only fall short of realizing the Truth of God, he or she will also fall short of realizing truths of man. That's because the objective is elevated at the expense of the subjective, and many human truths cannot be fully grasped without an appreciation of the subjective element.

Recall that it is from a higher purpose in mind that one becomes knowing, and it is from knowing that just and merciful ways are manifested on earth. So is it really necessary to appease those who make assertions and accusations concerning one's stance in faith in God? No. The real concern, though, is that when unjust and merciless behaviors become evident, even by those with strong religious convictions, such ways are manifestations of falsehoods of mind, even if touted to be true and on behalf of God.

> *Lie not one to another, seeing that ye have put off the old man*
> *with his deeds; And have put on the new [man],*
> *which is renewed in knowledge after the image of him that*
> *created him:*
> Colossians 3:9-10

While many West-leaning people are sought after for their intellect, speaking abilities, and commanding leadership skills, without faith in God they will be apt to mislead those who follow. In part they do this by distorting the image of those they profess to know all about, many times with condescension. Without faith, one will consistently be driven by the intellect, perceiving only what is explicit in works; this, instead of by beliefs, perceiving what is implicit in grace. This only skews one's perception of self-worth and what it means to be of good character. Simply put: A person who is not of good character (the result of being without true faith in God) will fail to be a good judge of good character. Thus, as poor judges of character, leaders such as these will typically overlook the best talent most capable to achieve the best course of action for the whole group. So what is the best course of action? That which permits a yoked response in the Northward constructive sense.

Those balanced by faith in God do know better. And because they know, they don't care to hold others in contempt just as they have been held in contempt. Why not? Invariably, it's because they want to help save others from their own contemptible behaviors. As with any misguided soul, time and patience is necessary. Believers of God are most apt to understand that all need to be shown mercy and forgiveness. These ways are not dictated first, they are shown first, so that with time God's love—as increasingly realized from one character-building experience to another—can ultimately weaken any proclivity for self-righteous and condescending ways.

vi. The Truth of the Story

> *[He that] speaketh truth sheweth forth righteousness:*
> *but a false witness deceit.*
> Proverbs 12:17

> *[For] the sin of their mouth [and] the words of their lips let*
> *them even be taken in their pride:*
> *and for cursing and lying [which] they speak.*
> Psalm 59:12

Let's go back to the command: *"Tell the truth!"* The context of truth can never be realized by command—it can only be realized and appreciated with time and patience by those who have a genuine interest and desire to learn about why. In other words, truth in its subjective form is difficult to learn about after the fact—that is, after one has already begun to judge another.

In order to avoid saying and doing things that are damaging or destructive, we must have had a sincere interest in knowing the true character of the person in question beforehand. As most people realize, though, it is not always possible to become acquainted with all others of interest on a first-name basis. So if we can't learn the truth about another's character on command, and fail to learn it before the fact, then how else can we learn it? According to the story, of course.

As most people know, the delivery of a story requires both a storyteller (the source) and an audience (the listener, reader, or viewer). The source can be an individual or a group of individuals; or it can be a movie, song, news article, etc., each based on an individual or group story. Some stories are inspirational in good ways, while others are inspirational in bad ways. The source may be driven by truth or falsehood, and the same is true of the listener.

This makes for some interesting dynamics between good and bad as stories are shared—that is, good as influenced by God through godly individuals, and bad as influenced by Evil through ungodly individuals. The main point here, though, is that such dynamics do exist when attempting to deliver the truth and/or attempting to get at or receive the truth.

What is 'True' is Not Always 'Truth'

When it comes to any sort of storytelling, the aim for the source is for the listener to acknowledge that his or her story is true. How to best go about the delivery of one's story, though, hangs in the balance. Even if the source says that his story is true, it isn't necessarily oriented by truth in its larger sense. Recall, there is more to truth than meets the eye.

There are stories that involve sorrow, hurt, hardship, and pain. Most of them need to be shared with trustworthy listeners. While there are some stories that pull on the heart-strings of the audience, there are others that seemingly lift the soul with inspiration and laughter. In practically all cases, though, a story is told for the sake of preserving or enhancing one's self-image and/or that of another. The other could be a friend, a group, or even God.

If the story is told for the sake of preserving the source's self-image, though, and most particularly when it is told in an attempt to enhance that image, there is usually a price to pay. That price is often the diminution or even the sacrifice of the image of a third party. That person may have acted poorly, but it just as likely that the story is deceptive, even if the source does not realize it. At the beginning of the story, the listener really doesn't know.

So while the listener must be entrusted with receiving such information, it is just as vital that the source be trusted to deliver the story in proper context. While context is an apprehension of the East of mind, when context is provided, the gap between linear facts and holistic truths is bridged. When this gap is bridged, one's overall grasp of the subject matter (as objectively and subjectively realized) becomes balanced and proper.

> *And he began again to teach by the sea side: and there was gathered unto him a great multitude, so that he entered into a ship, and sat in the sea; and the whole multitude was by the sea on the land.*
> Mark 4:1

Proper context relative to depth of matters of fact and of truth is vital to any story that is supposed to be altogether true. Depth of facts (West) is like layer upon layer of matters that are explicit, obvious, and provable. Depth of truths (East) is like layer upon layer of matters that are implicit, obscure, and difficult to explain. Learning facts (including how something is done) increases Western depths, while learning truth (including why it is done) increases Eastern depths.

Biblically speaking, passages that explicitly present facts will not contradict passages that contain implicit truths. The objective nature of facts will help clarify and even support the subjective truths.

Since depth of facts is linear in nature, think of this as soil that creates the land. Since depth of truths is holistic in nature, think of this as water that creates the sea. The Sea of Galilee and its surrounding lands (some mountainous) are a great example of this sort of imagery. This "sea" is a freshwater lake situated in the Northeast section of Israel. In essence, the human understandings that form land and sea are important matters to deepen and to balance.

While some true statements can be described as facts, and can even concern fiction (e.g., "It is true that he lied"), attempts to explain thoughts objectively can only be made sequentially or in snapshot form. Otherwise, matters of truth and even falsehoods are simultaneous and perpetually dynamic, as seen or derived by East of mind conceptions and perceptions.

With this understanding it's easy to see why movies, television shows, and other stories containing images of characters are popular sources for storytelling. While there are certainly some images that motivate viewers according to truth, many if not most motivate according to falsehoods. In other words, not only is it possible for such sources to deliver depth of fiction, such images in motion can also deliver depth of falsehoods.

Many will argue: "There's nothing wrong with movies and even books that provide escape and fulfill fantasies." This is, of course, is a personal decision, much dependent on the entertainment value of the source relative to what the underlying story really entails. But also consider that flooding the subjective side of the mind with fantasy only diminishes the desire to flood the mind with God's Truth.

An argument can also be made that audio and video recordings of actual events produced by man do little to reveal truths. Even if one's recording (seemingly) proves that someone has done something right, wrong, good, or bad, this does not mean that the recording presents truth in its larger sense. Much of the time such recordings are presented without context. Without context, it is difficult or impossible to know the motivations of those the story is about.

All in all, there is a difference between what a given recording reveals and whether it can be described as truth-oriented or false in the larger sense. While most recordings may be argued to be accurate or "true," the question is: Are the actions of characters the result of truths of mind or falsehoods? If the characters' motivation was not according to truth, then the recording will no doubt reveal falsehoods. Again, even if portions of the recording or even the recording itself can be described as factually true, the dynamics of characters in motion only reveals falsehoods, and thus teaches falsehoods.

It is these dynamics (e.g., the relational, simultaneous, holistic, etc.) that register in the Eastern mind. So the more the mind is engrossed with false teachings the less desirable truth becomes.

The negative impacts of recordings (as imaged and as presented in audio/video feeds) are compounded by the fact that many humans today have a false sense of justification for broadcasting them. Sure, most recordings are created for the sake of information-sharing and even entertainment. What's wrong with that? Nothing—that is, unless the motivation of the creator's mind is false. For example, there are those with the false compulsion to record what others have said and done in order to expose them, causing humiliation and scorn. Some even seem to believe that such a broadcast is justified because it seeks to prevent future acts of wrong-doing among the larger audience. However, if the premise of mind is false, then his or her production(s) will be false. Productions such as these do little to instill goodness among mankind. Instead, they do more to instill fear of breaking certain rules, laws, and sanctions. What most seem to disregard is that one does not become good by being subjected to fear-mongering tactics. One only becomes good by God's Grace!

In another example, those motivated by vindictiveness and deception may set up a scenario so that they can record the unexpected response of others. If creators and producers of such recordings tout them as "true" and yet falsehoods are the source's motivational basis, then more harm is done to the psyche of the audience than is done by the one recorded act. This is particularly the case when members of the audience replay this one recorded act time and again. When recordings are falsely justified, then the sources' own motivation will no doubt be for greed and/or notoriety. When truth in the subjective sense is dismissed for all involved, then (like a disease) falsehoods only beget falsehoods.

And not only [so], but we glory in tribulations also:
knowing that tribulation worketh patience;
And patience, experience; and experience, hope:
Romans 5:3-4

Proper context is crucial for any story to be oriented by truth. Without proper context the human response in itself (the effect) becomes the subject matter for a given story. Just like gossip, stories can become twisted by how they are delivered. Much of the time stories like these will be treated as the reason why a storyteller should be believed (in). In order to create and maintain interest in one's story, facts about certain others must be uncovered. For most listeners, the information unearthed represents context. While such approaches may explain the sequence of facts and circumstances, the true cause (as derived by the simultaneous of truths) will have yet to be negotiated by one's mind. Proper context involving subjective understandings typically comes much later. By that time, though, as the image of those presenting the story is (falsely) exalted, the image of character about those now reduced becomes further distorted and faded.

While a portion of this discussion deals with stories involving the image of one's character, what hasn't been discussed is what develops character. Generally speaking and in the Northward sense, depths of facts (land) and depth of truths (sea) are necessary apprehensions of mind as also evolved from one's personal experience (a.k.a., tried character). From such experience, each is better able to realize what works and what doesn't work during his walk in reality relative to (and in the balance of) idealisms and beliefs.

While much can be grasped from storytelling and the experience of others, realizations like these are only secondary to one's personal experience. By overcoming the afflictions of their experience, believers will ultimately become humbled, tempered, and good. Practically all humans will exhaust themselves in futility before finally realizing that God is indeed King! This is why it is vital for those who are loving, patient, and hopeful to help guide and even lift others in need. If those being guided are not allowed the freedom of trial and error, then how can they mature into a most pristine form of God? It would be difficult to say the least.

> *The first man [is] of the earth, earthy: the second man [is] the Lord from heaven. As [is] the earthy, such [are] they also that are earthy: and as [is] the heavenly, such [are] they also that are heavenly. And as we have borne the image of the earthy, we shall also bear the image of the heavenly.*
> 1 Corinthians 15:47-49

The image of one's character is important because it provides a sense of identity as affirmed in one's mind by what is seen in the eyes of others. This is even the case for believers of God who want to be viewed as good by those who are indeed good, and even for nonbelievers who care enough to learn more about God. If not for the character of the merciful, those who have erred along the way would find it difficult to recoup from their fallen state and be guided back onto the right path.

While some determine character by what a person does and how he does it (by depth of facts), others determine character by why the person does what he does (by depth of truths). As already mentioned, answers to questions concerning *why* are subjective in nature. Therefore, when we are seeking to determine the (pre- or post-manifested) cause of another's mind, it has less to do with deepening one's mind with facts (vs. fiction) and more to do with deepening the mind with truths (vs. falsehoods).

Proper context as balanced between facts and truths about one's character, even in relation to other characters, is vital for truth-oriented stories. In most cases, though, what makes a story most interesting is not simply what the characters in the story say and do in an ordinary way, it's the ways in which what they say and do differ from the listener's image of his or her own character.

> *He that hath my commandments, and keepeth them, he it is that loveth me: and he that loveth me shall be loved of my Father, and I will love him, and will manifest myself to him.*
> John 14:21

As "The Cause" Unfolds

What's also interesting about most quickly-shared stories, including news stories, is how they typically unfold. Details will usually begin in the West as fact-based deepened by objectivity, and (attempt to) unfold Eastward toward the subjective of truth (vs. falsehoods). Thus, a typical story begins with the headline (i.e., the attention-grabber, the assertion, charge, etc.), each based on a recent situation, event, and/or discussion. As human interest grows, the story prompts deepening questions as to what happened and how. Over time, as the pouring in of information begins to slow, the story enters subjective territory with questions attempting to arrive at the ultimate cause of the event. However, since many readers or listeners do not have the time, the patience, or the wherewithal to deal with matters of truth (vs. falsehoods), they will give the story only a limited time to develop in their minds. In large part this is because attention to one story is quickly displaced by attention to another more newsworthy story.

Human Understanding and Devotion

With only so much time each day to devote toward the surge of new stories, most people do not pause to reconsider their original judgment on yesterday's news. So while Eastern cause unfolds itself into Western action, stories that attempt to reveal the cause from the other direction (from West to East, as if unfolding) will typically fall short of truth. That's because these stories usually remain in objective territory with hardly any consideration for truths versus falsehoods of mind. Most think that objectivity alone is all that is necessary to understand the full extent of truth. This is simply not the case! Again, answers that involve the depth and breadth of truth (vs. falsehoods) as causation exist in the East, not in the West.

Deceit [is] in the heart of them that imagine evil:
but to the counsellors of peace [is] joy.
Proverbs 12:20

So does such a West to East approach pertain to how movies are made? No, not usually. People pay to be held as a captive audience for the two-hour span of a movie. This obviously provides greater opportunities for character development so the story can unfold from East to West.

The problem, though, is that while movies are created for the purposes of art and entertainment, most fall short in the area of character development according to truth. Why? Because many (perhaps most) people in the industry—from writers to producers to actors, etc.—are not motivated by the subjective of Truth. Their manmade creations go only as far (vertically North) as what they imagine, believe in, and stand for, individually and collectively.

Generally-speaking, those driven by the sequential of Logic (West) are naturally stimulated by the juicy parts of a story. Those driven by the simultaneous of Intuition (East) are naturally stimulated by the subjective process of image and character development.

So in the Southward sense, stories will unfold either from the West according to an elaboration on facts made into fiction; or from the East according to the character-building process of falsehoods – in such cases, not a buildup at all, but is one that is inherently destructive to one's soul.

Think about the impact that fiction and falsehoods have on the psyche. While one's greater interest could lean one way or the other, there are those whose temples are yoked Southward as a result of duality arising (hence: falling) from such purposeful stimuli. While many humans want to be liberated from life's captivity, most have little clue that these sorts of (wrongful) convictions end up hindering one's psyche from ever arising. So instead of seeking God in order to make a conscious decision to turn away from destructive influences, most choose to remain unconscious while tempting others to be similarly kindled by them.

While there are those who dedicate much time to watching movies and television shows, there are others who earnestly take the time to watch and listen to the stories of others. Some storytellers, though, find it easy to falsify the story and vilify the character of the person the story is about. In order to discourage this sort of behavior, those listening and with sound mind can encourage proper context and proper character development. To deliver truth, though—the result of one's inward goodness—is a subjective process that many storytellers are simply unaccustomed to. This process, however, is necessary before and/or during the process of attempting to prove the story true according to the facts. This not only makes sense, it's only fair, particularly since the source will naturally seek affirmation from the listener that his or her story is altogether true.

Therefore thou art inexcusable, O man,
whosoever thou art that judgest:
for wherein thou judgest another, thou condemnest thyself;
for thou that judgest doest the same things.
Romans 2:1

If there is affirmation that someone did act poorly or even badly, most people would think that person must pay a price for his or her misbehavior. In their mind the (common) enemy deserves every bit of indignation that he or she has coming, so even name-calling and labeling others as necessary should not be off limits. The compulsion to openly discredit, disgrace, and even judge those personally found to be guilty according to the facts seemingly helps to redeem and even lift those regarded as innocent.

In these cases, though, is the response of going on the offensive really drawn from truth? Hardly. The Truth of the New Testament does not teach "an eye for an eye,"[90] so even public ridicule and humiliation cannot be justified as good. Many bent on impugning others according to the (so-called) facts may be driven by logic relative to social norms and emotions, but even if everything is known about an alleged enemy, responses like these are still not guided by Truth.

With that said, reflect on those stories which diminish, obscure, or even contradict the truth about a person's character. This would not only skew the listeners' perception of the person the story is about, it also affects their perception of others who played influential roles in the story. In these cases, the listeners are not the only ones guided by the misguided storyteller: they may well go on to misguide others as they repeat the story to them.

Without proper context and proper character development, the source and listener have no choice but to use labels to explain various perceptions about given characters. While such usage certainly allows for the source to get to the point faster and even to make a stronger argument, it also provides much room to slant the story in one's favor, and against another. In these cases, instead of elaborating on the color of truth regarding certain characters, the source will end up elaborating on the black and white of facts. Embellishments like these end up as fiction (exaggerations, fabrications, etc.). When facts are blown out of proportion, the image of character of those placed into the defensive can more easily become tainted and distorted.

With greater distortions, it's much easier for the source and listener to agree on which labels should be pinned on the enemy. Without proper context, though, attempts to use labels to separate the bad from the good are subject to error as a result of misperception. This becomes particularly evident when the bad aspects of the situation are disproportionally emphasized and the good ignored.

---

[90] Matthew 5:38-39

People are innocent until proven guilty, or at least that's what "they" say. It seems, though, that many people try to get at the truth through objectivity, based simply on what was said and done. In these cases, attempts to explain underlying reasons only second-guess the motivations of those the story is about. In other words, instead of trying to understand motivation according to simultaneous truth (vs. falsehoods), many attempt to deepen their understandings about others of interest based on the sequence of (selective) facts (vs. fiction). Realize though that your behavioral response as driven by truths or falsehoods is subjective, circumstantial, and dynamic. You cannot know the subjective nature of another's motivation and behavior simply from an objective point of view.

Without access to God's Truth, many people see the scientific assessment of human responses (such as body language) as a form of truth that makes sense. People oriented to objectivity and knowledgeable about science will use this kind of information as a source of insight into the dynamics of an individual's thought and action. However, if the mind of such observers is not first balanced with true faith in God, their evaluations will consistently be misleading. That's because as one's Western objectiveness is (seemingly) honed, the more the holistic nature of another's subjective behavior is debased. What is consistently dismissed in one's analysis is Intuition – the Eastern subjectivity that underlies many human behaviors.

Without a greater appreciation of the motivations of those of interest before the fact (especially on the part of those who can help guide others onto better paths), one will only become suspicious about their intentions. This is especially the case after distance between one and another has been created. The more humans become scattered, the more proper context and proper character development are absent from their stories. Again, for many the process of distorting the image of another's character equates to increasing their own self-images.

Proper context, not simply the facts, is what makes a story true in the larger sense. Thankfully, the Holy Bible is a form of inspired art that objectivity alone cannot bear out. In order to have a better grasp on the context of Biblical understandings one must have a sincere interest in and desire to know more about the subjective nature of God's Truth. This is what balances the foundation of mind with the intellect—nothing else! With such understandings, each of His children is better able to realize and appreciate the subjective nature of truth in human stories as well.

Sure, it's easy to get carried away by what appears to be real in stories and even in dreams, but there are typically deeper meanings involved; meanings that oftentimes can become opportunities to learn why humans reason and respond as they do. It is the artful presentation of stories (as implicitly, figuratively, and inspirationally delivered) that humans ultimately learn from and are moved by.

It's the same with Biblical teachings. God's Truth serves as the inspirational basis or beginning for the believer's unfolding response. His story is the cause in one's mind for the effect as seen or manifested into reality. Again, it is the objective side of facts as seen in reality that helps clarify and even support the subjective side of (unseen) truths.

And are built upon the foundation of the apostles
and prophets, Jesus Christ himself being
the chief corner [stone];
Ephesians 2:20

Vitality According to Truth

Any properly laid foundation of stone in ancient times began with a "chief corner stone" (or cornerstone for discussion purposes). The cornerstone is the first stone laid; each successive stone placed alongside is aligned with the first. In essence, the cornerstone is the beginning. Since Christ Jesus is the cornerstone of faith for humanity, He exists as the beginning of mind for reasoning (an East to West process). For all those who then respond in faith (a vertical process), there is harmony with God and with others godly.

Before constructing one's temple Northward toward God Almighty, one must first build faith in Jesus Christ. By building faith in the One who best exemplified God's Truth while on earth, we become better prepared to reason from East to West, and according to Truth. The development of faith is a constructive process that we go through prior to and during the vertical response Northward. Throughout the temple building process, believers are provided by

God with the vitality for living today and for tomorrow. In other words, everything that is subjective (including righteousness) is a day-by-day constructive process that requires God's nurturing involvement. So indeed it is important for us to prepare our minds with the knowledge of God. By becoming more knowing and responding to Him in faith we as His Body can ultimately fulfill our Father's glory.

Biblically speaking, it is critical to progressively apprehend the context of God's story before the fact; that is, before our final judgment by God. With a greater appreciation for His story, we will understand the importance of grasping the context of any human story before we succumb to the natural human compulsion to judge.

Those who are not keenly aware of the importance of truth will consistently elaborate facts into fiction and according to falsehoods. An emotional appeal in support of such factual contentions seemingly helps to convince others of one's trust, worthiness, and innocence. So during the process of listening, one may hear statements like: "I do... (this or that)," or "I am... (this or that)." Because of the source's self-professed goodness, as passionate as he may be, the listener will oftentimes be inclined to believe him, and even stand by him. For those who often say "I do" or "I am," ask yourself: "What truly good person has to profess how good he or she is?" None that are spiritually mature, and that's the point.

> *And be not conformed to this world: but be ye transformed by*
> *the renewing of your mind, that ye may prove what [is] that*
> *good, and acceptable, and perfect, will of God.*
> Romans 12:2

Much of the confusion about the usages of *good* and *bad* has to do with a single-minded, blended approach toward reasoning. This is because many humans are unaware that—according to God's Truth—descriptive terms like *good, bad, right, wrong,* etc., have vertical implications.

Reasoning single-mindedly (as West leaning or East leaning, but particularly as upside-down), only leads to closed-mindedness. In these cases the upward vertical opportunities that exist for all to find the "king's [high] way"[91] go unnoticed. Responding with righteousness is the result of dual-mindedness fostered by faith in Jesus. So instead of striving to bring one's horizontal reasoning and response into the vertical (thus, awakening), there is no choice but for the psyche to reject the movement upward in order to become increasingly conformed to this world. Therefore, matters that are subjective in nature (e.g., those regarded as good, bad, right, wrong, etc.) will appear simply to be thoughts and opinions.

Here is an example: When driving on a road looking for a restaurant, a passenger says: "There's a good place to eat at." The question is: What is "good" about anything secular on earth, including a restaurant? Nothing! God is good, all that was created by God is good, and people of God are good. While members of the restaurant staff may be of good character, there are more fitting descriptions of the restaurant itself (hence: a fact or near fact, even if regarded as an opinion). For instance: "The atmosphere is lively and fun"; or "The service is prompt and courteous." In and of themselves, though, there is nothing *good* about anything created by man, unless it is of God (as stated above), or it is the result (or the effect) of an act of faith in God.

Another example deals with humans in competitive environments, such as sports, business, politics, etc. Many of those who work or play in these environments attempt to promote themselves by proclaiming how good they are; however, this can be very misleading. Even if such a person has incredible skills and talent, this does not mean that he or she is inwardly good, nor does it mean that his or her actions are good. All the audience really needs to know are the facts about his skills, talent, and experience. Unless offering a testimony about such a person's good character, why not stick to the facts? This way there is little compulsion to suggest in environments like these that one is good and another is bad.

They profess that they know God; but in works they deny [him], being abominable, and disobedient, and unto every good work reprobate.

Titus 1:16

---

[91] Numbers 20:17

The importance of appropriate word usages (particularly those involving the vertical) also carries over into the relationship-building process. Professing one's goodness is only indicative of a mindset that is driven by works instead of grace, and of willingness to falsify motives in order to project one's image as good. Only those of God are aware of the differences between good and bad. Such people realize and appreciate that goodness of heart is not judged according to works, but according to grace. While goodness may be argued to be self-evident, it is most evident to God's children. With true appreciation for what goodness entails, there is little to no compulsion to put others in the defensive position of having to demonstrate or prove themselves as worthy.

Of course humans will continue to use terms like *good, bad, right, wrong,* etc. to describe secular things. Realize, though, that one's soul is either constructed Northward or destroyed Southward as the result of how intangible things are perceived by the mind, and then used to prompt responses in others. As faith in God is increased, so is one's consciousness of the implied meanings of words, so that words are chosen with care.

Without an Eastern approach toward reasoning, your thinking will consistently be led from the West. In other words, the West of mind is essentially his or her mindful beginning for reasoning and response. So as certain facts (or fiction) about another are realized the mind will not only be led by such facts, but also by skepticism, control, and judgment. Without true faith and the gift of grace, most will be geared to find the faults in others as objectively realized, instead of seeing their goodness as subjectively realized. To be persistently led by the West only leads to an unreasonable approach to learning the truth and to presenting in a way that others will respond to.

While the West is the beginning of mind for many who are objectively inclined, without faith in God the process of reasoning and response will be out of harmony not only with godliness but also with perceived righteousness. This is because one's reasoning was not first guided by the East cornerstone. If and when building wholesome relationships with others does become important, God must be part of the equation.

The West dominant may dispute the notion that they are not as capable of perceiving the depth and breadth of Truth as others. That's because their perception of truth is consistently led linearly from West to East, according to logic, and not holistically from East to West according to love, grace, and mercy. The West dominant believe that these subjective qualities can be gained solely through objectivity. This is simply not the case. The more West-leaning a person is, the more logic plays into the reasoning process, as the person tends to inject his or her thoughts and opinions before truth is allowed time to reveal itself. If a person is unable to listen first, instead of speaking first, then what makes that person think that the truth in any story about a given character can be fully realized? If one's mind cannot reason out acts of goodness according to the subjective of Truth, then it is impossible! Subjective Truth is what first guides proper human responsiveness, not simply facts by way of objectivity.

For many, explaining one's intentions in advance seemingly helps to provide context for a future act (i.e., an undertaking, mission, quest, etc.)—an act that invariably prompts a story, as well as a forecast. Those West-leaning will insist on this sort of information so there can be a better understanding as to why such acts are necessary. Fact-driven information is important to those who are conformity-minded (Northward or Southward), especially when it seems to them that certain others (non-conformists) tend to do things differently.

Unless it is a joint effort with others who are Northward, though, explaining one's intentions to those who have yet to be aligned with the cornerstone does have its implications. Not only can explaining hamper the efforts of the responder to accomplish the greater according to God's will, many times it ends up placing others—many unknowing and impatient—in the middle of one's private response. So instead of just doing God's will—a process that requires time and patience—others are unwittingly placed into positions that can ultimately change the direction of one's response – that is, explaining one's intentions ends up confounding God's will with man's will.

Another problem with explaining one's intentions in advance is that doing so dismisses what a godly response is about. It has less to do with explaining to others what is about to be done (thus becoming measurable facts during the course of responding), and more to do with others evaluating one's true motivations by the fruit produced. If those West-leaning are not balanced by the non-conformity of truth-driven acts, then the context of stories about those under discussion will consistently fall short of propriety and balance.

Without proper context concerning the minds of character(s) that such stories are about, then the audience will only get caught up in responding to the facts. In these cases, even those who think they know right from wrong do so only as the result of facts. The more attention toward depth of facts the more depth of truths is disregarded, as each foolishly thinks he knew then and still knows now everything about the truth.

> *They gather themselves together against the soul of the righteous, and condemn the innocent blood.*
> Psalm 94:21

Some of those outcast and even branded as the enemy may indeed know better, and yet have had no compulsion to tell the truth after the fact, even under duress. Why? Because those who (falsely) assert and accuse them do not have the wherewithal to understand truth. In the mind of such accusers, those being condemned should instead become subject to them.

It takes time and patience, along with trust and mutual respect to gain greater understandings of matters of truth. Truth cannot be realized by condemning and vilifying—this only denies others the opportunity to respond by grace.

Even those who are easily overcome with the drama of emotions and yet think of themselves as faithful and good may be prone to deny others the freedom to respond by grace. While the subjective response of emotions is their mindful beginning, it may not be in unison with God's Truth. Think about it: Without a cornerstone, responders as these do not have proper guidance. Instead, their wants, passions, and desires will be for interests of self and/or for others on behalf of self. If the individual also lacks a sound grasp of reality, then at times he or she may become panic-stricken and unstable. As a result, they will place the blame for their emotional turmoil on others.

Without the time and patience to more fully realize the context of a given story, you will grasp just enough to frame the story out of context. This unavoidably distorts the image of character(s) the story is about, especially those who you have already, and perhaps unknowingly, judged.

Without context, everyone who is responsible for the story will naturally inject his or her opinions about the truth into it. If it is not first balanced with God's Truth, though, then no matter how many (so-called) facts are presented or how articulate or even educated the storyteller is, he or she will invariably spew fiction about certain characters. Interestingly, such fiction does not always track the falsehoods of the character's mind. It may actually track falsehoods of the storyteller's own mind. In these cases the psyche is bent on falsifying the image and character of another so as to enhance one's own image. This is similar to projecting one's weaknesses (fear, hatred, jealousy, revenge, and other wrongful behaviors) onto others so as to make these others appear to the larger group as the source of the problem. Sadly, those who project their own weaknesses in this manner usually believe what they say to be true. This makes the conflict resolution process (if any) that much more difficult to work through.

Listeners who see themselves as innocent of the kinds of offenses attributed to a character in a story can easily get caught up in impugning the (common) enemy. However, what if the story fails to properly develop each character according to truth? What if the purported enemy attempted to do what was right but was hindered as the result of outside pressures or requirements? What if no one cared enough, nor had the time and patience, nor had the aptitude to realize what truth really entails? What if the facts in the story were blown out of proportion or even fabricated in order to create an illusion of wrong-doing by the enemy? In each of these cases it is evident that subjective truth (most particularly God's Truth) remains deficient in those weak-minded and yet confident in their own superiority. Without the truest form of a cornerstone in one's mind there will rarely be any semblance of balance as his or her stories are shared with others, and as judgment is passed.

When a given story is revealed by those falsely driven, then it flawed at best, evil at worst. In these cases the story is not simply fiction—anyone can make up a lie. It is the storyteller's motivation, as evidenced by the lie that makes a story false and the storyteller falsely-driven. Think again about the vertical dynamics between good and bad for a moment, and the disastrous implications for trusting the influential stories of those who gossip become clear; whether the storytellers are passionate and yet misguided, or they offer false testimonies with malicious intent.

> *Many shall be purified, and made white, and tried; but the wicked shall do wickedly: and none of the wicked shall understand; but the wise shall understand.*
> Daniel 12:10

It is Evil—Satan (the adversary), the Great Whore, and their evil accomplices—that is more truly the common enemy. One way Evil compels humans to act out wrongly, immorally, and wickedly is to warp their judgment so that it follows fiction deemed to be fact, thus creating a perception of greater wrong-doing by those targeted, many of whom may be truly good. Even if not led from the West, the compulsion to pass judgment is oftentimes the result of a blended approach toward reasoning, especially if one's purpose is not Northward toward God. In other words, those purposed Southward toward self lack the (Northward) cognition of mind to reason with properness and balance between objectivity and subjectivity.

As those who are unknowing create distance from others perceived to be the enemy, so too do they experience the compulsion to intensify blame. As more become separated from others the more each must rely on his or her own testimony to convince those seemingly close of one's worthiness and even innocence. It's this instead of relying on others who are truly good to testify on one's behalf.

In large part, facts represent the past, while truth represents the future. All those fixated on the past of others are not and will never be driven by truth—that is, unless they come to have true faith in God. To be geared so much to the past only means that the mind is not preparing the soul for the future. That future includes becoming more naturally responsive to the (implicit) subtleties of God's will.

Those who think they know the truth and yet have false motives, and provide false testimonies do not necessarily mean to have such ways. For the most part they are simply unknowing. Because of their unknowing state they do more to influence divisiveness in the world than most of those found guilty on the basis of facts.

Without the balance of mind that only faith in God can provide, these unknowing people will assert their power, authority, and control over others in order to be the one to whom others respond. If those others do indeed respond to these demands and desires, then they will be exploited to serve these self-proclaimed authorities. In so-called "good times" self-serving behavior like this may be undetectable. As personal challenges come up, though, the power-driven conduct inherent to selfishness will undoubtedly surface.

Even so, many unbalanced people will already have convinced themselves that they are good as a result of how they perceive their own behavior relative to that of others. For instance, one may think of him- or herself as being nice or polite, but as will be discussed later, the ability to demonstrate politeness and even social graces does not mean that one is inwardly good.

It is when people lose control that their (not-so-good) hidden nature is revealed. Control (per se) isn't simply about losing one's composure—that could happen for any number of reasons, good or bad. It is when a given situation or circumstance doesn't go the way the person intended (usually the way of self); or when others fail to respond according to his or her will. When a person manifests these sorts of control behaviors, there's no question that he or she has more faith in self than in God.

Also consider how some people justify themselves to others. Much of their perception of self-worth is based on how others respond to their excuses and to their ways. Even if they are caught in a lie, they will claim that the lie is justified. The source can become so skilled at lying that he or she appears innocent even when falsely presenting his or her motives as good. The problem for such individual mindsets is that one does not become good by attempting to prove that others are bad. Justification of this sort is indicative of one's walk in self. This sort of walk cannot exist without control and blame. If it isn't one person to blame and prosecute, then it will be another; if not one group, then another.

Therefore, if there is ever a need to share one's personal story with others, can those without God-consciousness really be trusted with such information? Absolutely not! As well-meaning as they may be, their inability to listen first and be guided by Truth will only lead to further destruction for all involved. One's admissions or confessions will consistently be skewed, taken out of context, and even used for personal gain. If the gain is not financial, then it will be another form of gain. There are those who appear to listen and yet, as the result of having false motives, are naturally bent on being the one to whom others yield, respond, and even submit.

No one can build a heavenly temple on earth based on power, authority, and control—these are oppressive tendencies guided by Evil, not God. As parts of the whole in the Southward sense, each of those who are unknowing will attempt to influence others on behalf of Evil. People who oppress others do not and will never have the framework of mind to align with those who are truly good. If they did, they would recognize that everyone should be granted the opportunity to respond by faith and grace. Instead, they attempt to construct relationships with others based on works, not by grace. Works may seem justifiable at first, particularly in competitive environments. But when it comes to building wholesome social relationships, works are only a hindrance. That's because human relationships of the healthiest kind develop only as the result of all counterparts being under one higher authority.

Any relationship becomes strained when one party attempts to gain a superior edge over the other. Without the appreciation to be measured first according to faith and the gift of grace, then many will become subject to those who measure the before and after of works and performance. Those who do fall subject to such results-oriented schemes will consistently be bound by man according to Evil, instead of becoming liberated by God.

Evil exists on earth and within humans who have yet to repent and have true faith in God. While it's certainly the case that many people have made mistakes or have sinned, it is much worse to influence others to turn out of the way or commit wrong instead of right, and most particularly, to press down upon others so that they end up being held captive by their own sins. In either case, only those who already have the Spirit of God within will be able to overcome the power and influence of such Evil.

> *Judge not, and ye shall not be judged: condemn not, and ye shall not be condemned: forgive, and ye shall be forgiven:*
> Luke 6:37

At times commands, and even demands, are indeed necessary as wake-up calls for others, especially children, to respond in faith. Suggesting that certain behaviors are wrong is not judging per se, as most of those who are unknowing would think. Ultimate judgment comes from God, not from man. The intent of true believers of God is not to judge, nor to condemn others (to hell, for instance). There is a form of condemnation[92] that most of those who are faithless are unaware of. This form of condemnation comes from knowing persons who earnestly and yet prudently point out the wrongs in others' behavior in order to instill a new cause in their minds. That cause begins with the importance and value of God's love for us and our love for God. This is a higher cause, and it's only through this cause that those who are condemned can overcome their fallen state.

When believers assert that certain behaviors of others are wrong and yet themselves find it difficult to express the subjective qualities of God, those without God-consciousness will only perceive their claims as offensive. While this can be problematic for any relationship, the real concern is that Evil is the primary cause for nonbelievers to reject the love of God. Those of God know the way and want to share it, but it is especially difficult when so many people's minds are closed to the thoughts and opinions of even those who are truly good.

> *But speaking the truth in love, may grow up into him in all things, which is the head, [even] Christ:*
> Ephesians 4:15

---

[92] Isaiah 54:17

One cannot become a child of God if the mind/psyche rejects the righteousness of God, and is instead driven to do wrong. If not for those believers who stand up for what is right, nonbelievers would never be able to perceive the vertical contrast between right and wrong. So, indeed, there will be times when it does become necessary to point out the wrongs in others' behaviors that may influence others. The purpose of efforts like these is not to publicly humiliate individual wrong-doers, but rather to personally help them not to continue to hurt themselves and those they influence. This approach is the best way to convey love. It's impossible to convey love through open belittling or scorn, or the casting of stones.

When (according to one's conscience) criticism becomes a necessary duty, remember that such efforts can only be constructive in the Northward sense when used in tandem with the subjective qualities of God's Truth (love, grace, mercy, etc.). Only those who are Northward and balanced in their approach toward reasoning and response can truly help those in need of realizing the love of God. The point is that believers of God nurture each other as well as others in order to become Disciples of Christ.

Even so ye also outwardly appear righteous unto men,
but within ye are full of hypocrisy and iniquity.
Matthew 23:28

West-leaning people who claim to be faithful and righteous, and yet are unable to appreciate the significance of the subjective aspect of God's Truth will consistently be found to be self-righteous and hypocritical. An East-leaning person who seems to the objectively-minded to be lackluster in responsiveness is not necessarily falsely driven. If the person is East-leaning and yet God-loving, what he or she needs isn't greater faith in the subjective (although such faith will continue to evolve), but more of an objective grounding.

There is no doubt that there should be a greater level of conformity in Christendom, but according to whose standards -- those driven by objectivity, or those driven by subjectivity? Neither one nor the other, of course: Balance necessitates both as yoked, individually and collectively. Since Jesus is the cornerstone of faith, it is vital for believers to fill their minds with Biblical Truth. Increasing in Truth is what balances the foundation of mind. This is particularly important because in order for one's faith-driven response to be constructive, the human mind needs to balance Logic with the Intuitive.

As the result of seeking greater subjective depths of Truth, the reasoning process can be led from the East cornerstone. With this approach, believers are better able to frame thoughts, questions, and concerns from an Eastern (holistic) perspective. Once a believer is able to reason from East to West, judging becomes the last response, not the first, and mercy toward others is shown first (in response), not last.

All in all, what does this suggest? While rules, laws, and sanctions may prompt conformity, they do more to diminish non-conforming manifestations of faith and grace. In essence, manifestations of all that is good, including righteousness, are progressively weakened for citizens when earthly powers are guided by self-interest rather than interests of God. Therefore, during the course of building human-human and human-divine relationships, the optimal approach for reasoning (and response) is not from West to East according to (linear) law; it is reasoning from East to West according to (holistic) faith that ultimately fulfills The Law.

vii. The Response to Faith

The souls of believers can only be lifted and remain lifted by the love of and the love for God—*the* higher authority. This is why Jesus emphasized love for God as His "first and great commandment."[93] The inward goodness of children first comes about through faith in those who lovingly guide, such as good parents, mentors, and friends. However, unless the growing (spiritual) child advances from faith in good people to faith in God, then life's challenges will limit and ultimately exhaust his or her inward goodness.

If believers attempt to do good on earth without being first-purposed in God, they are effectually making Jesus' second commandment His first. This isn't really the right approach, but it's

---

[93] Matthew 22:37-38

important to recognize that such believers may be in the process of growing in faith. A person who does not truly aspire to know God so that He becomes the first purpose, will find that his or her attempt to adhere to even His second commandment will fall short.

> *But he that doeth truth cometh to the light, that his deeds may be made manifest, that they are wrought in God.*
> John 3:21

There's no question that doing good deeds feels good and will even improve your disposition, especially in the short-term. Without a higher purpose of mind and heart, though, such deeds will consistently miss the mark in achieving the ultimate goal: to have a personal relationship with our Divine Creator.

If God's Truth is progressively sown into the mind, then each of those who believe will be more apt to be one who "doeth truth" the right way. In this way "(good) deeds are made *manifest*"[94] on earth, as God is increasingly magnified. He is *the* source of love and all things good on earth. If you have faith in Him, your mind/psyche will accept Him as King. Again, it is not by one's own mindful conviction that goodness is accomplished on earth. Goodness is a manifestation of grace and the result of faith in God through Jesus Christ.

As discussed earlier, Jesus taught believers to pursue God with all of their hearts, souls, and minds—an exercise[95] in discernment, consciousness, and godliness—rather than first emphasizing practice as intellectually prescribed. This daily exercise (heart-inspired devotion that further develops the conscience) leads one to become spiritually mature and even intuitively prayerful from the heart, and not simply prayerful with the mind.

Keep in mind that the relationship between practice and exercise will vary from individual to individual, and from group to group—much of the time, again, depending on where God's Truth is drawn from, and where one's reasoning process is led from. For instance, the word *practise* (note the spelling variation) in the KJV is

---

[94] Ibid.
[95] Acts 24:16, Hebrews 5:14, 12:11, 1 Timothy 4:7-8

not used in the good sense (discussed below), while other Biblical translations do in-fact use the term in the (supposed) good sense, some more than others. Also consider that today's notions of what it means to practice (i.e., practice an instrument, a sport, etc.) has to do with becoming more accomplished in a given routine in the outward sense, much of the time in conjunction with exercise in the inward sense.

Faithfulness can be regarded as increasing with God's Truth inwardly so that the response to faith—as a manifestation of the inward spirit—produces fruit outwardly. While the notion of practice may make sense for many people, particularly for those who are objectively-minded and for those first coming to faith, the obvious goal is to become more God-centered and naturally responsive to Him with the heart. Again, this process will involve (inward) exercise as God is first-purposed.

The transformation from mind-induced to heart-induced responsiveness appears to correlate with how Jesus' two commandments are approached. Most converts will typically begin their faith-journey by attempting to adhere to His second commandment in practice. As the believer grows in faith and becomes more attuned to godliness, he or she will become more heart-responsive by exercise. Why is this important? It's because when one's heart does become intuitively responsive to His grace, the knowing mind will become more receptive toward executing its dominion over body (hence, mind over body).

Over time God becomes magnified in the minds and hearts of those who believe, making it more natural for them to adhere to Jesus' first commandment. As the result of loving Him first and foremost, we can also fulfill His second commandment earnestly and modestly.

Because there are so many forms of religious practice, worship styles, and spiritual discipline, believers must weigh in the balance of their own minds how such ways will help them to increase inwardly. The point here is that there are both good and bad forms of practice and of exercise. While both approaches can be regarded as good, they differ from each other in application.

> *LORD, thou hast heard the desire of the humble: thou wilt*
> *prepare their heart, thou wilt cause thine ear to hear:*
> *To judge the fatherless and the oppressed, that the man of the*
> *earth may no more oppress.*
> Psalm 10:17-18

Before continuing this discussion, though, let's pull back from the term *practice* as used in the good sense. Instead, let's think of this approach more in line with preparing the mind[96] in order to allow God to prepare the heart. In this way believers can become better at doing "(that which is) right."[97] There are two reasons for emphasizing preparing and doing over practice. First, this emphasis reestablishes the KJV as the source of Truth in our discussion; and second, inward goodness (if one has it at all) is only of God and revealed only in natural manifestations of faith and grace. In other words, true manifestations of inward qualities cannot be directly approached (as if by practice). Manifestations of God can only be revealed by one's natural response to faith, as increasingly evidenced by exercise.

When used in the good sense, the term *doing* is broader than *practice* and connotes a more immediate response to opportunity. With faith-based purpose in God there are no limits on what can be accomplished by doing what is right.

Preparing the mind with the knowledge of God increases one's faith and God-conscious state. This sets the stage for how the body—as increasingly influenced by the (prepared) mind and heart of the "inward (man)"[98]—will respond in exercise. "Doing truth"—initially a thought process between West and East of mind—is not only the result of one's preparedness and even readiness, it is an indication of mind over body as evidenced by proper action responses (righteousness). When the mind reigns over the body, the fruit of the spirit can naturally be produced. Progressively becoming better at doing right therefore conditions the mind and coordinates the body not only to respond to the will of mind, but even more significantly,

---

[96] Ephesians 6:14-16
[97] 1 Kings 11:33
[98] 2 Corinthians 4:16

to respond (by the heart) to the will of God. Recall that it is with the heart purposed in God that one more truly cleaves unto the Lord.

Without appealing to God first—whereby He becomes the reason why believers actually do good on earth—man will have no choice but to practice the acts of goodness without a sound reason for why. In other words, they will forego the manifestation process altogether and directly approach acts of goodness as the cause in order to (falsely) justify themselves in the eyes of others and to God.

viii. "I Am" Not

This brings up a quick point about manners, most specifically, etiquette. Generally speaking, students of etiquette are (objectively) taught how to appear (subjectively) good. Lessons learned will involve smiling, poise, charm, cordiality, well-mannered/polite behaviors, etc. The ability to demonstrate propriety and social graces is certainly appealing as such ways can even work in tandem with and be the result of inward goodness. While it can be argued that etiquette is important for a host of reasons, without a sound basis for why one should practice it (e.g., faith in God), teachings like these are practices (in the negative sense) geared only to increase the image of self for both teacher and student.

So if etiquette isn't always a sure sign of one's goodness, then this leaves many with no choice but to be the advocates of their own self-worth. A couple of phrases often used to persuade others of one's qualities include: "I am good" or "I am great" or any other "I am" that seemingly helps to convince others of one's worthiness or even innocence. When this doesn't work, the next line is usually: "Believe me!"

For children statements like these seem to be natural as a way to prove self-worth to just about anyone in doubt. As mentioned before, the testimonies of self also come at a price. For instance, the child may say, "I am good—he is bad," and then attempt to explain just how bad the other child is. Most parents will recognize that the child may be attempting to divert attention from himself, perhaps due to some form of guilt or shame. But out of curiosity, the parent will play along to find out just how far he will go in his attempt to assassinate the character of another. Unless they ultimately grow in honor and respect for the higher authority, and in mutual respect for others, we can expect children like these to be among the false accusers—future adults who aspire to be "believed in" while seeking greater authority and control.

> *And Moses said unto God, Behold, [when] I come unto the children of Israel, and shall say unto them, The God of your fathers hath sent me unto you; and they shall say to me, What [is] his name? what shall I say unto them? And God said unto Moses, I AM THAT I AM: and he said, Thus shalt thou say unto the children of Israel, I AM hath sent me unto you.*
> Exodus 3:13-14

It is one thing to be the best at what you can be, it's quite another to let it go to your head. The major problem with trumpeting "I am" this or that, and being full of selfish pride is that there is only one "I AM" and that is God—*this is His Name!* In other words, "I am" *nothing* until I have put on godly qualities from the great "I AM." And even when the gift of the Spirit has been inwardly received, to suggest "I am holy" or "I am perfect" will seem boastful—it certainly doesn't demonstrate humility.

While there are times that "I am" can express sorrow and regret, it is often used to influence the thoughts and behavior of others in order to advance the image of self. Many times such high notions of self are delivered with (so-called) good intentions, but actual achievement of goodness is rare. When people deem themselves to have achieved goodness, they usually become boastful, or else seek to blame others. While many people are responsive to the "I am" of others, not so with true Christians. That's because when we seek to glorify ourselves, it is evident that we do not know God.

We have all been asked: "What is it that you believe in?" or "What will you stand up for and fight for?" Whatever you believe in will also be what you stand for. No doubt about it, virtually all believers will say that they will stand up for God, but are they really as committed as this? That is, will they stand up for what's right, no matter the cost? Many will find it difficult to give up control to an intangible power, called "I AM." Instead, they may be more apt to place their faith and allegiance in tangible others who will stand on their behalf in return.

With so much discussion of who the new enemies of the day are, it really is no wonder that many find it difficult to stand up for anything that's right and to make themselves known for what they believe in. Keep in mind, though, it is one thing to stand up for what's right, and it's quite another to exalt oneself by sacrificing or destroying another. Tragically, many efforts to demonize and destroy others are unwarranted—tactics used to justify oneself as being good (as others are bad) and/or to simply save face.

If sinners are not justified by works and deeds, how can they become truly worthy to stand in the presence of God? The only answer is Jesus, the Christ! He alone atoned for the sins of humanity so that all might have the opportunity to be justified by faith in Him.

> *But the God of all grace, who hath called us unto his eternal*
> *glory by Christ Jesus, after that ye have suffered a while,*
> *make you perfect, stablish, strengthen, settle [you].*
> 1 Peter 5:10

The overarching goal for Christians is to become more Christ-like in thought and action. Indeed it can be an arduous task, and can even cause suffering, particularly in this upside-down world. However, if you are one of those who (as a Christian) also believes that it is impossible to walk in righteousness and in holiness, then let's revisit the question: "What is it that you *truly* believe in?" This is where many are perplexed. That's typically because they consider the relationship-building process with God as an ongoing struggle that is rarely fulfilling. The thoughts of those with this sort of mindset may parallel a view like this: "Why should I work so hard at becoming more like a saint when I know God will forgive my sins anyway? I am good, I am loving, and I am caring—that's all that matters!"

There are a number of problems with such beliefs. First of all, a work is not considered meaningless if the effort is (by desire) the result of increasing consciousness that Jesus Christ is indeed Savior and King. In other words, His people are saved because He has become the cause (of mind) for them to respond by in ways of grace.[99] Second, God is indeed forgiving but if He does not "know you"[100]—because of a reluctance to turn and know Him—then who or what name should be forgiven? Third, there is only one "I AM," so to have the propensity to offer testimonies about one's self is futile. One cannot be his or her own character witness when it comes to godly matters. Others who are godly, including the Spirit of God witness and testify on the believer's behalf.[101] These are only a few reasons why Christianity, as a faith to believe in and stand up for, is impeccably strong.

ix. To Be of God

Think about the discussions that have led up to this point regarding thought and action. Recall that we perceive reality with the West of mind and ideals and beliefs with the East of mind. Doing what's right is a characteristic and response drawn from the West of mind, but such notions are only as sound as the truths sown into the East. Is it not interesting how the integrity of one's walk is critically dependent on what truths exist in the East? Sure it is!

What we have yet to discuss, though, is one word that embodies the characteristic and response drawn from the East of mind and into the West; and then from thought to action. In order to have a better grasp of what this one word is let's begin with a simple question: "Who are you?" Most will answer this question by providing their own names, and then offering tidbits of information about family and ancestry. Others may provide details about their work experience and education, while still others may list all the (good) deeds they have accomplished. But do all of these things really explain who a person is now in the present? No! There is much more to know about a person besides that which can be objectively detailed.

"I am" is the first-person present form of the verb "to be." To accept God as the Head over one's person—the God whose name is

---

[99] Romans 11:5-6
[100] Luke 13:27
[101] John 5:31-32, Job 16:19, Romans 8:16

"I AM"—in part means to: repent and humbly submit to the King; let go of the sins of the past which weigh heavy on the soul; revere Him with glory, honor, and praise; and live confidently in the present and for the future.

> *And, behold, [there was] a man named Joseph, a counsellor;*
> *[and he was] a good man, and a just:*
> Luke 23:50

During the conversion process toward God the psyche/soul is progressively transformed from the being of self to the being of God. A person's inner *being*—the one word we were looking for—is both the source and the result of what has been revealed outwardly in actions.

Based on previous discussions we can surmise that there are two forms of mindful being—the linear (West) and the holistic (East). The linear form of being is cultivated by the body doing good. However, the manifestation of true goodness on earth can only be the result of (and in balance with) the holistic form of being cultivated by faith.[102] When the two forms of mindful being are yoked Northward, and as the body responds to the will of mind and even more to the will of God, then one's temple can be raised toward heaven.

We know people not simply by their (outward) doings, both past and present, but by their (inward) beings, both present and future. So to have a better sense of the whole of a person's individuality and character we must better understand the subjective nature of that person's being. Key indicators about what has been sown into a person's holistic being and then cultivated by doing will be revealed by his or her attitudes and behaviors. What is manifested on earth is evidence of one's faith in God, or one's faith in self.

For many, knowing more about the doings of another person is like having a more complete picture of his or her being. Entire industries—particularly those that are media and internet driven—have been created for the purpose of efficiently tapping into and sharing people's personal histories. Society is now accustomed to

---

[102] Mark 10:52

instant access to personal information, so much so that decisions are increasingly based on this information.

However, is society fooling itself to think that doings are the best way to know the being of another? Indeed it is! Approaches like these undermine the normal maturation process. This process is not simply a physical one that can be seen, but even more importantly, a spiritual one that cannot be seen. A person's being is subjective, circumstantial, and dynamic. A person's past doings may certainly be indicative of his or her current being, but consider that, irrespective of that past, the person may have had a change of heart about what his or her greater purpose in life is, a change that, at present, may not be outwardly apparent.

> *For they being ignorant of God's righteousness, and going about to establish their own righteousness, have not submitted themselves unto the righteousness of God.*
> Romans 10:3

A person who has the propensity to say I am... (this or that) will have a disposition of mind naturally bent on seeking greater authority and control over others and over circumstances. Could this be one reason why the internet has exploded in popularity? It most certainly can. Those who are not God-seekers are instead self-seekers. They seek to become a significant "I am" among the larger group in order to receive glory, honor, and praise.

Some self-seekers are easy to recognize because they simply exude evil. They openly seek greater power in order to exercise their authority. Then there are self-seekers who appear to be good, loving, and caring, and yet their being is not of God. So there are self-seekers who exercise power by holding others captive by demand, and then there are those who exercise it by holding others captive by desire. In either case a self-seeker strives to become an idol to be believed in while pressing upon others their own form of righteousness.

No question about it, as a communications tool, computers and the internet serve as a highly effective means to empower individuals to be the head over the virtual body of millions. If this isn't bad enough, consider the impact this has on the psyches of our youth today. It is one thing to spoil a child (which certainly has consequences of its own), it's quite another to tempt that self-seeking individual with the technological means to not only destroy his or her own reputation and character, but those of others as well, and to do so without much (earthly) repercussion.

If not recognized for what they are capable of doing, media (in general) can increasingly become a conduit for Evil. As a result, foolishness and disgrace will become even more prevalent on earth. During such exhibitions it becomes clear that the actor has yet to properly consider the consequence(s) of this kind of conduct, thus indicating a lack of conscious awareness.

Consider how spoiled children (irrespective of age) respond to what they think is right. These include (perhaps by no fault of their own) the coddled, and yet no matter how they justify their behavior, nor how much they play the victim card, these also include those who have a deep sense of privilege and entitlement. The more spoiled the child is, the more he or she seeks to influence the behavior of others to serve self.

Some of this discussion has, of course, dealt with the efforts of those who are falsely-driven to recruit others to serve self, but what about those who turn for the better? Think about recent converts who realize the importance of serving others on behalf of God, rather than for reasons of self. They may have done wrong in the past, but in these instances, do people of faith accept them as the beings of Christ that they are now; or will they have a greater compulsion to judge them even now for what they did then? True believers of God are repentant, caring most about remaining reconciled with Him and with others. Just as they have been forgiven in order to heal, they seek to forgive, not simply with words, but even more importantly (as fruits of the inward spirit) with true acts of mercy.

God transforms the minds and hearts of believers from the inside out through faith and grace, not from the outside in through works. If one is not motivated by the desire to appeal to the higher authority then one's efforts to do well on earth are simply works, no matter if such efforts are deemed by man to be good. Again, this is because efforts like these were not first conceived by faith and unearned grace. Humans, therefore, cannot do good nor be good without currently being good or becoming good as the result of faith and the gift of grace.

x. The Art of Goodness

That they do good, that they be rich in good works,
ready to distribute, willing to communicate;
1 Timothy 6:18

For our rejoicing is this, the testimony of our conscience, that
in simplicity and godly sincerity, not with fleshly wisdom,
but by the grace of God, we have had our conversation in the
world, and more abundantly to you-ward.
2 Corinthians 1:12

Perhaps one reason why many today are prone to scrutinize the doings of others is that much (so-called) faith has been placed in technologies and other innovations of man and what flows from them. It is easy to think of these things as tools for making life easier, but at what point does society go too far in its reliance on them? Let's see if a balance for this exists.

Before modern communications technologies came into existence, the primary ways people grew to know one another were face-to-face and through letters. Most people today recognize that there is no better way to get to know a person than to spend some quality time with that individual. As trust and mutual respect for each other are gained, so are the opportunities to become good friends, and perhaps more. As each unique relationship strengthens, disputes (if any) become much easier to resolve, both quickly and privately.

Being together is the optimal way to know the doings and being of another. This allows time to become better acquainted with the simultaneous of another's (whole) being rather than simply the sequence of their doings (e.g., doings via technologies such as email, texting, etc.). Countless books have been written about the art of communication, so it deserves much attention. However, it is mentioned here only to make the point that society seems to be consumed with replacing the art of communication with the science of communication.

There is no doubt that technologies have their place today, but the social ramifications are huge when people start to think that we are "connected" now more than ever before. It is certainly true that technologies are highly effective at keeping people in contact with one another, but they also have negative effects in that they deemphasize the need for togetherness and the human touch.

Knowing the being of another takes time and patience, and above all, his or her presence. In an age of instant messaging and instant gratification, though, people can be hard-pressed to find those who have the time to truly be a friend; that is, a true friend who can ultimately become a good witness to one's true character. It does seem that we have grown further apart, not only in proximity, but as a collective conscience. Ironically, the result of creating more distance has been to become even more engaged with emerging technologies to help bridge the ever-increasing gap.

The point is that each individual must assess how best to learn about the doings and being of others. While technologies do help with certain aspects of human connectivity, it is only through physical togetherness that the whole of another's character can be appreciated. Thus, the best way to bridge the ever-increasing gap between humans is not just through the science of communication, it is with greater emphasis on the art of all things good, including communication.

> *How God anointed Jesus of Nazareth with the Holy Ghost*
> *and with power: who went about doing good,*
> *and healing all that were oppressed of the devil;*
> *for God was with him.*
>
> Acts 10:38

Interestingly, the difference in approaches between the science-driven and the art-driven can also be seen in how humans typically seek treatment for a given ailment. For example, most people will seek the advice of a qualified medical professional when they have troublesome symptoms. In turn the doctor will diagnose the problem and make recommendations as necessary. As well-meaning and educated as most in the medical field are, though, their (objectively-driven) prognosis will be geared to treat only the manifested physical effect of one's condition and not the underlying cause.

As a result, the (inward) root of the problem, to the extent that it resides in false cause, will continue to fester within. Systemically, this cause can work itself into other mental and physical health disorders. With the understanding that bad things (i.e., the unpreventable) even happen to 'good' people, and that age and genetics can also be factors, many if not most health conditions are principally the result of a physiological lower cause. What is meant by lower cause? If the person has not sought after God as the higher cause of mind for healing and restoration, then he or she will only be driven by the lower cause of mind for such healing. While it makes sense that those with pressing health concerns should seek medical attention, in the balance, it is also important to involve God.

Understand that while there are certainly those doctors who take the time to treat more than a condition, it should come as no surprise that many in the medical profession are not motivated by way of or in accordance with the art of faith and grace. If they were, there would be greater appreciation by the science community for an East to West approach to reasoning and response: hence, a holistic approach to healing one's overall physiological condition from the inside out. As the result of holistic faith development the believer is poised for healing and restoration according to and by the grace of God: the Great Healer.

xi. Summary

And he said unto him, Arise, go thy way:
thy faith hath made thee whole.
Jesus, Luke 17:19

Being filled with the fruits of righteousness, which are by
Jesus Christ, unto the glory and praise of God.
Philippians 1:11

Most realize that every good cause compels a good story. As a form of linguistic art, it is the subjective nature of Truth nestled within Biblical stories that is the cause (or basis) for reasoning and responding with greater purpose. Again, truth in the subjective sense (the holistic, implicit) is what ultimately makes the objective of truth a fact (the linear, explicit).

If not for God's Story and placing Him first and foremost, the psyche/soul will only fail to be lifted. Until there is a vertical change in one's significant purpose in life, then his or her suffering will be an ongoing battle. This is why the story of Jesus is vital for eternal salvation. His story trumps all others in the holistic ways of faith and grace. He was then and is now the epitome of the Word becoming flesh. To restate: Those with faith-based purpose in God not only believe differently from those without faith, they also reason and respond differently.

By the grace of God Almighty those who truly believe in Him can arise into God-inspired consciousness. By God's Spirit each is made wise, righteous, sanctified, and redeemed.[103] From such gifts believers are humbled to realize that it is only because of Him that "I am" any good at all. As a result of such gifts one gains a fervent yet modest appreciation that: I am good because of God, I am loving because of God, and I am caring because of God. His Being is the cause for who I am today and what I am able to share with others on His behalf (the effect).[104]

Over time the conviction of mind and heart becomes intuitively responsive to and on behalf of God. As fruits of the inward spirit graced by God, "good works" are evidenced of a person who: "doeth righteousness", "doeth truth", and "doeth good."[105] Thus, children of God first come to be, so that as the result of their inner being, they then come to do, in His name and for His glory.

As the prominence of God grows in the believer's mind so does the heart-felt desire for and appreciation of becoming more beholding of God's majesty, and more beautiful in His sight. As more decide that God is indeed the greater "I AM," then it can be said that the Law of God has the greatest opportunity to be fulfilled, both realistically and naturally.

So what is the best way for believers to become lovingly obedient to our heavenly Father? Emphasize togetherness and continue to teach from the Holy Bible—an inspired work of art—about why it is good to be becoming to our Lord and Savior. As a result, truths about God and truths about love, grace, and holiness become evident on earth, even to nonbelievers. These qualities are

---

[103] 1 Corinthians 1:30-31

[104] Reflect on the *'be'* in *beatitudes* of Jesus' teachings found in Matthew 5:3-12 and Luke 6:20-22.

[105] 1 John 2:29, John 3:21, and 3 John 1;11, respectively

central to the (intuitive) learning process, and are the gifts of God to be inwardly received for all who, in response to faith, believe on His name.

> *And he called [unto him] the twelve,*
> *and began to send them forth by two and two;*
> *and gave them power over unclean spirits;*
> Mark 6:7

> *For we [being] many are one bread, [and] one body:*
> *for we are all partakers of that one bread.*
> 1 Corinthians 10:17

One day more believers of God will see that it is by using two perspectives (Western and Eastern) that a unified, integrated Christian understanding can be realized. Even while each group/denomination may maintain its unique characteristics, WE as His Body and His Church will become increasingly and lovingly yoked into one accord by the commonality of faith.

Just like a marriage between man and woman, or any other two people side by side committed toward God first, it is the difference that attracts and unites. If each continues to resist what the other stands for, then the strength of both will be jeopardized. The key is for each side to recognize and appreciate that their differences are minor relative to their greater strength when they come together. In other words, their combined strength—or synergy—will be greater than the sum of what the two could do alone, and that's because the Holy Spirit is more effective when two are of one accord. When the Church does achieve greater unity, then the pillar of Christianity will become even more strong and vertical, thus, balancing the foundation of mind, individually and collectively.

g. Summary

God does not want His children to live with guilt and shame. Such weights arise from one's own devices as the exalted id continues to trick the mind into decisions of foolishness and disgrace. It is Satan and his cohorts (including the Great Whore) who further tempt the id-driven mind and body, and it is man's (unforgiving) system that empowers those Southward to use information as a weapon to persecute those attempting to rise from the pit.

> *Then the people rejoiced, for that they offered willingly, because with perfect heart they offered willingly to the LORD: and David the king also rejoiced with great joy.*
> 1 Chronicles 29:9

Humans must resist Evil, but in order to overcome its strong influence, each must first repent and humbly increase in faith toward God. Individually and collectively, as the foundation of the mind becomes yoked into one Northward accord, and as the Lord reciprocates His Grace within, then will the Temple of God become progressively raised.

2. Functional Alignments Table

> *For this [is] the covenant that I will make with the house of*
> *Israel after those days, saith the Lord; I will put my laws into*
> *their mind, and write them in their hearts: and I will be to*
> *them a God, and they shall be to me a people:*
> *And they shall not teach every man his neighbour, and every*
> *man his brother, saying, Know the Lord:*
> *for all shall know me, from the least to the greatest.*
> Hebrews 8:10-11

The Functional Alignments Table (see below) integrates all of the previous discussions while demonstrating that Democracy (e.g., a democratic republic) is superior to Fascism, and that the State and the Church should exist as two separate functions. In this way, the citizens who form the Valley may more easily aspire toward God. As the passage above suggests, the Law of God (through Moses) is written into the hearts of believers because of their faith in Jesus. Thus, there's little reason why the Church (of any religion) should attempt to directly affect law.

Recall the discussion in the *Great Commandment* section whereby the law and the prophets hang on love for God first, others second.[106] Jesus is not simply making a clear distinction between law and prophets in the minds of believers. He is also suggesting that there are functional distinctions between the State (law) and the Church (prophets), so that the Valley below (collectively instilled with love) may be allowed to freely prosper while coexisting between these two great pillars. Thus, when all three major groups are in Northward alignment toward God, then there will be peace and harmony.

This table is discussed and illustrated only from the perspective of Northward aspirations. The hope is to identify the best functional condition for the light and love of God to shine upon the Valley.

---

[106] Matthew 22:37-40

Table 4

SOLIDUS
Functional Alignments Table ©

GOD THE TRINITY
KING OVER KINGS
✡
Then shall the righteous shine forth as the sun in the kingdom of their Father. Who hath ears to hear, let him hear.
Matthew 13:43

THE STATE		*Every valley shall be exalted, and every mountain and hill shall be made low: and the crooked shall be made straight, and the rough places plain:* Isaiah 40:4	THE CHURCH	
Judicial	Legislative		Western Church	Eastern Church
Justice		**THE VALLEY OR PLAIN**		*Mercy*
		CAPITALISM	SOCIALISM	
		Civics, Economics, Science, Sociology, etc.	*Culture, Art, Music, Humanities, etc.*	
	LOGIC (Civic-Economic Tendencies)		INTUITION (Socio-Cultural Tendencies)	
Knowledge				

It was important to incorporate the *devotional elements* of the triquetra (Knowledge, Justice, and Mercy) into this table since these action elements are necessary for any house to become stable and strong. So imagine circle-elements that expand beyond this house and you will see that this table reflects the Northward HUHD

Model. Now we can more easily discuss the roles of Institutions and that of the Valley on a grander scale between thought and action.

The bottom of the table identifies the (left-right) spectrum of the collective mind: those more West-dominant (Logic) toward the left and those more East-dominant (Intuition) toward the right. As previously discussed, it is from the (holistic) Eastern mind that mankind best understands the subjective aspect of truths, while then interpreting such truths from the objective side using the (linear) Western mind. The strength of the foundation relies largely on the consensus that forms Knowledge. Those more West-leaning will tend to have more Civic-Economic aspirations whereas those more East-leaning will tend to have more Socio-Cultural aspirations. Then there will be those who are balanced between the two tendencies.

Notice that the State is positioned on the West side of the table and the Church is positioned on the East side. In a sense these two institutions form pillars that those in the Valley can use as supports to guide the righteous along the way. The State is best suited for Judicial matters and the Church is best suited for Merciful matters. While these pillars serve specific West and East functions, those in the Valley region are capable of exhibiting both Just and Merciful ways.

The Functional Alignments Table illustrates the State (Judicial and Legislative) as a Northward pillar, but depending on its leaders' purpose, such an upward expression may be questionable, particularly when one also considers State differences among all nations. To reiterate a previous point, dual-control and yoke are not the same. Dual-control is a conformity-driven measure that is designed to prevent one side or the other from falling (i.e., the reason for separation of powers between branches of government), but this has nothing to do with arising. In contrast, to be yoked with another encourages the rise or forward motion for two of one accord and against a certain resistance.

> *Jesus saith unto them, Did ye never read in the scriptures,*
> *The stone which the builders rejected,*
> *the same is become the head of the corner:*
> *this is the Lord's doing , and it is marvellous in our eyes?*
>
> Matthew 21:42

As we noted in the section *The Church*, the Western and Eastern Churches will become further yoked into one accord, thus forming the united Christian Church, an Eastern pillar on the side of Intuition. As to the State, most would agree that one man should not be empowered to lead all nations. While every denomination of the Church has the prerogative to be led by one leader or a group of leaders, the same argument may be similarly applied to the future Church. In essence, unless it is Jesus after His Second Coming, most would likely object to having one person lead the collective of all Christian groups. Why would this be a reasonable response? Is it not because until He comes again in physical form, Christ Jesus (in the spirit) will continue to be the East cornerstone of faith for the growing collective? Is it not because the collective element of Purpose for the Valley and for the visible Church should remain intangible as more believers become instilled with the strength of His loving Spirit? If the Valley becomes purposed into the leadership of one visible Church instead of God, would this not frustrate the direct union between the Godhead and His Body—that is, the invisible church, the collective of Northward temples found in the Valley? Think about how Jesus worshipped His Father—in a direct unmediated relationship.

> *Ye shall observe to do therefore as the LORD your God hath commanded you: ye shall not turn aside to the right hand or to the left. Ye shall walk in all the ways which the LORD your God hath commanded you, that ye may live, and [that it may be] well with you, and [that] ye may prolong [your] days in the land which ye shall possess.*
> Deuteronomy 5:32-33

Based on a previous discussion, turning to the left or the right connotes either:

- Being first-purposed in tangible earthly matters, instead of the intangible divinity of God (above);
- Rejecting the strengths and qualities that others Northward offer; and/or
- Being engaged in conflict with others, even to the point of extreme behavior.

Consider how people tend to respond when captivating leaders rise into prominent positions of State, Church, or any other group that may find itself in an intermediary position. They often let the leader mediate the relationship between the individual and the higher power. Though there is nothing wrong with following sound leaders, the problem arises when followers become purposed in such leaders (hence, turning toward them). In these cases, instead of building faith in intangible God one would find it easier to build faith in tangible man and/or in the institutions created by man. Unless we learn how to arise with our own sense of conviction and accomplishment (the result of being first-purposed in God), then how will we ever learn how to move according to His will? It simply cannot be done.

> *Now he that planteth and he that watereth are one: and every man shall receive his own reward according to his own labour. For we are labourers together with God: ye are God's husbandry, [ye are] God's building.*
> 1 Corinthians 3:8-9

Notice that The Valley identifies two categories that may also become yoked into one accord (by individual choice) – Capitalism and Socialism. There are obviously many different Western and Eastern classifications that may become yoked, but these two were identified since they are driven by ideology. Below the terms Capitalism and Socialism are interests of those N-West and N-East that are better represented within the Valley section as opposed to the State or the Church. (For the rationale of using the terms Capitalism and Socialism in the Northward sense, refer back to the section *Those Who Persecute*).

Note in the Table that both the State and the Church have their respective functions while the Valley below serves as the foundation and has its own function. The model depicts a certain affinity between the State and Capitalism (both out of the West) and the Church and Socialism (both out of the East). Consider the possible implications of one pillar or the other deciding to broaden its functional role over the Valley. For instance, the State may strive to be more involved with issues of Mercy, while the Church may strive to be involved with issues of Justice. This may seem fine to some, but the question becomes: At what point does the issue of simple affinity turn into an issue of authority over one's affinity group in order to stretch into areas in which each pillar has proven to be ineffective?

The Issue of Affinity

As a general rule there is a certain affinity of interest between the State and Capitalism (both out of the West) and between the Church and Socialism (both out of the East). The point here is that Capitalism and Socialism are best instigated and managed by those in the Valley. It is common knowledge that there have been persistent efforts (past/present) by leaders of the State and/or the Church to increase the institution's functional role over the Valley. Again, when does the issue of simple affinity turn into an issue of authority over one's affinity group? The answer may come to light in the following discussion.

Should the State ever forego simple affinity with capitalism in order to pursue areas of Mercy? And should the Church ever forego simple affinity with social issues in order to pursue areas of Justice? Some will not see a problem with either, particularly with the State's becoming involved with issues of Mercy since the State is regarded as a tax collector with deep pockets and no face. Assuming one does not live under fascist rule that mandates State-conformity, could this view be a result of having grown to rely less upon the Church and others in the Valley while growing more dependent upon the State? Of course it is. Then there are those who see nothing wrong with the Church becoming involved with issues of Justice. Again, assuming one does not live under fascist rule that mandates religious conformity, could this be because they have grown to rely less upon the State and others in the Valley while growing more dependent upon the Church? In other words, those who have forsaken the Church will build faith (or believe) in government, whereas those who have forsaken the State will use religion as a means for prosecution.

As for merciful expenditures by the State, recall Jesus' words, Let not thy left hand know what thy right hand doeth.[107] On the institutional level, if the right hand represents just ways and the left

---

[107] Matthew 6:1-4

hand represents merciful ways, then it appears that the State should not be involved in matters of mercy. While there are many reasons to suggest why this makes sense, it is inarguable that many political figures are naturally boisterous about the merciful good that has been accomplished in one's own name or as a group during the course of spending other people's money.

Let's now assume that the State and the Church are attempting to broaden their functional role over the Valley even more greatly. In order to accomplish this they must increase power, authority, and control over their respective affinity group. Thus, in order for the State to become more involved with issues of Mercy it must gain greater control over Capitalism, and in order for the Church to become more involved with issues of Justice it must gain greater control over Social issues. The more such pillars stretch over the Valley to reach the other side, the more of a shadow they cast over the Valley region. Even worse, what if one pillar is so committed to do it all that its next goal is to overtake the role of the other pillar, and thus become one formidable pillar? In either case the Valley below becomes increasingly separated from the premier source of light and life—God above! Therefore, instead of further empowering the State and/or the Church, would it not be wiser for these institutions to empower the Valley? Of course it would. In this way the State and the Church (as separate and distinct pillars) can stand strong and vertical, while the Valley below is blessed with a greater opportunity to freely aspire toward God Almighty!

And he did [that which was] right in the sight of the LORD,
and walked in the ways of David his father,
and declined [neither] to the right hand, nor to the left.
2 Chronicles 34:2

The critical point is that in order for the Valley to become upright and liberated, it must be allowed to be in direct union with God Almighty, not in groups or institutions, nor in anything else tangible. The State and the Church are extremely vital, but if those in the Valley become purposed in such pillars they will become increasingly reliant upon them physically (for their livelihood) and even spiritually. Thus, the role of the visible Church should be to help all believers aspire directly toward God, not necessarily through the (visible) Church itself, but aside from the Church and especially aside from the State.

While it may have been necessary for the State or the Church to be an authority over the Valley in the past (particularly prior to the Age of Enlightenment), it is widely accepted that the functions of State and Church should be separate and distinct. That's because all humans are endowed by our Creator with unalienable rights—life, liberty, and the pursuit of happiness—which the Church helps to teach and the State helps to secure for the benefit of all citizens. This is why the United States Constitution is so significant, and why most citizens have a heartfelt willingness to honor and defend it.

> *Surely I have behaved and quieted myself, as a child that is weaned of his mother: my soul [is] even as a weaned child.*
> Psalm 131:2

The main reason society should resist becoming purposed in institutions is that each pillar has had a tendency in the past to empower its leadership instead of empowering the Valley. Yes, it can be argued that each sincerely attempts to help those in need, but just like some parents who become purposed in their children, they may actually be doing more harm than good. Some parents simply cannot restrain themselves from being the child's decision-maker even after the child reaches adulthood. Many leaders have done likewise with the Valley. This effectively redirects the individual's attention from intangible God to the tangible institution of man.

As the State makes more long-term social programs available, the less motivated people in the Valley will become to do well on their own, even to the point of becoming complacent with respect to the Church. So instead of weaning the Valley to become independently viable, the State will have no choice but to assert more authority and control over the Valley. Then consider how some in the State such as judges are eager to suppress free speech and diminish laws of the land with bench rulings of their own. It is not only the State that consistently attempts to broaden its functional role over the Valley, there are also (wealthy) elitist-minded and attorney-led groups that will use any legal means possible to enforce their own socio-ideological and political agendas.

The functional roles of the State and the Church should be to allow the Valley to aspire toward and come into communion with God instead of being required to turn to the left or the right. God needs pillars formed by righteousness to help guide the objects of His affection—His children who exist in the Valley. The following are some other questions pertaining to the State to reflect upon:

- If the State stretches Eastward toward issues of mercy, will it not be required to impose more taxes both on businesses and on those deemed wealthy in order to fund social endeavors?
- If those in the Valley are taxed more by the State, are they as able to give alms and gifts to the Church and to social efforts that they independently deem worthy?
- If the State (whose leaders are overwhelmingly attorneys) does broaden its role over the Valley into areas of mercy, would it not find it necessary to legislate morality and ethical behavior?
- If the State becomes so purposed in giving toward the Valley while the Valley reciprocates that affection with votes, is this not similar to a (false) act of communion?
- If the consensus is that the State is not functionally reliable in transferring wealth among its citizens, then why is it allowed to be generous with the people's money for the benefit of other nations? The real question here is: Would the humanitarian needs of other nations not be best managed by those in the Valley as also directed by the Church?

Is it really possible for leaders of the State to reduce or even repeal legislation to diminish governmental oversight? Realize that most elected officials run for office because they aspire to help in grand ways. So to suggest a decrease in the role of government is similar to suggesting a reduction in their own influence. The only way a valid course correction can occur is for more leaders to understand that all have a higher authority so that doing what's right is the result of faith-based purpose in God.

Obviously, similar questions can be posed regarding the Church, but since the Church is recognized in so many different ways, I encourage you to ponder this issue from your own denominational/religious perspective. One question, though, can be asked regarding the righteous efforts of any faith-based group seeking to broaden its functional role Westward. Is it really possible for any group to be more effective than the (Northward) democratic State when attempting to properly resolve and prosecute issues of justice? Recall that justice and mercy are devotional elements as fostered by a higher purpose (e.g., that in God Almighty), and that neither justice nor mercy can be directly approached (as if by practice), even at the institutional level. Both are manifestations of faith and grace by God through each of those responsive to the greater "I AM". So, it is impossible for any religious group which takes on the issue of mercy earnestly and modestly to be more effective than the (Northward) democratic State when dealing with issues of justice.

Recall that natural conformity is the effect of a loving God-first relationship (the cause), which the Church helps instill by proclaiming the Word as written and as heard. Thus, the Church, which has a natural affinity for social issues stands as a strong East pillar maintaining truth; while the State (Justice) with a natural affinity for capitalism stands as a strong West pillar maintaining facts. When the State (secular, standing for justice) and the Church (religious, standing for mercy) both stand as strong vertical pillars and support individual liberty, then those in the Valley have greater opportunities to become yoked Northward toward God and thus to be freed.

While the overall argument supports the notion of State and Church as separate, there is an interesting oneness that occurs within the minds and hearts of believers in the Valley. It is in this collective house that those in the Valley can weigh for themselves the motivations for laws and the words of the prophets, both good and bad, in true democratic fashion.

In summary, the Functional Alignments Table demonstrates that neither pillar alone can accomplish what the Valley was designed by God to do. If one pillar or the other does stretch beyond its functional role then it will have no choice but to legislate and oversee its affinity group. If one pillar or the other becomes purposed as the provider by those in the Valley, then the increasing collective of citizens will have no choice but to turn out of the way from God. All in all, the Table demonstrates that there is a blessed opportunity for believers to become yoked between conformity on Civic-Economic issues on one hand, and non-conformity on Socio-Cultural issues on the other hand, individually and collectively.

So just as believers become yoked with Christ in order to balance the house of mind, each can now realize that in order to balance the collective house, the Valley (below) must become empowered by such pillars to do what it knows best. Because most individuals want to receive salvation, they will naturally seek to become yoked with others if only given a bona fide chance to freely aspire toward God Himself.

3. Church & State as Parents: Fatherhood & Motherhood

In this section, I argue that the pillars of Church and State parallel the pillars of fatherhood and motherhood, respectively. In each case, the child aspires toward a higher authority: first, according to the will of parents as the child is being introduced to God; and second, according to the will of God as the child aspires further toward Him alongside both parents.

If the parents increasingly regulate the maturing child, they will only stifle the child's natural desire to become happy, healthy, and prosperous. Thus, in order for the child to transition from earthly pillars as the higher authority toward God (the overarching authority), the parents must exercise diminishing authority and control over the life of the child. As control is released, freedoms are increased, along with personal responsibility and care for others.

Only by virtue of the functional strength of two parents can children develop to achieve balance. If one parent falls, it only means that the child must rely upon the other for attributes that it likely does not possess (just as mother and father have different qualities). Both parents are needed, as are both Church and State, but in each case, in order for harmony to exist, all involved in the process must be sound of mind and follow after the preeminence of God as the higher authority.

Human Understanding and Devotion

And he answered and said unto them, Have ye not read, that he which made [them] at the beginning made them male and female, And said, For this cause shall a man leave father and mother, and shall cleave to his wife: and they twain shall be one flesh? Wherefore they are no more twain, but one flesh. What therefore God hath joined together, let not man put asunder.

Jesus, Matthew 19:4-6

Assume that a man and a woman have found each other and fall in love. Each is physically mature, emotionally secure, and Northward in Christ. Keep in mind that spiritual maturity comes with time, so it is quite possible that though both are physically mature, they may not yet be spiritually mature. Each will likely have strengths of mind and of character that the other does not possess. This makes their mutual attraction that much stronger and more fascinating.

Recalling the Socio-Ideological Tendencies Table and realizing that opposites attract, we can predict that one will likely exemplify more N-West qualities (practicality, sensibility, and responsibility) while the other will exemplify more N-East qualities (kindness, compassion, and character). Vertically speaking, also consider how one will likely exemplify more wisdom while the other will exemplify more grace. Since each found the other while walking with Northward Purpose, this natural attraction may ultimately lead into marriage and then children. Thus, without any forced acts of submission, these two different mindsets with the same purpose will join and become one even more perfected in the sight of God.

Note that this does not suggest that each partner loses his or her unique spirit when becoming united in this way. It suggests that when two Northward individuals are yoked together their combined spirit and strength are greater than the sum of what each could do alone. (This is a parallel to the discussion of the branches of the Christian Church in the section called *The Church*.)

Each child born from this naturally-formed union will have a greater opportunity to offer good fruit as he or she is nurtured in the best possible light. I am not suggesting that those who have only one parent or are in foster care will not bear good fruit, but it does mean that the road to healthy development will be more difficult for the child. Even so, anyone may overcome difficult challenges of life when shown the Northward path toward God.

> *Jesus saith unto them, Fill the waterpots with water.*
> *And they filled them up to the brim.*
> John 2:7

While maintaining the individuality of each parent, the union of father and mother is the epitome of perfection when it is formed from a God-first relationship. God is the source of love instilled within each vessel, and in this vertical union each is more capable of expressing true love not only toward the other but toward their children as well. It is important to note that the parents do not have children as their first purpose—their purpose is the loving procreation of more souls for God's creation.

If one pillar (or parent) maintains that it can do it all, this only prompts notions of functional expansion that effectively leads into greater authority and control over the Valley (or child); hence, a road made more difficult for all. If the Valley dismisses the value of one pillar or the other, then there will be a foundational imbalance that will prompt a turn. If all dismiss the higher authority, then all will be turned out of the way, as purpose of a darker kind emerges. Thus, both pillars and the Valley below are instrumental in helping all resist the fall while encouraging the rise.

V. Conclusion

*Now set your heart and your soul to seek the LORD your
God; arise therefore, and build ye the sanctuary of the LORD
God, to bring the ark of the covenant of the LORD,
and the holy vessels of God,
into the house that is to be built to the name of the LORD.*
1 Chronicles 22:19

It is amazing how the complexities of life issues are better understood when approached from a God-first perspective, one that (in this case) I hope you have found to be balanced. This book was written to help empower the Valley by explaining why God is so important during one's time on earth. The fundamental goals were twofold: (1) to provide reasons to support the idea that those with faith-based purpose in God not only believe differently from those without faith, they also reason and respond differently; and (2) to affirm God's existence and humanity's position within His creation.

I hope that the illustrations, tables, and discussions presented have helped demonstrate the nature of human beings relative to one another on the horizontal plane, and relative to and in communion with God on the vertical plane. The main objective of the study was to spotlight the functional distinctions between the two parts of mind (and resulting behaviors) that may become yoked into one accord, individually and collectively.

We began with the issue of diversity and a sense of belonging and ended with who each of us is, why we exist, and why we need strong pillars in our lives. I hope by now it is evident that in order to be in direct union with our Lord and Savior one must increase in faith, respond to His call, and with the gift of grace, arise into God-inspired consciousness.

The dual function and capacity of the mind allows humans to strengthen and balance both objective and subjective reasoning processes. Thus, the efforts of the West realize (by integration) the efforts of the East, so that the independent functionality of each is optimized and strengthened when both have the same purpose.

Children of God first come to be, so that by their inner being they then come to do, in His name and for His glory. With devotion (the response to faith) those who truly believe in Him can cleave unto the Lord with the heart. From such a union then can God's goodness—as fruits of man's inward spirit—become manifest from the spiritual realm to the physical realm.

> *Till we all come in the unity of the faith, and of the knowledge of the Son of God, unto a perfect man, unto the measure of the stature of the fulness of Christ:*
> Ephesians 4:13

The fundamental basis of the model is revelation from both Old and New Testaments coalesced into one Truth (as taught and exemplified by the East pillar). Our Father best represents issues of Justice and Christ Jesus best represents issues of Mercy – together Father and Son are yoked into perfection with the Holy Spirit proceeding downward toward His (upward) perfected Body.

True believers of God are inherently Northward and need no help in affirming His existence—they would grow in their faith and trust in our Lord with or without this book. For those who needed to be shown why faith in God is vital, I hope that this book has helped pinpoint the reasons for various types of behavioral tendencies, and especially what happens when He is not factored into social practices and policy.

Sadly, I am aware that even after this demonstration that He is our higher divine authority, our love, and that we all are His children in need of conversion and in healing, some will choose to continue to fight within the horizontal plane and will fall rather than take flight into the vertical.

Only with a God-first approach toward life itself can we better understand and appreciate our existence. As each temple heightens, it becomes apparent that purposes of any other kind—i.e., those without God high in mind first—will only lead to wrong paths and futility. The most effective means to help lift the souls of those who are fallen is to teach the (upright) vertical principle of understanding and devotion that Jesus instructed and exemplified. This will enable each person to humbly decide to respond with faith in Him from the basis of love, righteousness, and holiness.

The hope is that as more people become capable of discerning from the arisen state, they will naturally forego thoughts and

Human Understanding and Devotion

behaviors that are in direct conflict with their moral and right standing with God—the Supreme Being. Having said that, though, let me restate that one is justified not by works, but by grace, according to measure of the gift of Christ.[108] Loving God with all their hearts (the result of a sound mind) is what positions believers not only to receive the gifts of hope, peace, joy, and love,[109] but in turn, to share such gifts with others in His name. In this light we find that it is not up to those who are heart-driven to convince or prove to anyone that they are righteous and holy; rather, it is up to others to recognize them as such by their natural goodness, and by their fruits.[110]

Because of Jesus' two commandments WE (individually as parts of a greater whole) better understand how to weigh the motivations for law(s) and the prophets, those good and bad, each of which becomes subject to love, grace, and truth. By His divine example, believers more easily apprehend the importance of becoming yoked into one Northward accord (or one collective conscience), as the strength of our Father's loving Spirit is further instilled into each of His children—those Christ-like. With Jesus as the "chief corner stone" of faith, the foundation of one's house becomes more level, stable, and strong so that greater temple height can be achieved. In the process of building up the temple, believers are spiritually cleansed, sustained, and strengthened by heaven's holy water.[111]

> *At that day ye shall know that I [am] in my Father,*
> *and ye in me, and I in you.*
> Jesus, John 14:20

All who choose to grow in their faith and believe in God can now appreciate that it is by two that WE become perfected toward Him; and because of the love for God first, then—in reciprocating fashion—the spiritual land of Israel will become magnified, a land

---

[108] Romans 11:6, 2 Timothy 1:9, Ephesians 4:7
[109] During Advent season the inward qualities of *hope, peace, joy, and love* are of special meaning to reflect upon and share with others in His name.
[110] Matthew 7:12-20
[111] Mark 1:8, John 3:5

created in part by the Godhead and in part by true believers—the commonality among the diverse—that form His Body.

VI. Epilogue

> *And every one that hath forsaken houses, or brethren, or sisters, or father, or mother, or wife, or children, or lands, for my name's sake, shall receive an hundredfold, and shall inherit everlasting life.*
> Jesus, Matthew 19:29

This book required a certain amount of thought and research on my part, but I confess that I have not had the depth of understanding of these issues for most of my life. I wrote this book because I wanted to respond to His appeal the best way I knew how. Be reminded, though, I make no claim that I am better than anyone else, yet it is amazing what can be accomplished when one keeps his feet moving while God becomes progressively purposed.

An important point to consider is that this book asks both the State and the Church to back away from strict oversight and allow the Valley to grow and prosper directly toward God as it was designed to do. However, there is something interesting that must be shared among believers. Suggesting that the Church's function is more in tune with Mercy exposes it more to malicious attack as we see in many quarters today.

Most believers understand that the Church should not have to conform to man's standards. At the same time, however, others have backed away from the Church because they were, at times, expected to conform to man's standards as driven by the institution of the Church (just reflect on the discussion involving edicts of conformity). For a moment, put aside all conformity-driven measures and expectations. Remember that natural, loving conformity among the Body of Christ can be sustainably achieved only as the result of a God-first approach toward life itself, individually and collectively.

The onus of protecting the invisible and visible Church is on the Valley. This does not mean that there should be attacks on others who don't agree with Christianity, because all have the right to free speech and freedom of religion. It means that the collective Christian voice (as also shaped the Church and by the Northward consensus) should be allowed to justly, yet peacefully defend itself against oppressors, particularly against those who proactively seek to silence Christians.

The aim of this book was not simply to identify what the enemy is and what is not, it is to help empower the individual, not one individual, nor one group of individuals, but the collective of those in the Valley who choose to increase with faith in Christ.

> *Wherefore the rather, brethren, give diligence to make your calling and election sure: for if ye do these things, ye shall never fall: For so an entrance shall be ministered unto you abundantly into the everlasting kingdom of our Lord and Saviour Jesus Christ.*
> 2 Peter 1:10

So why are these things mentioned? Each and every person has a skill or talent and a contribution to make. Perhaps he or she has not yet realized what it is. The State has its leaders and so does the Church—each vitally important, but most people (including myself) do not have aspirations to lead in either capacity. Still, each of us has a calling of one kind or another. I have come to understand that my skills and talents involve administrative tasks. While I may be challenged to serve in other ways from time to time, it is in this area that I hope to become even more proficient. Functionally speaking, God needs for all to realize their calling, so that as parts of a greater whole each may then be instrumental in helping accomplish God's plan for achieving true peace, harmony, and liberty for all.

VII. Appendices

The tables in Appendices A-C, are compilations of selected Strong's Lexicons (as driven by the KJV) retrieved from the *BlueLetterBible.org* website first sorted by Hebrew and Greek, then by Part of Speech and Strong's Number. Because the column for *Pronunciation* has been replaced with *Part of Speech*, each table will be considered as "compiled." The *Part of Speech* information was found through a link for each Strong's Number. I hope that such groupings will help satisfy questions that may arise in the reader's mind.

Remember that Old Testament scripture includes books that lead up to the coming of Jesus whereas New Testament scripture includes books that recount the time during and after the earthly life of Jesus. One will find both similarities and differences in the categorical groupings in the Old and New Testament passages.

Appendix A – Noteworthy Terminology

1. Contents

TABLE	PAGE	DESCRIPTION
TABLE 5	220	PURPOSE
TABLE 6	221	HEART
TABLE 7	222	SOUL
TABLE 8	224	FAITH
TABLE 9	225	BELIEVING
TABLE 10	225	OBJECTS OF KNOWING

2. Purpose

Purpose

Table 5

Strong's Number	Heb/Greek Word	Part of Speech	English Equivalent
Old Testament (Hebrew)			
H2656	chephets	masc noun	pleasure, desire, delight, PURPOSE, acceptable, delightsome, matter, pleasant, willingly
H6640	tsĕbuw (Aramaic)	masc noun	PURPOSE
H7385	riyq	masc noun	vain, vanity, no PURPOSE, empty, vain thing
H8356	shathah	masc noun	foundations, PURPOSES
H4284	machashabah	fem noun	thought, device, PURPOSE, work, imaginations, cunning, devised, invented, means
H6098	`etsah	fem noun	counsel, counsels, PURPOSE, advice, counsellors, advisement, counsel <> <>, counsellor
H2154	zimmah	verb	lewdness, wickedness, mischief, lewd, heinous crime, wicked devices, lewdly, wicked mind, PURPOSES, thought
H2161	zamam	verb	thought, devise, consider, PURPOSE, imagine, plot

Appendix A – Noteworthy Terminology

H2803	chashab	verb	count, devise, think, imagine, cunning, reckon, PURPOSE, esteem, account, impute, forecast, regard, workman, conceived, misc
H3289	ya`ats	verb	counsel, counsellor, consult, give, PURPOSEd, advice, determined, advise, deviseth, taken, misc
H3335	yatsar	verb	form, potter, fashion, maker, frame, make, former, earthen, PURPOSEd
H7997	shalal	verb	spoil, take, fall, prey, PURPOSE
New Testament (Greek)			
G1106	gnōmē	fem noun	judgment, mind, PURPOSE, advice, will, agree
G4286	prothesis	fem noun	PURPOSE, shewbread
G1013	boulēma	neuter noun	PURPOSE, will
G1011	bouleuō	verb	consult, be minded, PURPOSE, determine, take counsel
G4255	proaireō	verb	PURPOSE
G4388	protithēmi	verb	PURPOSE, set forth

Source for *compilation*: BlueLetterBible.org. Retrieved March 3, 2009

3. Heart and Soul

Heart

Table 6

Strong's Number	Heb/Greek Word	Part of Speech	English Equivalent
Old Testament (Hebrew)			
H1079	bal (Aramaic)	masc noun	HEART
H3820	leb	masc noun	HEART, mind, midst, understanding, hearted, wisdom, comfortably, well, considered, friendly, kindly, stouthearted, care, misc
H3821	leb (Aramaic)	masc noun	HEART
H3824	lebab	masc noun	HEART, consider, mind, understanding, misc
H3825	lĕbab (Aramaic)	masc noun	HEART

Strong's Number	Heb/Greek Word	Part of Speech	English Equivalent
H4578	*me'ah*	masc noun	bowels, belly, HEART, womb
H7907	*sekviy*	masc noun	HEART
H3826	*libbah*	fem noun	HEART
H5315	*nephesh*	fem noun	soul, life, person, mind, HEART, creature, body, himself, yourselves, dead, will, desire, man, themselves, any, appetite, misc
H3823	*labab*	verb	ravished my HEART, make, made cakes, be wise
New Testament (Greek)			
G2588	*kardia*	fem noun	HEART, broken hearted
G5590	*psychē*	fem noun	soul, life, mind, HEART, heartily, not tr
G674	*apopsychō*	verb	HEART failing
G1282	*diapriō*	verb	be cut to the HEART, be cut

Source for *compilation*: BlueLetterBible.org. Retrieved March 3, 2009

Soul

Table 7

Strong's Number	Heb/Greek Word	Part of Speech	English Equivalent
Old Testament (Hebrew)			
H5082	*nědiybah*	fem noun	SOUL
H5315	*nephesh*	fem noun	SOUL, life, person, mind, heart, creature, body, himself, yourselves, dead, will, desire, man, themselves, any, appetite, misc
H5397	*něshamah*	fem noun	breath, blast, spirit, inspiration, SOULS
New Testament (Greek)			
G5590	*psychē*	fem noun	SOUL, life, mind, heart, heartily, not tr

Source for *compilation*: BlueLetterBible.org. Retrieved March 3, 2009

Notice above that there are two English Equivalents for *soul* as both mind *and* heart: one is in the Old Testament as *nephesh* and the other in the New Testament as *psyche*. If one further examines these two terms then it's easy to see how broad the definition of *soul* really is. The following is a summary of how *nephesh* and *psyche* are used in the Bible. This is from the "Outline of Biblical Usage" section as driven from Gesenius' and Thayer's Lexicon:

Soul as *Nephesh*[112] H5315 (Old Testament):
1) soul, self, life, creature, person, appetite, mind, living being, desire, emotion, passion
    a) that which breathes, the breathing substance or being, soul, the inner being of man
    b) living being
    c) living being (with life in the blood)
    d) the man himself, self, person or individual
    e) seat of the appetites
    f) seat of emotions and passions
    g) activity of mind
        1) dubious
    h) activity of the will
        1) dubious
    i) activity of the character
        1) dubious

Soul as *Psyche*[113] G5590 (New Testament):
1) breath
    a) the breath of life
        1) the vital force which animates the body and shows itself in breathing
            a) of animals
            b) of men

---

[112] Blue Letter Bible. "Dictionary and Word Search for nephesh (Strong's 5315)." Blue Letter Bible. 1996-2009. 3 Mar 2009. < http://www.blueletterbible.org/lang/lexicon/lexicon.cfm?strongs=H5315 >
[113] Blue Letter Bible. "Dictionary and Word Search for psychē (Strong's 5590)." Blue Letter Bible. 1996-2009. 2 Mar 2009. < http://www.blueletterbible.org/lang/lexicon/lexicon.cfm?strongs=G5590 >

b) life

c) that in which there is life

   1) a living being, a living soul

2) the soul

   a) the seat of the feelings, desires, affections, aversions (our heart, soul etc.)

   b) the (human) soul in so far as it is constituted that by the right use of the aids offered it by God it can attain its highest end and secure eternal blessedness, the soul regarded as a moral being designed for everlasting life

   c) the soul as an essence which differs from the body and is not dissolved by death (distinguished from other parts of the body)

4. Faith and Believing

Faith

Table 8

Strong's Number	Heb/Greek Word	Part of Speech	English Equivalent
Old Testament (Hebrew)			
H529	'emuwn	masc noun	faithful, truth, FAITH
H530	'emuwnah	fem noun	Faithfulness, truth, faithfully, office, faithful, FAITH, stability, steady, truly, verily
New Testament (Greek)			
G1680	elpis	fem noun	hope, FAITH
G4102	pistis	fem noun	FAITH, assurance, believe, belief, them that believe, fidelity

Source for *compilation*: BlueLetterBible.org. Retrieved March 3, 2009

Appendix A – Noteworthy Terminology

Believe

Table 9

Strong's Number	Heb/Greek Word	Part of Speech	English Equivalent
Old Testament (Hebrew)			
H539	'aman	verb	BELIEVE, assurance, faithful, sure, established, trust, verified, stedfast, continuance, father, bring up, nurse, be nursed, surely be, stand fast, fail, trusty
H540	'aman (Aramaic)	verb	BELIEVE, sure, faithful
New Testament (Greek)			
G4102	pistis	fem noun	faith, assurance, BELIEVE, belief, them that BELIEVE, fidelity
G4103	pistos	adjective	faithful, BELIEVE, believing, true, faithfully, BELIEVEr, sure not tr
G3982	peithō	verb	persuade, trust, obey, have confidence, BELIEVE, be confident, misc
G4100	pisteuō	verb	BELIEVE, commit unto, commit to (one's) trust, be committed unto, be put in trust with, be commit to one's trust, BELIEVEr

Source for *compilation*: BlueLetterBible.org. Retrieved March 3, 2009

5. Objects of Knowing

Table 10

Strong's Number	Hebrew Word	Part of Speech	English Equivalent
H7922	sekel	masc noun	understanding, wisdom, wise, prudence, knowledge, sense, discretion, policy
H8394	tabuwn	masc noun	Understanding, discretion, reasons, misc
H1847	da'ath	masc/fem noun	knowledge, know, cunning, unwittingly, ignorantly, unawares
H998	biynah	fem noun	understanding, wisdom, knowledge, meaning, perfectly, understand
H2451	chokmah	fem noun	wisdom, wisely, skilful man, wits
H4209	mĕzimmah	fem noun	discretion, wicked device, device, thought, intents, mischievous device, wickedly, witty inventions, lewdness, mischievous

Source for *compilation*: BlueLetterBible.org. Retrieved March 10, 2009

- Exd 35:31 And he hath filled him with the spirit of God, in wisdom^{H2451}, in understanding^{H8394}, and in knowledge^{H1847}, and in all manner of workmanship;
- Pro 2:6 For the LORD giveth wisdom^{H2451}: out of his mouth [cometh] knowledge^{H1847} and understanding^{H8394}.
- Pro 3:21 My son, let not them depart from thine eyes: keep sound wisdom and discretion^{H4209}:
- Pro 9:10 The fear of the LORD [is] the beginning of wisdom^{H2451}: and the knowledge^{H1847} of the holy [is] understanding^{H998}.
- Pro 19:11 The discretion^{H7922} of a man deferreth his anger; and [it is] his glory to pass over a transgression.
- Isa 11:2 And the spirit of the LORD shall rest upon him, the spirit of wisdom^{H2451} and understanding^{H998}, the spirit of counsel and might, the spirit of knowledge^{H1847} and of the fear of the LORD;

One Lexicon entry that the reader may find out of place when reviewing the English Equivalent column is the Hebrew word *mězimmah* H4209, which appears to have negative connotations that parallel purpose in a Southward sense. In the Proverbs 3:21 passage above, this same word is used in a positive sense – here discretion is equivalent to "counsel, prudence, or craftiness."[114]

Other Lexical entries for *discretion* are consistently shown in a positive light. Thus, the words *knowledge, understanding, discretion,* and *wisdom* can be characterized in noun form each having positive connotations and, thus, regarded as good to possess.

---

[114] Blue Letter Bible. "Dictionary and Word Search for mězimmah (Strong's 4209)." Blue Letter Bible. 1996-2009. 17 Nov 2009. < http://www.blueletterbible.org/lang/lexicon/lexicon.cfm?Strongs=H4209&t=KJV&sf=4 >

Appendix B – HUHD Model

1. Contents

TABLE	PAGE	DESCRIPTION
Descriptions of Northward Elements as driven by Purpose		
TABLE 11	227	PURPOSE
TABLE 12	228	KNOWLEDGE (KNOW, KNOWN)
TABLE 13	229	JUSTICE (JUST)
TABLE 14	229	MERCY (MERCIFUL)
Descriptions of Perfected Elements		
TABLE 15	230	WISDOM, WISE
TABLE 16	230	UNDERSTANDING, UNDERSTAND
TABLE 17	231	GRACE, GRACIOUS
Descriptions of Southward Elements as driven by Purpose		
TABLE 18	232	PURPOSE (AND DISCRETION IN THE NEGATIVE SENSE)
TABLE 19	232	KNOWLEDGE (UNKNOWING)
TABLE 20	233	JUSTICE (UNJUST)
TABLE 21	233	MERCY (MERCILESS)
Descriptions of Non-Perfected Elements		
TABLE 22	234	FOOLISHNESS, FOOL
TABLE 23	235	MIS-UNDERSTANDING, MIS-UNDERSTAND
TABLE 24	235	DISGRACE, VILE

2. Northward

a. Trichotomy Group

i. Purpose

Purpose (n,v)

Table 11

Strong's Number	Heb/Greek Word	Part of Speech	English Equivalent
H2656	*chephets*	masc noun	pleasure, desire, delight, PURPOSE, acceptable, delightsome, matter, pleasant, willingly

H6098	`etsah	fem noun	counsel, counsels, PURPOSE, advice, counsellors, advisement, counsel <> <>, counsellor
G4286	prothesis	fem noun	PURPOSE, shewbread
G4255	proaireō	verb	PURPOSE

Source for *compilation*: BlueLetterBible.org. Retrieved March 8, 2009

b. Triquetra Group

i. Knowledge

Know (n,v), Known (adj,v)

Table 12

Strong's Number	Heb/Greek Word	Part of Speech	English Equivalent
H1843	dea`	masc noun	opinion, KNOWledge
H4093	madda`	masc noun	KNOWledge, thought, science
H1847	da`ath	masc/fem noun	KNOWledge, KNOW, cunning, unwittingly, ignorantly, unawares
H1844	de`ah	fem noun	KNOWledge
G1108	gnōsis	fem noun	KNOWledge, science
G1922	epignōsis	fem noun	KNOWledge, acKNOWledging, acKNOWledgement
G1110	gnōstos	adjective	KNOWn, acquaintance, notable
G1990	epistēmōn	adjective	endued with KNOWledge
H3045	yada`	verb	KNOW, KNOWn, KNOWledge, perceive, shew, tell, wist, understand, certainly, acKNOWledge, acquaintance, consider, declare, teach, misc
H5234	nakar	verb	KNOW, acKNOWledge, discern, respect, KNOWledge, KNOWn, feign to another, misc [nakar has both positive and negative connotations]
G1097	ginōskō	verb	KNOW, perceive, understand, misc
G1107	gnōrizō	verb	make KNOWn, declare, certify, give to understand, do to wit, wot
G1231	diaginōskō	verb	enquire, KNOW the uttermost
G1921	epiginōskō	verb	KNOW, acKNOWledge, perceive, take KNOWledge of, have KNOWledge of, KNOW well

Source for *compilation*: BlueLetterBible.org. Retrieved March 8, 2009

ii. Justice

Justice (n,v), Just (n,adj,v,adv)

Table 13

Strong's Number	Heb/Greek Word	Part of Speech	English Equivalent
H6664	tsedeq	masc noun	righteousness, JUST, JUSTice, righteous, righteously, right, righteous cause, unrighteousness, misc
H6666	tsĕdaqah	fem noun	righteousness, JUSTice, right, righteous acts, moderately, righteously
H3477	yashar	adjective	right, upright, righteous, straight, convenient, Jasher, equity, JUST, meet, meetest, upright ones, uprightly, uprightness, well
H6662	tsaddiyq	adjective	righteous, JUST, righteous man, lawful
H8003	shalem	adjective	perfect, whole, full, JUST, peaceable, misc
G1342	dikaios	adjective	righteous, JUST, right, meet
H6663	tsadaq	verb	JUSTify, righteous, JUST, JUSTice, cleansed, clear ourselves, righteousness
G1346	dikaiōs	adverb	JUSTly, righteously, to righteousness

Source for *compilation*: BlueLetterBible.org. Retrieved March 8, 2009

iii. Mercy

Mercy (n), Merciful (n,adj,v)

Table 14

Strong's Number	Heb/Greek Word	Part of Speech	English Equivalent
H2617	checed	masc noun	MERCY, kindness, lovingkindness, goodness, kindly, MERCIFUL, favour, good, goodliness, pity, reproach, wicked thing [*checed* is primarily of positive connotation]
H7356	racham	masc noun	MERCY, compassion, womb, bowels, pity, damsel, tender love
G3628	oiktirmos	masc noun	MERCY
H2551	chemlah	fem noun	MERCIFUL, pitiful
G1656	eleos	neuter noun	MERCY

G4698	*splagchnon*	neuter noun	bowels, inward affection, tender MERCY
G1655	*eleēmōn*	adjective	MERCIFUL
H2603	*chanan*	verb	MERCY, gracious, MERCIFUL, supplication, favour, besought, pity, fair, favourable, favoured, misc
H7355	*racham*	verb	... MERCY, ...compassion, pity, love, MERCIFUL, Ruhamah, surely
G1653	*eleeō*	verb	have MERCY on, obtain MERCY, show MERCY, have compassion, have compassion on, have pity on, have MERCY, have MERCY upon, receive MERCY

Source for *compilation*: BlueLetterBible.org. Retrieved March 8, 2009

c. Wisdom and Grace

Wisdom (n), Wise (v)

Table 15

Strong's Number	Heb/Greek Word	Part of Speech	English Equivalent
H2451	*chokmah*	fem noun	WISDOM, WISEly, skilful man, wits
H2452	*chokmah* (Aramaic)	fem noun	WISDOM
H2454	*chokmowth*	fem noun	WISDOM, every WISE
H8454	*tuwshiyah*	fem noun	WISDOM, enterprise, thing as it is, that which is, substance, working
G4678	*sophia*	fem noun	WISDOM
G5428	*phronēsis*	fem noun	WISDOM, prudence
H7919	*sakal*	verb	understand, WISE, prosper, WISEly, understanding, consider, instruct, prudent, skill, teach, misc

Source for *compilation*: BlueLetterBible.org. Retrieved March 8, 2009

Understanding (n), Understand (v)

Table 16

Strong's Number	Heb/Greek Word	Part of Speech	English Equivalent
H3820	*leb*	masc noun	heart, mind, midst, UNDERSTANDing, hearted, wisdom, comfortably, well, considered, friendly, kindly, stouthearted, care, misc
H3824	*lebab*	masc noun	heart, consider, mind, UNDERSTANDing, misc

Strong's Number	Heb/Greek Word	Part of Speech	English Equivalent
H7922	sekel	masc noun	UNDERSTANDing, wisdom, wise, prudence, knowledge, sense, discretion, policy [sekel is primarily of positive connotation]
H8085	shama'	masc noun	hear, hearken, obey, publish, UNDERSTAND, obedient, diligently, shew, sound, declare, discern, noise, perceive, tell, reported, misc
H8394	tabuwn	masc noun	UNDERSTANDing, discretion, reasons, misc
G3563	nous	masc noun	mind, UNDERSTANDing
H998	biynah	fem noun	UNDERSTANDing, wisdom, knowledge, meaning, perfectly, UNDERSTAND
H999	biynah (Aramaic)	fem noun	UNDERSTANDing
H7924	soklĕthanuw (Aramaic)	fem noun	UNDERSTANDing
G1271	dianoia	fem noun	mind, UNDERSTANDing, imagination [dianoia has both positive and negative connotations]
G4907	synesis	fem noun	UNDERSTANDing, knowledge
H995	biyn	verb	UNDERSTAND, UNDERSTANDing, consider, prudent, perceive, regard, discern, instruct, misc.

Source for *compilation*: BlueLetterBible.org. Retrieved March 8, 2009

Grace (n), Gracious (n,adj,v)

Table 17

Strong's Number	Heb/Greek Word	Part of Speech	English Equivalent
H2580	chen	masc noun	GRACE, favour, GRACIOUS, pleasant, precious, wellfavoured
H8467	tĕchinnah	fem noun	supplication, favour, GRACE
G2143	euprepeia	fem noun	GRACE
G5485	charis	fem noun	GRACE, favour, thanks, thank, thank, pleasure, misc
H2587	channuwn	adjective	GRACIOUS
G5543	chrēstos	adjective	kind, easy, better, goodness, good, GRACIOUS
H2603	chanan	verb	mercy, GRACIOUS, merciful, supplication, favour, besought, pity, fair, favourable, favoured, misc

Source for *compilation*: BlueLetterBible.org. Retrieved March 8, 2009

3. Southward

a. Trichotomy Group

i. Purpose

Purpose (n,v), Discretion (n)

Table 18

Strong's Number	Heb/Greek Word	Part of Speech	English Equivalent
H7385	riyq	masc noun	vain, vanity, no PURPOSE, empty, vain thing
H4284	machashabah	fem noun	thought, device, PURPOSE, work, imaginations, cunning, devised, invented, means
H4209	mězimmah	fem noun	DISCRETION, wicked device, device, thought, intents, mischievous device, wickedly, witty inventions, lewdness, mischievous
H2154	zimmah	verb	lewdness, wickedness, mischief, lewd, heinous crime, wicked devices, lewdly, wicked mind, PURPOSEs, thought
H2803	chashab	verb	count, devise, think, imagine, cunning, reckon, PURPOSE, esteem, account, impute, forecast, regard, workman, conceived, misc
H7997	shalal	verb	spoil, take, fall, prey, PURPOSE

Source for *compilation*: BlueLetterBible.org. Retrieved March 8, 2009

b. Triquetra Group

i. Knowledge

Unknowing (n,adj,v)

Table 19

Strong's Number	Heb/Greek Word	Part of Speech	English Equivalent
H7922	sekel	masc noun	understanding, wisdom, wise, prudence, KNOWledge, sense, discretion, policy [*sekel* has both positive and negative connotations]
G56	agnōsia	fem noun	not the KNOWledge, ignorance
G57	agnōstos	adjective	unKNOWn

Appendix B – HUHD Model

H5234	nakar	verb	KNOW, acKNOWledge, discern, respect, KNOWledge, KNOWn, feign to another, misc [nakar has both positive and negative connotations]
G50	agnoeō	verb	be ignorant, ignorant, KNOW not, understand not, ignorantly, unKNOWn

Source for *compilation*: BlueLetterBible.org. Retrieved March 8, 2009

ii. Justice

Unjust (n,adj,v)

Table 20

Strong's Number	Heb/Greek Word	Part of Speech	English Equivalent
H205	'aven	masc noun	iniquity, wicked(ness), vanity, affliction, mischief, unrighteous, evil, false, idol, mourners, mourning, nought, sorrow, unJUST, vain
H2555	chamac	masc noun	violence, violent, cruelty, wrong, false, cruel, damage, inJUSTice, oppressor, unrighteous
H5767	'avval	masc noun	wicked, unJUST, unrighteous
H5766	'evel	masc/fem noun	iniquity, wickedness, unrighteousness, unJUST, perverseness, unJUSTly, unrighteously, wicked, wickedly, variant
G93	adikia	fem noun	unrighteousness, iniquity, unJUST, wrong
G94	adikos	adjective	unJUST, unrighteous
H5765	'aval	verb	deal unJUSTly, unrighteous
G91	adikeō	verb	hurt, do wrong, wrong, suffer wrong, be unJUST, take wrong, injure, be an offender, vr hope

Source for *compilation*: BlueLetterBible.org. Retrieved March 8, 2009

iii. Mercy

Merciless (adj)

Table 21

Strong's Number	Heb/Greek Word	Part of Speech	English Equivalent
G415	aneleēmōn	adjective	UNMERCIFUL

Source for *compilation*: BlueLetterBible.org. Retrieved March 8, 2009

c. Foolishness and Disgrace

Foolishness (n,adj), Fool (n,adj,v)

Table 22

Strong's Number	Heb/Greek Word	Part of Speech	English Equivalent
H1198	ba`ar	masc noun	brutish, FOOLish
H3684	kĕciyl	masc noun	FOOL, FOOLish
H5530	cakal	masc noun	FOOL, FOOLish, sottish
H5531	cikluwth	masc noun	folly, FOOLishness
H200	'ivveleth	fem noun	folly, FOOLishness, FOOLish, FOOLishly
G877	aphrosynē	fem noun	FOOLishly, FOOLishness, folly
G3472	mōria	fem noun	FOOLishness
G3473	mōrologia	fem noun	FOOLish talking
H191	'eviyl	masc adj	FOOL(s), FOOLish (man)
H5036	nabal	adjective	FOOL, FOOLish, vile person, FOOLish man, FOOLish women
H6612	pĕthiy	adjective	simple, simple ones, FOOLish, simplicity
H8602	taphel	adjective	untempered, FOOLish, unsavoury
G453	anoētos	adjective	FOOLish, FOOL, unwise
G801	asynetos	adjective	without understanding, FOOLish
G878	aphrōn	adjective	FOOL, FOOLish, unwise
G3474	mōros	adjective	FOOLish, FOOL, FOOLishness
H3688	kacal	verb	FOOLish
H5034	nabel	verb	fade, fade away, wear away, wither, disgrace, surely, dishonoureth, fall down, esteemed, falling, FOOLishly, come to nought, fall off, surely, make vile
H5528	cakal	verb	done FOOLishly, turn into FOOLishness, make FOOLish, play the FOOL
G3471	mōrainō	verb	lose savour, become a FOOL, make FOOLish

Source for *compilation*: BlueLetterBible.org. Retrieved March 8, 2009

Mis-understanding (n), Mis-understand (v)

Table 23

Strong's Number	Heb/Greek Word	Part of Speech	English Equivalent
G1271	dianoia	fem noun	mind, UNDERSTANDing, imagination [dianoia has both positive and negative connotations]
G801	asynetos	adjective	without UNDERSTANDing, foolish
G50	agnoeō	verb	be ignorant, ignorant, know not, UNDERSTAND not, ignorantly, unknown

Source for *compilation*: BlueLetterBible.org. Retrieved March 8, 2009

Disgrace (n,v), Vile (n,adj)

Table 24

Strong's Number	Heb/Greek Word	Part of Speech	English Equivalent
H5039	nĕbalah	fem noun	folly, villany, VILE
G819	atimia	fem noun	dishonour, VILE, shame, reproach
G5014	tapeinōsis	fem noun	low estate, humiliation, VILE, be made low
H2151	zalal	verb	flow down, VILE, glutton, riotous eaters, riotous
H5034	nabel	verb	fade, fade away, wear away, wither, DISGRACE, surely, dishonoureth, fall down, esteemed, falling, foolishly, come to nought, fall off, surely, make VILE
H5217	naka'	verb	VILEr
H7034	qalah	verb	seem VILE, shall be condemned, lightly esteemed, despised, base, settest light

Source for *compilation*: BlueLetterBible.org. Retrieved March 8, 2009

Appendix C – Quadra-Circumplex Model

1. Contents

TABLE	PAGE	DESCRIPTION
TABLE 25	237	OT: JUST, WEIGHT, BALANCE, SCALES
Falling		
TABLE 26	238	OT: PATHS, WAYS, TURNED ASIDE
TABLE 27	239	OT: FALL, BOWED DOWN, CAST DOWN, BROUGHT LOW, UPSIDE-DOWN
TABLE 28	240	NT: TURNED, BOWED DOWN, SUBVERT
TABLE 29	240	NT: HOUSE
TABLE 30	241	NT: CONSCIENCE
TABLE 31	241	OT: LEAN, UPHOLD
TABLE 32	242	OT: TABERNACLE, SANCTUARY
TABLE 33	242	OT: VESSEL, EMPTY
TABLE 34	243	OT: PIT, CAPTIVITY
TABLE 35	243	NT: CAPTIVE, CAPTIVITY
TABLE 36	244	OT: CROOKED
Arising		
TABLE 37	244	OT: CROOKED
TABLE 38	245	NT: CROOKED
TABLE 39	245	OT: BROUGHT UP, CAST UP, RAISED, UPRIGHT
TABLE 40	246	NT: AWAKE, ARISE, CONVERTED
TABLE 41	246	OT: WAY, HIGHWAY, STRAIGHT
TABLE 42	247	NT: WAY, STRAIGHT, STRAIT
TABLE 43	248	OT: HOUSE, TEMPLE
TABLE 44	249	NT: HOUSE, TEMPLE
TABLE 45	249	OT: LEAN, UPHOLD
TABLE 46	250	NT: LEAN
TABLE 47	250	NT: CONSCIOUS
TABLE 48	251	OT: TABERNACLE, SANCTUARY
TABLE 49	251	NT: TABERNACLE, SANCTUARY
TABLE 50	252	NT: VESSEL, FILLED
TABLE 51	252	OT: PERFECT, INTEGRITY
TABLE 52	253	NT: PERFECT, SOUND

Appendix C – Quadra-Circumplex Model

2. Just, Weight, Balance, Scales

OT: Just, Weight, Balance, Scales

Table 25

Strong's Number	Hebrew Word	Part of Speech	English Equivalent
H3599	Kiyc	masc noun	bag, purse, variant
H3976	mo'zen	masc noun	balances
H4941	mishpat	masc noun	judgment, manner, right, cause, ordinance, lawful, order, worthy, fashion, custom, discretion, law, measure, sentence, misc
H4657	miphlas	masc noun	balancings
H6425	Pelec	masc noun	weight, scales
H6664	tsedeq	masc noun	righteousness, just, justice, righteous, righteously, right, righteous cause, unrighteousness, misc
H68	'eben	fem noun	stone(s), weight(s), divers weights, hailstones, stony, carbuncle, hailstones, hailstones, headstone, masons, plummet, slingstones
H8254	shaqal	verb	weigh, pay, throughly, receive, receiver, spend

Source for *compilation*: BlueLetterBible.org. Retrieved February 23, 2009

- Lev 19:36 Just[H6664] balances[H3976], just[H6664] weights[H68], a just ephah, and a just hin, shall ye have: I [am] the LORD your God, which brought you out of the land of Egypt.
- Job 31:6 Let me be weighed[H8254] in an even[H6664] balance[H3976], that God may know mine integrity.
- Job 37:16 Dost thou know the balancings[H4657] of the clouds, the wondrous works of him which is perfect in knowledge?
- Pro 16:11 A just[H4941] weight[H6425] and balance[H3976] [are] the LORD'S: all the weights[H68] of the bag[H3599] [are] his work.
- Isa 40:12 Who hath measured the waters in the hollow of his hand, and meted out heaven with the span, and comprehended the dust of the earth
- in a measure, and weighed[H8254] the mountains in scales[H6425], and the hills in a balance[H3976]?

- Eze 45:10 Ye shall have just[H6664] balances[H3976], and a just ephah, and a just bath.

3. Falling

a. Wrong Paths, Ways

OT: Paths, Ways, Turned Aside

Table 26

Strong's Number	Hebrew Word	Part of Speech	English Equivalent
H734	'orach	masc noun	way, path, highway, wayfaring man, manner, race, ranks, traveller, troops
H1870	derek	masc noun	way, toward, journey, manner, misc
H7635	shabiyl	masc noun	path, variant
H5410	nathiyb	masc/fem noun	path, way, byways, pathway
H3782	kashal	verb	fall, stumble, cast down, feeble, overthrown, ruin, bereave, decayed, faileth, utterly, weak, variant
H3943	laphath	verb	take hold, turn aside, turn

Source for *compilation*: BlueLetterBible.org. Retrieved February 23, 2009

- Job 6:18   The paths[H734] of their way[H1870] are turned aside[H3943]; they go to nothing, and perish.
- Job 30:12   Upon [my] right [hand] rise the youth; they push away my feet, and they raise up against me the ways[H734] of their destruction.
- Pro 2:13   Who leave the paths[H734] of uprightness, to walk in the ways[H1870] of darkness;
- Pro 4:14   Enter not into the path[H734] of the wicked, and go not in the way[H1870] of evil [men].
- Jer 18:15   Because my people hath forgotten me, they have burned incense to vanity, and they have caused them to stumble[H3782] in their ways[H1870] [from] the ancient paths[H7635], to walk in paths[H5410], [in] a way[H1870] not cast up;

OT: Fall, Bowed Down, Cast Down, Brought Low, Upside-Down

Table 27

Strong's Number	Hebrew Word	Part of Speech	English Equivalent
H3721	kaphaph	verb	bow down, bow
H3766	kara`	verb	bow, ...down, fell, subdued, brought low, couched, feeble, kneeling, very
H5307	naphal	verb	fail, fall down, cast, cast down, fall away, divide, overthrow, present, lay, rot, accepted, lie down, inferior, lighted, lost, misc
H5791	`avath	verb	pervert, crooked, bow, bow down, falsifying, overthrown, perversely, subvert
H7164	qarac	verb	stoop
H7817	shachach	verb	bow down, cast down, bring down, brought low, bow, bending, couch, humbleth, low, stoop

Source for *compilation*: BlueLetterBible.org. Retrieved February 23, 2009

- Psa 38:6 I am troubled; I am bowed down[H7817] greatly; I go mourning all the day long.
- Psa 42:6 O my God, my soul is cast down[H7817] within me: therefore will I remember thee from the land of Jordan, and of the Hermonites, from the hill Mizar.
- Psa 42:11 Why art thou cast down[H7817], O my soul? and why art thou disquieted within me? hope thou in God: for I shall yet praise him, [who is] the health of my countenance, and my God.
- Psa 57:6 They have prepared a net for my steps; my soul is bowed down[H3721]: they have digged a pit before me, into the midst whereof they are fallen[H5307] [themselves]. Selah.
- Psa 146:9 The LORD preserveth the strangers; he relieveth the fatherless and widow: but the way of the wicked he turneth upside down[H5791].
- Psa 107:39 Again, they are minished and brought low[H7817] through oppression, affliction, and sorrow.
- Pro 28:18 Whoso walketh uprightly shall be saved: but [he that is] perverse [in his] ways shall fall[H5307] at once.
- Isa 46:2 They stoop[H7164], they bow down[H3766] together; they could not deliver the burden, but themselves are gone into captivity.

NT: Turned, Bowed Down, Subvert

Table 28

Strong's Number	Greek Word	Part of Speech	English Equivalent
G384	anaskeuazō	verb	subvert
G654	apostrephō	verb	turn away, turn away from, put up again, turn from, bring again, pervert
G1612	ekstrephō	verb	subvert
G1624	ektrepō	verb	turn aside, avoid, turn, turn out of the way
G2827	klinō	verb	lay, bow, bow down, be far spent, turn to fight, wear away

Source for *compilation*: BlueLetterBible.org. Retrieved February 23, 2009

- Luk 24:5 And as they were afraid, and bowed down^{G2827} [their] faces to the earth, they said unto them, Why seek ye the living among the dead?
- Act 15:24 Forasmuch as we have heard, that certain which went out from us have troubled you with words, subverting^{G384} your souls, saying, [Ye must] be circumcised, and keep the law: to whom we gave no [such] commandment:
- 1Ti 1:6 From which some having swerved have turned aside^{G1624} unto vain jangling;
- 1Ti 5:15 For some are already turned aside^{G1624} after Satan.
- Tts 1:14 Not giving heed to Jewish fables, and commandments of men, that turn^{G654} from the truth.
- Tts 3:11 Knowing that he that is such is subverted^{G1612}, and sinneth, being condemned of himself.

b. House

NT: House

Table 29

Strong's Number	Hebrew Word	Part of Speech	English Equivalent
G3614	oikia	fem noun	house, at home, household, from the house

Source for *compilation*: BlueLetterBible.org. Retrieved March 14, 2009

- Luk 6:49 But he that heareth, and doeth not, is like a man that without a foundation built an house^{G3614} upon the earth; against which the stream did beat vehemently, and immediately it fell; and the ruin of that house was great.

c. Conscience

NT: Conscience

Table 30

Strong's Number	Hebrew Word	Part of Speech	English Equivalent
G4893	syneidēsis	fem noun	conscience

Source for *compilation*: BlueLetterBible.org. Retrieved March 14, 2009

- Jhn 8:9   And they which heard [it], being convicted by [their own] conscience^{G4893}, went out one by one, beginning at the eldest, [even] unto the last: and Jesus was left alone, and the woman standing in the midst.
- 1Cr 8:7   Howbeit [there is] not in every man that knowledge: for some with conscience^{G4893} of the idol unto this hour eat [it] as a thing offered unto an idol; and their conscience^{G4893} being weak is defiled.
- 1Cr 8:12   But when ye sin so against the brethren, and wound their weak conscience^{G4893}, ye sin against Christ.
- Tts 1:15   Unto the pure all things [are] pure: but unto them that are defiled and unbelieving [is] nothing pure; but even their mind and conscience^{G4893} is defiled.
- 1Pe 3:16   Having a good conscience^{G4893}; that, whereas they speak evil of you, as of evildoers, they may be ashamed that falsely accuse your good conversation in Christ.

d. Lean Upon

OT: Lean, Uphold

Table 31

Strong's Number	Hebrew Word	Part of Speech	English Equivalent
H8172	sha'an	verb	lean, stay, rely, rest, lieth

Source for *compilation*: BlueLetterBible.org. Retrieved February 23, 2009

- Job 8:15   He shall lean^{H8172} upon his house, but it shall not stand: he shall hold it fast, but it shall not endure.

e. Tabernacle, Sanctuary

OT: Tabernacle, Sanctuary

Table 32

Strong's Number	Hebrew Word	Part of Speech	English Equivalent
H4720	miqdash	masc noun	sanctuary, holy place, chapel, hallowed part
H4908	mishkan	masc noun	tabernacle, dwelling, habitation, dwellingplaces, place, dwelleth, tents
H6944	qodesh	masc noun	holy, sanctuary, (holy, hallowed,...) things, most, holiness, dedicated, hallowed, consecrated, misc

Source for *compilation*: BlueLetterBible.org. Retrieved March 14, 2009

- Num 19:20 But the man that shall be unclean, and shall not purify himself, that soul shall be cut off from among the congregation, because he hath defiled the sanctuary[H4720] of the LORD: the water of separation hath not been sprinkled upon him; he [is] unclean.
- Psa 74:7 They have cast fire into thy sanctuary[H4720], they have defiled [by casting down] the dwelling place[H4908] of thy name to the ground.
- Eze 44:8 And ye have not kept the charge of mine holy things: but ye have set keepers of my charge in my sanctuary[H6944] for yourselves.
- Dan 8:11 Yea, he magnified [himself] even to the prince of the host, and by him the daily [sacrifice] was taken away, and the place of his sanctuary[H4720] was cast down.

f. Vessel, Empty

OT: Vessel, Empty

Table 33

Strong's Number	Hebrew Word	Part of Speech	English Equivalent
H3627	kĕliy	masc noun	vessel, instrument, weapon, jewel, armourbearer, stuff, thing, armour, furniture, carriage, bag, misc

Source for *compilation*: BlueLetterBible.org. Retrieved March 16, 2009

- Jer 14:3 And their nobles have sent their little ones to the waters: they came to the pits, [and] found no water; they returned with their vessels[H3627] empty; they were ashamed and confounded, and covered their heads.
- Jer 51:34 Nebuchadrezzar the king of Babylon hath devoured me, he hath crushed me, he hath made me an empty vessel[H3627], he hath

swallowed me up like a dragon, he hath filled his belly with my delicates,he hath cast me out.

g. Captivity

OT: Pit, Captivity

Table 34

Strong's Number	Hebrew Word	Part of Speech	English Equivalent
H7628	shĕbiy	fem noun	captivity, captive, prisoners, taken away, taken
H7845	shachath	fem noun	corruption, pit, destruction, ditch, grave
H7882	shiychah	fem noun	pit, variant

Source for *compilation*: BlueLetterBible.org. Retrieved February 23, 2009

- Psa 57:6   They have prepared a net for my steps; my soul is bowed down: they have digged a pit^{H7882} before me, into the midst whereof they are fallen [themselves]. Selah.
- Psa 119:85 The proud have digged pits^{H7882} for me, which [are] not after thy law.
- Isa 46:2   They stoop, they bow down together; they could not deliver the burden, but themselves are gone into captivity^{H7628}.

NT: Captive, Captivity

Table 35

Strong's Number	Greek Word	Part of Speech	English Equivalent
G163	aichmalōtizō	verb	bring into captivity, lead away captive
G2221	zōgreō	verb	catch, take captive

Source for *compilation*: BlueLetterBible.org. Retrieved February 23, 2009

- 2Cr 10:5   Casting down imaginations, and every high thing that exalteth itself against the knowledge of God, and bringing into captivity^{G163} every thought to the obedience of Christ;
- 2Ti 2:26   And [that] they may recover themselves out of the snare of the devil, who are taken captive^{G2221} by him at his will.

h. Crooked

OT: Crooked

Table 36

Strong's Number	Hebrew Word	Part of Speech	English Equivalent
H1281	*bariyach*	adjective	crooked, piercing, nobles
H6618	*pěthaltol*	adjective	crooked
H5791	*`avath*	verb	iniquity, perverse, perversely, perverted, amiss, turn, crooked, bowed down, troubled, wickedly, wrong
H6140	*`aqash*	verb	perverse, pervert, crooked

Source for *compilation*: BlueLetterBible.org. Retrieved February 23, 2009

- Deu 32:5 They have corrupted themselves, their spot is not the spot of his children: they are a perverse and crooked[H6618] generation.
- Job 26:13 By his spirit he hath garnished the heavens; his hand hath formed the crooked[H1281] serpent.
- Ecc 7:13 Consider the work of God: for who can make that straight, which he hath made crooked[H5791]?
- Isa 59:8 The way of peace they know not; and there is no judgment in their goings: they have made them crooked[H6140] paths: whosoever goeth therein shall not know peace.

4. Arising

a. Crooked

OT: Crooked

Table 37

Strong's Number	Hebrew Word	Part of Speech	English Equivalent
H4625	*ma`aqash*	masc noun	crooked things
H6121	*`aqob*	adjective	crooked, deceitful, polluted

Source for *compilation*: BlueLetterBible.org. Retrieved February 23, 2009

- Isa 40:4 Every valley shall be exalted, and every mountain and hill shall be made low : and the crooked[H6121] shall be made straight, and the rough places plain:
- Isa 42:16 And I will bring the blind by a way that they knew not; I will lead them in paths that they have not known : I will make darkness light

before them, and crooked[H4625] things straight. These things will I do unto them, and not forsake them.

NT: Crooked

Table 38

Strong's Number	Greek Word	Part of Speech	English Equivalent
G4646	*skolios*	adjective	crooked, untoward, froward

Source for *compilation*: BlueLetterBible.org. Retrieved February 23, 2009

- Luk 3:5 Every valley shall be filled, and every mountain and hill shall be brought low; and the crooked[G4646] shall be made straight, and the rough ways shall be made smooth;
- Php 2:15 That ye may be blameless and harmless, the sons of God, without rebuke, in the midst of a crooked[G4646] and perverse nation, among whom ye shine as lights in the world;

b. Raised, Awaken

OT: Brought Up, Cast Up, Raised, Upright

Table 39

Strong's Number	Hebrew Word	Part of Speech	English Equivalent
H3477	*yashar*	adjective	right, upright, righteous, straight, convenient, Jasher, equity, just, meet, meetest, upright ones, uprightly, uprightness, well
H8549	*tamiym*	adjective	without blemish, perfect, upright, without spot, uprightly, whole, sincerely, complete, full, misc
H2210	*zaqaph*	verb	raise
H5549	*calal*	verb	cast up, raise up, exalt, extol, made plain
H5927	`alah	verb	(come, etc...) up, offer, come, bring, ascend, go, chew, offering, light, increase, burn, depart, put, spring, raised, arose, break, exalted

Source for compilation: BlueLetterBible.org. Retrieved February 23, 2009

- Psa 15:2 He that walketh uprightly[H8549], and worketh righteousness, and speaketh the truth in his heart.
- Psa 30:3 O LORD, thou hast brought up[H5927] my soul from the grave: thou hast kept me alive, that I should not go down to the pit.

- Psa 84:11 For the LORD God [is] a sun and shield: the LORD will give grace and glory: no good [thing] will he withhold from them that walk uprightly^{H8549}.
- Psa 145:14 The LORD upholdeth all that fall, and raiseth^{H2210} up all [those that be] bowed down.
- Psa 146:8 The LORD openeth [the eyes of] the blind: the LORD raiseth^{H2210} them that are bowed down: the LORD loveth the righteous:
- Pr 16:17 The highway of the upright^{H3477} is to depart from evil: he that keepeth his way preserveth his soul.
- Isa 57:14 And shall say, Cast ye up^{H5549}, cast ye up, prepare the way, take up the stumblingblock out of the way of my people.

NT: Awake, Arise, Converted

Table 40

Strong's Number	Greek Word	Part of Speech	English Equivalent
G450	anistēmi	verb	arise, rise, rise up, rise again, raise up, stand up, raise up again, misc
G1453	egeirō	verb	rise, raise, arise, raise up, rise up, rise again, raise again, misc
G4762	strephō	verb	turn, turn (one's) self, turn (one), turn again, turn back again, turn (one) about, be converted

Source for *compilation*: BlueLetterBible.org. Retrieved February 23, 2009

- Mat 18:3 And said, Verily I say unto you, Except ye be converted^{G4762}, and become as little children, ye shall not enter into the kingdom of heaven. [stated by Jesus]
- Eph 5:14 Wherefore he saith, Awake thou^{G1453} that sleepest, and arise^{G450} from the dead, and Christ shall give thee light.

c. Right Paths, Ways

OT: Way, Highway, Straight

Table 41

Strong's Number	Hebrew Word	Part of Speech	English Equivalent
H1870	derek	masc noun	way, toward, journey, manner, misc
H4334	miyshowr	masc noun	plain, equity, straight, even place, right, righteously, uprightness
H4547	macluwl	masc noun	Highway

Appendix C – Quadra-Circumplex Model

| H4546 | *mĕcillah* | fem noun | highway, causeway, path, way, courses, terraces |
| H3474 | *yashar* | verb | please, straight, direct, right, well, fitted, good, make straight, meet, upright, uprightly |

Source for *compilation*: BlueLetterBible.org. Retrieved February 23, 2009

- 2Ki 22:2 And he did [that which was] right in the sight of the LORD, and walked in all the way^{H1870} of David his father, and turned not aside to the right hand or to the left.
- Psa 101:2 I will behave myself wisely in a perfect way^{H1870}. O when wilt thou come unto me? I will walk within my house with a perfect heart.
- Pro 16:17 The highway^{H4546} of the upright [is] to depart from evil: he that keepeth his way^{H1870} preserveth his soul.
- Isa 35:8 And an highway^{H4547} shall be there, and a way^{H1870}, and it shall be called The way of holiness; the unclean shall not pass over it; but it [shall be] for those: the wayfaring men, though fools, shall not err [therein].
- Isa 40:3 The voice of him that crieth in the wilderness, Prepare ye the way^{H1870} of the LORD, make straight^{H3474} in the desert a highway^{H4546} for our God.
- Isa 42:16 And I will bring the blind by a way^{H1870} [that] they knew not; I will lead them in paths [that] they have not known: I will make darkness light before them, and crooked things straight^{H4334}. These things will I do unto them, and not forsake them.
- Isa 62:10 Go through, go through the gates; prepare ye the way^{H1870} of the people; cast up, cast up the highway^{H4546}; gather out the stones; lift up a standard for the people.
- Eze 44:4 Then brought he me the way^{H1870} of the north gate before the house: and I looked, and, behold, the glory of the LORD filled the house of the LORD: and I fell upon my face.

NT: Way, Straight, Strait

Table 42

Strong's Number	Greek Word	Part of Speech	English Equivalent
G3598	*hodos*	fem noun	way, way side, journey, highway, misc
G2117	*euthys*	adjective	straight, right, immediately, straightway, anon, by and by, forthwith
G3717	*orthos*	adjective	upright, straight
G4728	*stenos*	adjective	strait

Source for *compilation*: BlueLetterBible.org. Retrieved February 23, 2009

- Mat 3:3   For this is he that was spoken of by the prophet Esaias, saying, The voice of one crying in the wilderness, Prepare ye the way^{G3598} of the Lord, make his paths straight^{G2117}.
- Mat 7:14 Because strait^{G4728} [is] the gate, and narrow [is] the way^{G3598}, which leadeth unto life, and few there be that find it. [stated by Jesus]
- Mar 1:3   The voice of one crying in the wilderness, Prepare ye the way of the Lord, make his paths straight^{G2117}.
- Luk 3:4   As it is written in the book of the words of Esaias the prophet, saying, The voice of one crying in the wilderness, Prepare ye the way^{G3598} of the Lord, make his paths straight^{G2117}.
- Jhn 14:6 Jesus saith unto him, I am the way^{G3598}, the truth, and the life: no man cometh unto the Father, but by me.
- 1Th 3:11 Now God himself and our Father, and our Lord Jesus Christ, direct our way^{G3598} unto you.
- Hbr 12:13 And make straight^{G3717} paths for your feet, lest that which is lame be turned out of the way; but let it rather be healed.

d. House, Temple

OT: House, Temple

Table 43

Strong's Number	Hebrew Word	Part of Speech	English Equivalent
H1964	heykal	masc noun	temple, palace
H1004	bayith	proper partial adjective	house, household, home, within, temple, prison, place, family, families, dungeon, misc

Source for *compilation*: BlueLetterBible.org. Retrieved March 14, 2009

- Psa 5:7   But as for me, I will come [into] thy house^{H1004} in the multitude of thy mercy: [and] in thy fear will I worship toward thy holy temple^{H1964}.
- Psa 49:11 Their inward thought [is, that] their houses^{H1004} [shall continue] for ever, [and] their dwelling places to all generations; they call [their] lands after their own names.
- Psa 65:4 Blessed [is the man whom] thou choosest, and causest to approach [unto thee, that] he may dwell in thy courts: we shall be satisfied with the goodness of thy house^{H1004}, [even] of thy holy temple^{H1964}.
- Zec 8:9   Thus saith the LORD of hosts; Let your hands be strong, ye that hear in these days these words by the mouth of the prophets, which [were] in the day [that] the foundation of the house^{H1004} of the LORD of hosts was laid, that the temple^{H1964} might be built.

Appendix C – Quadra-Circumplex Model

NT: House, Temple

Table 44

Strong's Number	Hebrew Word	Part of Speech	English Equivalent
G3624	*oikos*	masc noun	house, household, home, at home, misc
G3614	*oikia*	fem noun	house, at home, household, from the house
G2411	*hieron*	neuter noun	temple

Source for *compilation*: BlueLetterBible.org. Retrieved March 14, 2009

- Luk 6:48   He is like a man which built an house[G3614], and digged deep, and laid the foundation on a rock: and when the flood arose, the stream beat vehemently upon that house[G3614], and could not shake it: for it was founded upon a rock. [stated by Jesus]
- Luk 21:38 And all the people came early in the morning to him in the temple[G2411], for to hear him.
- Jhn 8:2   And early in the morning he came again into the temple[G2411], and all the people came unto him; and he sat down, and taught them.
- Act 2:36   Therefore let all the house[G3624] of Israel know assuredly, that God hath made that same Jesus, whom ye have crucified, both Lord and Christ.
- Act 2:46   And they, continuing daily with one accord in the temple[G2411], and breaking bread from house to house, did eat their meat with gladness and singleness of heart,
- Act 5:42   And daily in the temple[G2411], and in every house[G3624], they ceased not to teach and preach Jesus Christ.
- 1Pe 2:5   Ye also, as lively stones, are built up a spiritual house[G3624], an holy priesthood, to offer up spiritual sacrifices, acceptable to God by Jesus Christ.

e. Lean, Uphold

OT: Lean, Uphold

Table 45

Strong's Number	Hebrew Word	Part of Speech	English Equivalent
H5564	*camak*	verb	lay, uphold, put, lean, stay, sustained, holden up, borne up, established, stand fast, lieth hard, rested, set
H8172	*sha`an*	verb	lean, stay, rely, rest, lieth

Source for *compilation*: BlueLetterBible.org. Retrieved February 23, 2009

- Psa 37:24 Though he fall, he shall not be utterly cast down: for the LORD upholdeth[H5564] [him with] his hand.
- Psa 54:4 Behold, God [is] mine helper: the Lord [is] with them that uphold[H5564] my soul.
- Psa 145:14 The LORD upholdeth[H5564] all that fall, and raiseth up all [those that be] bowed down.
- Pro 3:5 Trust in the LORD with all thine heart; and lean[H8172] not unto thine own understanding.

NT: Lean

Table 46

Strong's Number	Hebrew Word	Part of Speech	English Equivalent
G345	*anakeimai*	verb	sit at meat, guests, sit, sit down, be set down, lie, lean, at the table
G377	*anapiptō*	verb	sit down, sit down to meat, be set down, lean

Source for *compilation*: BlueLetterBible.org. Retrieved February 23, 2009

- Jhn 13:23 Now there was leaning[G345] on Jesus' bosom one of his disciples, whom Jesus loved.
- Jhn 21:20 Then Peter, turning about, seeth the disciple whom Jesus loved following; which also leaned[G377] on his breast at supper, and said, Lord, which is he that betrayeth thee?

f. Conscience

NT: Conscience

Table 47

Strong's Number	Hebrew Word	Part of Speech	English Equivalent
G4893	*syneidēsis*	fem noun	conscience

Source for *compilation*: BlueLetterBible.org. Retrieved March 14, 2009

- 2Cr 1:12 For our rejoicing is this, the testimony of our conscience[G4893], that in simplicity and godly sincerity, not with fleshly wisdom, but by the grace of God, we have had our conversation in the world, and more abundantly to you-ward.
- 2Cr 4:2 But have renounced the hidden things of dishonesty, not walking in craftiness, nor handling the word of God deceitfully; but by manifestation of the truth commending ourselves to every man's conscience[G4893] in the sight of God.
- 1Ti 1:5 Now the end of the commandment is charity out of a pure heart, and [of] a good conscience[G4893], and [of] faith unfeigned:

g. Tabernacle, Sanctuary

OT: Tabernacle, Sanctuary

Table 48

Strong's Number	Hebrew Word	Part of Speech	English Equivalent
H168	'ohel	masc noun	tabernacle(s), tent(s), dwelling, place(s), covering, home
H4720	miqdash	masc noun	sanctuary, holy place, chapel, hallowed part
H4908	mishkan	masc noun	tabernacle, dwelling, habitation, dwellingplaces, place, dwelleth, tents

Source for *compilation*: BlueLetterBible.org. Retrieved March 14, 2009

- 1Ch 22:19 Now set your heart and your soul to seek the LORD your God; arise therefore, and build ye the sanctuary^{H4720} of the LORD God, to bring the ark of the covenant of the LORD, and the holy vessels of God, into the house that is to be built to the name of the LORD.
- Psa 43:3 O send out thy light and thy truth: let them lead me; let them bring me unto thy holy hill, and to thy tabernacles^{H4908}.
- Pro 14:11 The house of the wicked shall be overthrown: but the tabernacle^{H168} of the upright shall flourish.

NT: Tabernacle, Sanctuary

Table 49

Strong's Number	Hebrew Word	Part of Speech	English Equivalent
G4633	skēnē	fem noun	tabernacle, habitation
G4636	skēnos	neuter noun	tabernacle
G39	hagion	adjective	sanctuary, holy place, holiest of all, holiness

Source for *compilation*: BlueLetterBible.org. Retrieved March 14, 2009

- Act 15:16 After this I will return, and will build again the tabernacle^{G4633} of David, which is fallen down; and I will build again the ruins thereof, and I will set it up:
- 2Cr 5:1 For we know that if our earthly house of [this] tabernacle^{G4636} were dissolved, we have a building of God, an house not made with hands, eternal in the heavens.
- Hbr 8:2 A minister of the sanctuary^{G39}, and of the true tabernacle^{G4633}, which the Lord pitched, and not man.
- Hbr 9:2 For there was a tabernacle^{G4633} made; the first, wherein [was] the candlestick, and the table, and the shewbread; which is called the sanctuary^{G39}.

- Hbr 9:11 But Christ being come an high priest of good things to come, by a greater and more perfect tabernacle[G4633], not made with hands, that is to say, not of this building;

h. Vessel, Filled

NT: Vessel, Filled

Table 50

Strong's Number	Hebrew Word	Part of Speech	English Equivalent
G4632	skeuos	neuter noun	vessel, goods, stuff, sail

Source for *compilation*: BlueLetterBible.org. Retrieved March 16, 2009

- 2Cr 4:7 But we have this treasure in earthen vessels[G4632], that the excellency of the power may be of God, and not of us.
- 1Th 4:4 That every one of you should know how to possess his vessel[G4632] in sanctification and honour;
- 2Ti 2:21 If a man therefore purge himself from these, he shall be a vessel[G4632] unto honour, sanctified, and meet for the master's use, [and] prepared unto every good work.

i. Perfect, Whole, Sound, Integrity

OT: Perfect, Integrity

Table 51

Strong's Number	Hebrew Word	Part of Speech	English Equivalent
H8537	tom	masc noun	integrity, upright, uprightly, uprightness, venture, full, perfect, perfection, simplicity
H8537	tummah	fem noun	integrity
H8003	shalem	adjective	perfect, whole, full, just, peaceable, misc
H8535	tam	adjective	perfect, undefiled, plain, upright
H8549	tamiym	adjective	without blemish, perfect, upright, without spot, uprightly, whole, sincerely, complete, full, misc

Source for *compilation*: BlueLetterBible.org. Retrieved February 23, 2009

- Deu 25:15 [But] thou shalt have a perfect[H8003] and just weight, a perfect and just measure shalt thou have: that thy days may be lengthened in the land which the LORD thy God giveth thee.

Appendix C – Quadra-Circumplex Model

- 1Ki 8:61   Let your heart therefore be perfect^{H8003} with the LORD our God, to walk in his statutes, and to keep his commandments, as at this day.
- 1Ki 9:4   And if thou wilt walk before me, as David thy father walked, in integrity^{H8537} of heart, and in uprightness, to do according to all that I have commanded thee, [and] wilt keep my statutes and my judgments:
- 2Ch 19:9   And he charged them, saying, Thus shall ye do in the fear of the LORD, faithfully, and with a perfect^{H8003} heart.
- Job 8:20   Behold, God will not cast away a perfect^{H8535} [man], neither will he help the evil doers:
- Job 9:20   If I justify myself, mine own mouth shall condemn me: [if I say], I [am] perfect^{H8535}, it shall also prove me perverse.
- Job 31:6   Let me be weighed in an even balance, that God may know mine integrity^{H8538}.
- Psa 19:7   The law of the LORD [is] perfect^{H8549}, converting the soul: the testimony of the LORD [is] sure, making wise the simple.
- Psa 26:11   But as for me, I will walk in mine integrity^{H8537}: redeem me, and be merciful unto me.
- Psa 37:37   Mark the perfect^{H8535} [man], and behold the upright: for the end of [that] man [is] peace.
- Psa 78:72   So he fed them according to the integrity^{H8537} of his heart; and guided them by the skilfulness of his hands.
- Psa 101:2   I will behave myself wisely in a perfect way. O when wilt thou come unto me? I will walk within my house with a perfect^{H8537} heart.
- Pro 11:1   A false balance [is] abomination to the LORD: but a just^{H8003} weight [is] his delight.

NT: Perfect, Sound

Table 52

Strong's Number	Greek Word	Part of Speech	English Equivalent
G3647	holoklēria	fem noun	perfect soundness
G5046	teleios	adjective	perfect, man, of full age
G5199	hygiēs	adjective	whole, sound
G2675	katartizō	verb	perfect, make perfect, mend, be perfect, fit, frame, prepare, restore, perfectly joined together
G5048	teleioō	verb	make perfect, perfect, finish, fulfil, be perfect, consecrate
G5198	hygiainō	verb	sound, be sound, be whole, whole, wholesome, be in health, safe and sound

Source for *compilation*: BlueLetterBible.org. Retrieved February 23, 2009

- Mat 5:48 Be ye therefore perfect^{G5046}, even as your Father which is in heaven is perfect^{G5046}. [stated by Jesus]
- Jhn 5:9 And immediately the man was made whole^{G5199}, and took up his bed, and walked: and on the same day was the sabbath.
- Jhn 5:15 The man departed, and told the Jews that it was Jesus, which had made him whole^{G5199}.
- Act 3:16 And his name through faith in his name hath made this man strong, whom ye see and know: yea, the faith which is by him hath given him this perfect soundness^{G3647} in the presence of you all.
- Act 4:10 Be it known unto you all, and to all the people of Israel, that by the name of Jesus Christ of Nazareth, whom ye crucified, whom God raised from the dead, [even] by him doth this man stand here before you whole^{G5199}.
- Rom 12:2 And be not conformed to this world: but be ye transformed by the renewing of your mind, that ye may prove what [is] that good, and acceptable, and perfect^{G5046}, will of God.
- 2Cr 13:11 Finally, brethren, farewell. Be perfect^{G2675}, be of good comfort, be of one mind, live in peace; and the God of love and peace shall be with you.
- Col 1:28 Whom we preach, warning every man, and teaching every man in all wisdom; that we may present every man perfect^{G5046} in Christ Jesus:
- 2Ti 1:13 Hold fast the form of sound^{G5198} words, which thou hast heard of me, in faith and love which is in Christ Jesus.
- Tts 1:9 Holding fast the faithful word as he hath been taught, that he may be able by sound^{G5198} doctrine both to exhort and to convince the gainsayers.
- Tts 2:2 That the aged men be sober, grave, temperate, sound^{G5198} in faith, in charity, in patience.
- Hbr 9:11 But Christ being come an high priest of good things to come, by a greater and more perfect^{G5046} tabernacle, not made with hands, that is to say, not of this building;
- Jam 1:17 Every good gift and every perfect^{G5046} gift is from above, and cometh down from the Father of lights, with whom is no variableness, neither shadow of turning.
- 1Jo 4:12 No man hath seen God at any time. If we love one another, God dwelleth in us, and his love is perfected^{G5048} in us.
- 1Jo 4:18 There is no fear in love; but perfect^{G5046} love casteth out fear: because fear hath torment. He that feareth is not made perfect in love.

Selected Bibliography

Armstrong, Karen. *A History of God: The 4,000-Year Quest of Judaism, Christianity, and Islam*. New York: Ballantine Books, an imprint of The Random House Publishing Group, 1993.

DeMint, Senator Jim and Professor J. David Woodward. *Why We Whisper: Restoring Our Right to Say It's Wrong*. Lanham, MD: Rowman & Littlefield Publishers, Inc., 2008.

Gellman, Rabbi Marc, Monsignor Thomas Hartman. *Religion for Dummies®*. New York: Wiley Publishing, Inc., 2002.

Goettmann, Alphonse and Rachel. *Prayer of Jesus—Prayer of the Heart*. Translated by Theodore and Rebecca Nottingham. Greenwood, IN: Inner Life Publications, 1996.

Griffith-John, Robin. *The Four Witnesses: the Rebel, the Rabbi, the Chronicler, and the Mystic*. New York: HarperCollins® Publishers, 2001.

Keller, Timothy. *The Reason for God: Belief in an Age of Skepticism*. New York: Dutton, a member of Penguin Group (USA) Inc., 2008.

LeTourneau, R. G. *Mover of Men and Mountains*. Old Tappan, NJ: Prentice-Hall, Inc., reprinted by special arrangement with Moody Press. 1972

Lockyer, Herbert. *All the Apostles of the Bible*. Grand Rapids, MI: Zondervan, 1972.

McGee, Robert S. *The Search for Significance: Seeing Your True Worth through God's Eyes*. Nashville, TN: W Publishing Group, a division of Thomas Nelson, Inc., 2003.

Miller, Stephen M. *Who's Who and Where's Where in the Bible*. Uhrichsville, OH: Barbour Publishing, Inc., 2004.

Montgomery, Ph.D., Stephen. *People Patterns: A Modern Guide to the Four Temperaments*. Del Mar, CA: Archer Publications, 2002.

Neal, Gregory S. *Grace Upon Grace*. Richardson, TX: Koinonia Press, 2000.

Omartian, Stormie. *The Power of Praying® Through the Bible*. Eugene, OR: Harvest House Publishers, 2008.

Richardson, Beth A. *The Uncluttered Heart: Making Room for Advent and Christmas*. Nashville, TN: Upper Room Books®, a Ministry of GBOD®, 2009

Tobin, Greg. *The Wisdom of St. Patrick: Inspirations from the Patron Saint of Ireland*. Barnes & Noble, Inc., by arrangement with The Reference Works, Inc. 2004.

Wuthnow, Robert. *Christianity in the Twenty-first Century: Reflections on the Challenges Ahead*. New York: Oxford University Press, 1993.

www.ingramcontent.com/pod-product-compliance
Lightning Source LLC
Chambersburg PA
CBHW070557300426
44113CB00010B/1293